AF714603

Medical Law in Greece

Medical Law in Greece

Vasileios Th. Koniaris
Eleni S. Konstantinidou

This book was originally published as a monograph in the International Encyclopaedia of Laws/Medical Law.

Founding Editor: Roger Blanpain
General Editor: Frank Hendrickx
Volume Editor: Herman Nys; Associate Editor: Tom Goffin

Wolters Kluwer

Published by:
Kluwer Law International B.V.
PO Box 316
2400 AH Alphen aan den Rijn
The Netherlands
E-mail: lrs-sales@wolterskluwer.com
Website: www.wolterskluwer.com/en/solutions/kluwerlawinternational

Sold and distributed by:
Wolters Kluwer Legal & Regulatory U.S.
920 Links Avenue
Landisville, PA 17538
United States of America
E-mail: customer.service@wolterskluwer.com

DISCLAIMER: The material in this volume is in the nature of general comment only. It is not offered as advice on any particular matter and should not be taken as such. The editor and the contributing authors expressly disclaim all liability to any person with regard to anything done or omitted to be done, and with respect to the consequences of anything done or omitted to be done wholly or partly in reliance upon the whole or any part of the contents of this volume. No reader should act or refrain from acting on the basis of any matter contained in this volume without first obtaining professional advice regarding the particular facts and circumstances at issue. Any and all opinions expressed herein are those of the particular author and are not necessarily those of the editor or publisher of this volume.

ISBN 978-94-035-3486-2

e-Book: ISBN 978-94-035-3926-3
web-PDF: ISBN 978-94-035-3936-2

This title is available on www.kluwerlawonline.com

© 2023 Kluwer Law International BV, The Netherlands

All rights reserved. No part of this publication may be reproduced, stored in a retrieval system, or transmitted in any form or by any means, electronic, mechanical, photocopying, recording, or otherwise, without the prior written permission of the publisher.

Permission to use this content must be obtained from the copyright owner. More information can be found at: www.wolterskluwer.com/en/solutions/legal-regulatory/permissions-reprints-and-licensing

The Authors

Dr Vasileios Th. Koniaris holds a PhD in International and European Studies (University of Macedonia, 2017, a BA in International and European Studies (University of Macedonia, 2007), an MA in Accounting and Finance (University of Macedonia, 2009) and an MA in General Management (Vlerick Leuven Management School, 2010). Since 2010, he has been managing Operational Programmes for Education and Initial Vocational Training in the Medical School of the Aristotelian University of Thessaloniki and the AHEPA Hospital in Thessaloniki, Greece, concerning the relations between physicians and patients with Alzheimer's and Parkinson's and a EUROPEAID project on Forensics between the Medical School of EKPA (Athens) and the Forensics Institute of St Cyril and Methodius University of Northern Macedonia. He currently researches issues concerning the rights and marginalization of persons with disabilities, labour and industrial relations in Europe and Greece. He is the co-author of *European Works Council, Greece and Labour Law, Greece in the International Encyclopaedia of Laws*, Kluwer. He is currently a senior researcher in the University of Macedonia in Thessaloniki, Greece.

Eleni S. Konstantinidou, born in 1990, is of Greek nationality. She obtained her LLB from the Democritus University of Thrace (2013) and thereafter obtained her Master's (LLM) in International Business Law from the University of Rennes I in France (2015). She has been a member of Thessaloniki's Bar Association since 2016 and is today a lawyer at the Court of Appeal. She has worked in law firms in Brussels and in Thessaloniki, where she obtained significant practical experience in the fields of civil law, commercial law, public law, Data Protection Law and other practice areas. She provided legal advice and has litigated in the field of medical liability, representing businesses and individuals. She has participated as a speaker in numerous seminars organized by law firms in Thessaloniki. During the COVID-19 pandemic, she participated in a project advising health services to overcome problems caused by the requisition of private hospitals. She contributed strongly to various youth volunteering organizations, such as Europe Direct Greece (Komotini). She speaks fluently English and French and has a good knowledge of Spanish.

Table of Contents

List of Abbreviations

AEI	Universities
APSI	Supreme Medical Disciplinary Council
CC	Civil Code
CD	Compulsory Degree
CDMAR	Code of Deontology for Medically Assisted Reproduction
CPME	Standing Committee of European Doctors
CPP	Code of Penal Procedure
DOATAP	Hellenic National Academic Recognition Information Centre
DYPE	Regional Health Care Administration
EFKA	Single Institution of Social Security
EFY	Single Health Care Body
EINAP	Hospital Physicians of Athens and Piraeus
EKAB	National First Aid Centre
EKEA	National Blood Donation Centre
EKEY	National Centre for Health Research
ENE	Union of Nursing Personnel of Hellas
EOF	National Organization of Medicines
EOM	National Transplantation Organization
EOO	Hellenic Dental Federation
EOPYY	National Agency for the Provision of Health Services
ESIHD	National Council of Medical Ethics and Deontology
ESY	National Health Care System
ESYKA	National System of Health Care and Social Solidarity
EU	European Union
FEK	Official Journal of the Government
GDP	Gross Domestic Product
GDPR	General Data Protection Regulation
IEEPYY	Institute for Health Service Quality Research and Control
IKA	Institute of Social Insurance for Employees
ISA	Medical Association of Athens

List of Abbreviations

KEDY	Central Public Health Laboratory
KESY	Central Health Council
LD	Legislative Decree
MA	Mandatory Act
MAR	Medically Assisted Reproduction
NMA	National Medical Association
NPO	National Pharmaceutical Organization
NSSG	National Statistical Service of Greece
OKANA	Organization Against Drugs
PC	Penal Code
PD	Presidential Decree
PFY	First-Level Health Care
PIS	Panhellenic Medical Association
RD	Royal Decree
SDCD	Supreme Disciplinary Council for Dentists
SKEIOPNI	Councils for the Assessment and Selection of Medical and Dental Personnel in Care Institutions
StE	The Council of State, The Supreme Administrative Court
SYPE	Regional Health Care Council
SYSEDYPY	Council for the Coordination of Unified Action by Health Services
TEI	Tertiary Technical Colleges
TEKA	Supplementary Capitalization Insurance Fund
UN	United Nations
WHO	World Health Organization
WMA	World Medical Association
YA	Ministerial Decision
YSEM	Service for the Coordination and Control of Transplantation

General Introduction

Chapter 1. The General Background of the Country

§1. Geography and Climate

1. Hellas, a relatively small Western European country, lies at the southern end of the Balkan Peninsula. Hellas is bordered to the north by Albania, the Republic of Northern Macedonia and Bulgaria; to the east by Turkey and the Aegean Sea; to the south by the Mediterranean and to the west by the Ionian Sea. Hellenic territory now covers an area of 131,957 square kilometres, of which the islands cover 24,042 square kilometres. The population, according to the last census of March 2011, is 9,903,268. Although this number was projected to be more than 10,000,000 inhabitants in 2011, this difference is mainly attributed to a change in the statistical method used to calculate the population and to immigration caused by the economic crisis in 2009. Athens is the capital, and there are about 228 urban agglomerations and cities with more than 10,000 inhabitants.

2. Ever since the revolution of 1821 against the Turkish occupation, the Hellenes had the dream of liberating all the European and Asia Minor territories which had a large Hellenic population and had been the centre of Hellenic civilization. This 'Great Idea' had been considered as the dream and the duty of all generations of Hellenes. For its realization, the Hellene people suffered many hardships, which delayed the economic and cultural development of their country.[1]

3. The Hellenes, in spite of the opposition of the rest of Europe, liberated some Hellenic territory, but the split of 1915–1922 destroyed the dream of the complete realization of national ambition. According to the London Protocol of 1830 and the Constantinople Convention, the first territory of the independent Hellenic State comprised 47,516 square kilometres.[2]

4. The territory grew after the Protocol of London of 1864 to 50,211 square kilometres, while after the Balkan Wars, in accordance with the Protocols of London and Bucharest of 1913 and the arbitration of the Big Powers in 1914, the territory

1. V. Markezini Sp., *Political History of Modern Hellas*, Vol. 12, Papyros Press EPE, 1966, 73 et seq.
2. K. Paparrigopoulou, *History of the Hellenic Nation*, Vol. 7, N.D. Nikas AE, 2007, 227–229; M. Apostolopoulou & K. Hatziantoniou, *History of the Hellenic Nation 1821–1941*, Pelekanos, 70 et seq.

grew to 121,794 square kilometres. After the Lausanne Convention of 30 January 1923, Hellenic territory grew to 129,794 square kilometres, while Hellenes totalling 1,222,000 (according to the census of 1928, five years later) had moved into Hellenic territory from the agricultural lands of Asia Minor, Eastern Thrace, the Black Sea territories, Constantinople and other places. Lastly, after the decision of the Allied Powers in Paris of 27 June 1946, which was ratified by the Hellenic-Italian Convention of 10 February 1947, the territory grew to what it is today.

5. Hellas generally enjoys a moderate, Mediterranean climate, though summer temperatures occasionally exceed 40°C, and winters can be cold in the north and centre, with strong northerly winds and snow on high ground. Average temperatures are between 19°C and 31°C.[3]

§2. Cultural Composition

6. In Hellenic society, there is a continuity of cultural, religious, political and philosophical thought. Science, worship and *logos* have coexisted in the same place from the Hellenic city states, through its evolution until and through the communes under the Turkish occupation, and during the early industrial period when Hellas achieved independence as a nation-state. *Tragodia*, the conception and praxis of *'democratia'*, and the emergence of the praxis of *philosophia*, i.e., the purely philosophical conception of *logos* as a radical openness to the question, are highlights of Hellenic civilization: the power of *logos* in the healing arts, from Homeric[4] literature to the positions held by Plato (*c.* 427–347 BC), Aristotle (384–322 BC) or the Hippocratic school, is well known in philosophy. The Homeric tradition presents a *logos-physis* relationship, i.e., nature and humans as coextensive. Plato's *epode* is found centrally in *logotherapeia*. Aristotle presents the therapeutic power of *logos* in rhetoric and dramatic *katharsis* and the effects of the power on morality, psychological disposition and health. The practices of Hippocratic physiological physicians, on the quest to rid *dismetria* of individual *physis*, give prominence to the psychotherapeutic and physically curative powers of *logos*.[5]

7. The Stoic conception of *logos* as a constitutive feature of the cosmos provides a model of ecological thinking and a basis for judgments in the attempt to determine the proper place of humans in the management of the environment.[6] The three saints of Orthodoxy, Vasilios the Great, Grigorios the Theologian and Ioannis

3. Source: National Meteorological Service, in NSSG, CSY 2011.
4. From Hellenic Homeros. Homer is the Hellene epic poet believed to have been author of the works Iliad, and Odyssey.
5. Dr Philip L. Drew, Jr (The George Washington University) 'Logos' in: 7th International Conference on Greek Philosophy ed., *The Philosophy of Logos*, Samos-Patmos, August 1995, 56.
6. N. Galanopoulou, *Environment and Its Relation with Health*, Iatriko Vima, June–February 1994, 42–48.

the Goldenmouth, were among the first to bring together Hellenic *logos* and Christian *logos* in reference to the management of the environment, and this conception is promoted now for implementation by the Orthodox Ecumenical Patriarch of Constantinople.

8. The Hellenic language reached the peak of its development in dialect form, mainly Ionian, with the poetry of Homer (*c.* 900 BC). This was the final stage of a single living vernacular language, not an amalgam of dialect elements. This language, in turn, was the starting point for the emergence of the Attic Koine, which was spoken and written in the extended area of Hellenic rule following the conquests of Alexander the Great. This evolved into the Hellenistic Koine, which is preserved in the New Testament and in medical documents on papyrus. The Hellenic language has journeyed for more than 4,000 years and still maintains the vigour and euphony of music, its poetic quality and its flexibility in lexico-semantic reformulation, as exemplified in the New Testament. The orthography, much of the syntactic structure, and a very large amount of lexis have remained essentially the same for thousands of years. Hellenic has contributed an extensive part of the lexis of other modern languages, some of which have relied on it for the formation of scientific and technical terms.[7]

9. The meeting of Christianity with the Hellenic language and culture was an extraordinary thing. The inclination of the Hellenic spirit was to theorize, to use the intellect to attend to phenomena. Christianity adopted the basic thought and theory of Hellenic culture. The incarnation of the word is the meeting of Hellenic thought with Christian faith that prevailed under the name of Orthodoxy. The Hellenic language became the vehicle for the ecumenical ideal, formerly in Homeric epic, later in the New Testament.

10. General clauses in documents of all periods refer to such concepts as freedom, autonomy, justice, equality, equity, good faith, concord, solidarity and good health. Byzantine Philanthropy was the organized effort of the Byzantine Empire to implement, among other protective institutions, the practice of medicine and the protection of health.[8] During the second half of the eighteenth century, Hellenic society, at a communal level and under *mercantile collectivism*, continued to have institutions of health care which astonished travellers from abroad.[9]

---

7. Prof V. Mandilaras, *In a Brochure for the Philatelic Office of Hellenic Post*, 1966; G. Papazahos, *Hellenic: The Language of Medicine*, Iatriko Vima, July–August 1995, 56–57.
8. D.J. Constantelos, *Byzantine Philanthropy and Social Welfare*, Rutgers University Press, 1968, 152 et seq.
9. H. Holland, *Travellers in the Ionian Isles ... During the Years 1812 and 1813*, Longman, 1815. W.M. Leak, *Travels in Northern Greece*, Hurst, 1835, 387 (de) F. Beaujour, *Tableau du Commerce de la Grèce*, Vol. I, Rees, 1800, 287; E. Dodwell, *A Classical and Topographical Tour Through Greece*, Vol. II, Orme, 1819, 108; H. Tozer, *Researches in the Highlands of Turkey*, Brown, 1869, 62; D. Urquhart, *Turkey, Its Resources, Its Municipal Organization, Its Commerce etc.*, Vol. B, 1835, 75, 100 et seq.; F. Boulanger, *Ambelakia ou les Associations et les Municipalités Helléniques*, 1875.

§3. Political and Judicial System

11. Modern Hellas has been a Republic, a democratic constitutional monarchy, with a short interval of dictatorship, and a Presidential Democracy since 1975. In the past, there have been military movements, *coup d'états* and dictatorships. The first Governor of Hellas was I. Kapodistrias (1828–1831). After 1832, Hellas became a kingdom and passed through the stages of absolute monarchy to democracy with a monarch. The Kingdom of Hellas lasted until the Declaration of Republic by A. Papanastasiou in 1924, after a period of unrest and military movements, the most important of which were on 15 August 1909, by which E. Venizelos was introduced and on 15 September 1922 by N. Plastiras. New military movements followed, but finally a *coup d'état* by I. Metaxas restored the king and led to a dictatorial State from 1936 until the German occupation.

12. Hellas was a kingdom again after World War II and survived as such during the communist guerrilla war that lasted until the summer of 1949. In 1967, an 'updated' *coup d'état* took place 'to avert the danger of a communist threat against the nation'. A referendum took place under the military regime in 1973, and Hellas became a Republic. A new *coup d'état* took over from 1973 until the final collapse of the military dictatorship on 23 July 1974. On 8 December 1974, a new referendum on the Republic was proclaimed, and 69.2% of the valid votes attested the preference of the electorate for the republican regime.

13. Since 1844, the principle of separation between legislative power, executive power and judicial power has been in all the Constitutions of modern Hellas. The Constitution of 1975 as revised on 6 March 1986, in the Spring of 2001 by the parliamentary resolution of 6 April 2001 of the VII Revisionary Parliament in 2008, and recently in 2019, in Article 26 promulgates:

(1) The legislative powers shall be exercised by the Parliament and the President of the Republic.
(2) The executive powers shall be exercised by the President of the Republic and the government.
(3) The judicial powers shall be exercised by courts of law, the decisions of which shall be executed in the name of the Hellene people.

14. General public elections are normally held every four years for all the seats of the Parliament (300). The most recent elections were on 7 July 2019. Besides the election of 300 seats of the National Parliament, the electors in a further election cast their votes for the 24 seats Hellas holds in the European Parliament. There had been, until the financial crisis of 2009, three major national parties which under different names have dominated the Hellenic political scene: rightists and liberals, now under the party of New Democracy; socialists or/and social democrats, now the Panhellenic Socialist Movement, and communists; or the Communist Party. In the current Parliament, New Democracy (right-wing, liberal) holds the majority.

15. The Supreme Court in Hellas is the *Areios Pagos*. The judicial power in Hellas is entrusted to courts having regular judges. Article 87 of the National Constitution mandates that:

(1) justice shall be administered by courts composed of regular judges who shall enjoy functional and personal independence;
(2) in the discharge of their duties, judges shall be subject only to the Constitution and the laws; in no case whatsoever shall they be obliged to comply with provisions enacted in violation of the Constitution;
(3) regular judges shall be inspected by judges of a superior rank, as well as by the Public Prosecutor and the Deputy Prosecutor of the Supreme Civil and Criminal Court; Public Prosecutors shall be inspected by the Supreme Civil and Criminal Court judges and Public Prosecutors of a superior rank, as specified by law.

16. The courts are distinguished into Administrative, Civil and Criminal courts, and they are organized by particular laws. The courts are bound not to apply laws, the contents of which are contrary to the Constitution. Thus, the courts in Hellas have the power not to apply Laws passed by the legislature if they rule them non-constitutional. According to Article 94 of the National Constitution:

(1) the Supreme Administrative Court and ordinary administrative courts shall have jurisdiction on administrative disputes, as specified by law, without prejudice to the competence of the Court of Audit;
(2) civil courts shall have jurisdiction on private disputes, as well as on cases of non-contentious jurisdiction, as specified by law;
(3) in special cases and in order to achieve an unified application of the same legislation, law may assign the hearing of categories of private disputes to administrative courts or the hearing of categories of substantive administrative disputes to civil courts;
(4) any other competence of an administrative nature may be assigned to civil or administrative courts, as specified by law. These competences include the adoption of measures ensuring compliance of the Public Administration with judicial decisions. Judicial decisions are subject to compulsory enforcement also against the public sector, local government agencies and public law legal persons, as specified by law.

17. According to Article 95 of the Constitution:

(1) The jurisdiction of the Supreme Administrative Court (Council of State or *Symvulion tis Epikratias*, StE) pertains mainly to the following:
   (a) The annulment upon petition of enforceable acts of the administrative authorities for excess of power or violation of the law.
   (b) The reversal upon petition of final judgments of ordinary administrative courts, as specified by the law.

(c) The trial of substantive administrative disputes submitted thereto as provided by the Constitution and the statutes.
(d) The elaboration of all decrees of a general regulatory nature.

(2) The provisions of paragraphs 2 and 3 of Article 93 shall not be applicable in the exercise of the competence specified under subparagraph (d) of the preceding paragraph.

(3) The trial of categories of cases that come under the Supreme Administrative Court's jurisdiction for annulment may by law come under ordinary administrative courts, depending on their nature of importance. The Supreme Administrative Court has the second instance jurisdiction, as specified by law.

(4) The jurisdiction of the Supreme Administrative Court shall be regulated and exercised as specifically provided by law.

(5) The Public Administration shall be bound to comply with judicial decisions. The breach of this obligation shall render liable any competent agent, as specified by law. Law shall specify the measures necessary for ensuring the compliance of the Public Administration.

§4. Population and Other Basic Statistics

18. While during 1828 the population was 753,400 according to the census of that year, in 1920, it was 5,017,000, and in 1971, the population was 8,769,000, which means an annual rate of increase of 1.10%. Beyond the natural increase, additional factors contributed to this rate. During the period 1920–1928, Hellas saw an annual increase of 2.7%, while during the war years and until 1947 this fell to 0.25%. The national rate of increase in population averaged 1.20% between 1955 and 1960. A decrease to 0.45% during the period 1961–1971, unusually low in comparison with international averages, was mainly caused by emigration.

19. Emigration rose rapidly in the 1950s and early 1960s to more than 71,500 per annum (average 1961–1962) and reached a peak during 1965 (117,167 according to the National Statistical Service of Greece (NSSG)), while during 1970 emigration reached a figure of 92,681. Earlier, from 1901 to 1921, 398,767 Hellenes emigrated overseas (95% to the US). The number 398,000 compared with the total Hellenic population of 1901, about 2,500,000, was bound to do permanent damage to the size of the Hellene population.

20. Until 1974, the real increase in population was lower than the natural increase. It was higher only in the district of Greater Athens (where Athens, the capital of the country, is located) and in the districts of Central and Western Macedonia. All other areas of the country did not retain the increase in population due to the natural rate of increase because emigration left a negative balance. It was only in 1977 that the real increase became 0.88% due to the increase in immigration compared with emigration.

21. Calculating the recent rates of natality and mortality, the population in Hellas, under the precondition of balanced migration, will increase at a very slow rate, the annual birth rate will diminish progressively and the death rate will increase relatively. This will mainly be the consequence of an increase in the population over the age of 65 years:[10]

	1971	*1981*	*1991*	*2001*	*2009*	*2011*	*2021*
0–19 years	33.0	31.4	26.8	24.2	19.4	19.6	14.1
20–64 years	56.1	56.8	59.5	59.6	61.7	60.2	63.3
65 years and over	10.9	11.8	13.7	16.2	18.8	19.9	22.5

22. In 2021, the density of population was 80.9 inhabitants per square kilometre. But Hellas manifests what is perhaps an exceptional phenomenon, namely the accumulation of about 60% of the whole increase in the country's population, since 1961, in the area of Greater Athens. This area contains more than half of the inhabitants of the Hellenic cities and more than a quarter of the total Hellenic population.[11]

23. Based on population forecasts of the Hellenic Statistical Authority, the population structure per age group will be rather different in the upcoming decades due to adverse demographic changes, the mass influx of economic immigrants in the country and the trends of low birth rate and population ageing.

§5. Social and Cultural Values Regarding Health

24. The state of a country's health can provide a measure of the success of its efforts in health care. An overview of the country's health reflects the health problems of a country, such as malfunction, disease, abnormality and other qualitative factors, for which no social indicators exist. It is necessary to try to agree on evaluative criteria for health. In Hellas, basic demographic statistical data on natality, mortality, etc., are available, but there is a difficulty of specific data, e.g., on mortality by socio-professional category. We also lack health-related data on measurements such as the flow of welfare (related to the level of health) and the state of welfare (related to health at any given time).

25. Hygiene is here defined as the science of health and the prevention of disease. Disease is an abnormal condition of the body or part of the body, especially as a consequence of infection, inherent weakness or environmental stress that impairs normal physiological functioning. The above three factors, at least, are combined in the aetiology of health or disease.

26. Infection is the invasion by pathogenic organisms of part of the body when conditions are favourable for their growth, the production of toxins and consequent

10. *See* Hellenic Statistical Authority, 2012, 37 and Hellenic Statistical Authority Bulletin 2021
11. *See* Hellenic Statistical Authority, 2012, II: 14, 47.

injury to tissue. Infectious disease is commonly the object of the collection of statistical data, especially when dealing with immunization coverage or the spread of a transmissible disease. In Hellas, malaria and tuberculosis have been eliminated, and immunization coverage of children against poliomyelitis, diphtheria, tetanus and pertussis approaches 100%.

27. Inherent weakness, or 'constitutional' weakness as it used to be called, shows a falling trend in Hellas, to judge by data on growth, height and weight, which may be considered as indicators of inherent health.

28. Living and working conditions play a major determining role in the state of health of a population. It is worth mentioning the high average expectation of life in Hellas (among the highest in the world). An adequate public water supply, sewage disposal, public hygiene, and housing conditions, as well as public baths, have been recognized as health factors since ancient times. These days, our progress in ameliorating some of the environmental determinants of health may be called into question, with negative factors including traffic noise, high mortality in traffic accidents, urban living conditions, the social and psychosocial environment, environmental pollution and working conditions.

29. There are strong correlations between tobacco consumption,[12] alcohol consumption, and diet, and the occurrence of certain diseases. Hellas has the highest consumption of cigarettes in Europe, and the third highest in the world, at 3,640 cigarettes per capita per year; among Hellenes of 18 years of age and over, 43% were smokers in 1994.[13] However, this trend is decreasing, and in 2014, the percentage of smokers was 27% of the adult population, still being the highest percentage in the European Union (EU).[14] Recent researches nowadays set this percentage at 10% of the adult population, signifying the biggest decrease among European countries. Law 3420/2005 ratified the World Health Organization (WHO) Framework Agreement on the control of tobacco in order that Hellas might meet its obligations to the WHO and participate in its meetings as a full voting member. A striking difference between the Hellenic diet and that of Northern Europe is the high consumption of olive oil in place of fats considered more dangerous to health. Alcohol consumption represents a low percentage of the total calorific intake in both men and women.

---

12. *See* completed research of 1996 by the group of the Cardiological Clinic of Athens University, headed by Professors P. Toutouzas & H. Stafanadis, *The Undesirable Results of Tobacco Consumption on the Flexibility of the Aorta,* 1996; also published in *Circulation* by the American Heart Association. *See also* Decision No. Y3d/econ. 4322/1993 of the Minister of Health, Social Insurance and Social Solidarity.
13. European Environment State and Outlook 2005, 582. Research on the impact of smoking on the expired C.O. in kiosk workers in central Thessaloniki, one of the most polluted cities of EU, in *Elliniki Iatriki*, 2006.
14. Eurostat, Tobacco consumption statistics, 2014 available at http://ec.europa.eu/eurostat/statistics-explained/index.php/Tobacco_consumption_statistics, accessed 8 Feb. 2018.

Chapter 2. General Description of Health Care

§1. The Historical Background

I. Ancient Time

30. The origins of healthcare systems are ancient, and it is appropriate to review what is known about health care in Ancient Hellas. The social structure of Hellas in antiquity played an important role in the development of healthcare systems in the Hellenic cities, particularly in the democracies, from about 1600 BC. The concentration of wealth in the hands of the few led to a reaction by the working class (free agricultural workers, artisans), with notable social and economic consequences. The lower classes were placated and the socially disadvantaged relieved by the state provision of medical care as a legally enforceable right. The Cretan and Mycenean civilizations developed systems of health protection. They developed water supply and sewage systems as well as introduced the bathroom. Cretan texts on pharmacology and therapy refer to aromatic and curative herbs and mention the therapeutic properties of mineral waters. Surviving texts show that priests dispensed medication (theurgic or hierurgic medicine), including infusions and ointments made from fruit juices, oil, honey and water.[15] Hippocrates (460?–*c.*377 BC), the great Hellene physician, was the first who collated, systematized and added to the empirical and theoretical knowledge of his predecessors, so creating medical science in the sense in which we understand it today. Decades before Hippocrates, Alkmeon of Kroton had made important discoveries in the fields of anatomy and physiology. Erasistratos, active in Alexandria in the late fourth century, may be considered the first pathological anatomist. His contemporary Herophilos may be considered the founder of anatomy; his instruments were admired nearly five hundred years later by Galen (Latin name: Claudios Galinos, AD *c.*130–*c.*201), Hellene anatomist, physiologist and physician.[16] According to Galen, medicine is not a science, that is to say, a body of certain knowledge which may not be changed by *logos,* but an art, that is a system of accomplishments regarding quality and quantity directed to an end which is useful for living.[17]

31. In Hellas in antiquity, there were three categories of doctor:[18] the priest, the State doctor and the private doctor. Private doctors were well rewarded, but priests even better. State doctors were employed by the city state, as is explained below.

15. Fabbri, Giovanni Battista, *History of Medicine,* Milano, Fratelli Fabbri Editory, 1968, 19–20. G. Rigatos, *The Medicine of Antiquity in Our Popular Traditions* 1999, 7 et seq. M. Lang, *Cure and Cult in Ancient Corinth*, Princeton, 1977.
16. *History of Medicine*, *supra*, 30 et seq.
17. M. Arvaniti-Sotiropoulou, *Medicine as a Civil Practice Within the Hippocratic Criteria*, Iatriko Vima, March 1993, 34–37. Ph. Argenti & H.T. Rose, *The Folk-lore of Chios*, Vol. I, II, Cambridge University Press, 1949. R. Kotansky, *Greek Magical Amulets: The Inscribed Gold, Silver, Copper and Bronze Lamellae*, Part I. Published text of known provenance, Westdeutscher Verlag, Opladen, 1994.
18. Th. Tampakis, *Categories of Doctor and Their Rewards in Ancient Hellas*, Iatriko Vima, May–June 1995, 58–59.

The priests of the temples of Asclepios[19] offered medical care, and their concern was as much to uplift the spirit as to heal the body. At the temple of Asclepios, treatment involved diet, spa waters, herbs, diuretics, light purgatives and emetics. Therapeutic efforts were not concentrated only on those able to pay high fees or bring expensive presents to the temple of Asclepios.[20]

32. A recognition by the city state of health as central to the well-being of its citizens led not only to the protection of health by the treatment of illness but also to a new view of the problems of the citizen as being the concern of the whole of society. Legislation began to deal with such matters as the hygiene of public places, the care of the needy and the physical education of the young.

33. The first known State provision of medical care came with the institution of 'public doctors', elected by the citizen body in the city assembly, and rewarded with a stipend from public funds. This institution is known to have existed in Athens from 425 BC, and was subsequently adopted, in imitation of the metropolis, by the other cities and by the colonies in Greater Hellas. Public doctors and their assistants were obliged to treat anyone, citizen, resident, present in the area, or servant, and to undertake the protection of public health. They were elected for a year, a term which could be extended for further years, and the number of doctors depended on the size of the population and the prevalence of the disease. In case of an epidemic, additional doctors were taken on to meet the increased needs of the population.[21]

34. Care was provided in Public Medical Offices[22] for those able to get there, and house calls were made to those unable to move. Any medication prescribed was normally dispensed by the public doctor himself as part of his duties. Public provision was restricted to the attempt to restore patients to health: it did not extend, for example, to the replacement of lost income.

35. Hippocrates was the first, besides making medicine a real science, to put forward the idea that health might be protected by following a code of humanistically based rules. The Hippocratic writings are a collection of treatises by Hippocrates himself and by his pupils, which laid the foundations not only of scientific medicine but also of a positive orientation towards the maintenance of good health, stressing the importance of environment, nutrition and personal habits in the prevention of disease.[23]

36. Health-related matters were clearly of some importance in the intellectual life of Ancient Hellas. The works of philosophers and historians, such as Plato,

19. Asclepios, Apollo's son, the god of medicine, is identified with the Roman Aesculapius; Chr. Oikonomopoulou, *From the Temples of Asclepios to the Modern Hospitals*, Iatriko Vima, September–October 1993, 46–52.
20. *History of Medicine, supra*, 26 et seq.
21. X. Thomaidi, *Research on Social Protection Institutions in Hellenic Territories from Antiquity to Hellenic Revolution of 1921*, 1973, 34 et seq.
22. Plato, *Politeia III*, 405.
23. *History of Medicine, supra*, 22 et seq.

Embedokleous, Herodotus and Anaximander, and of poets, such as Aeschylus, Sophocles and Euripides, all touch on medicine, on related research, and on the theories both of Hippocrates and of the pre-Socratic philosophers on health and the nature of humankind.

37. Health care was also the object of collective action by private individuals acting together. The 'charitable collectives' and the 'troupes', which were organizations of citizens formed for mutual assistance and welfare, collected regular subscriptions from which large sums were dedicated to keeping doctors on salary for the protection of members' health.[24]

38. The Hippocratic Oath is widely considered to be the original guide to medical ethics and propriety. It dates from the second half of the fourth century, a hundred years after Hippocrates, and many experts believe that it was influenced, or even composed, by the followers of Pythagoras. It stipulates respect for life, for the patient, for medicine and for its practitioners. The art and science of medicine are to be practised honourably. The Hippocratic Oath includes the following:[25]

> I swear before Apollo the Healer, and Asklepios, and Health, and Panacea, and before all the gods and all the goddesses, whom I call in witness, that I shall keep this oath and this agreement, to the best of my power and my judgment. I shall honour as a father he who taught me this art, openly, as long as I shall live, and should he fall into need, I shall provide for him from my own. His sons shall be as brothers to me and, should they so wish, I shall teach them this art without payment or written contract. They have the right to written instruction, to teaching by word-of-mouth, and to every other kind of guidance, which I shall pass on only to my sons, to the sons of my teacher, or to pupils who are bound to me by contract and by oath, as is the way of doctors: to no others. I shall give only prescriptions that are beneficial to the patient, insofar as this is within my power and my judgment, and I shall guard against giving prescriptions for evil purposes or that do harm. I shall not provide a lethal drug, nor advice to this end, though I be asked; neither shall I give to a woman any drug to procure an abortion. I shall keep my life and my art pure and clean. I shall not operate for the removal of stones, a task I shall leave to those suitably experienced. When I enter a house, it will be for the good of the sufferer. I shall avoid every kind of wilful wrongdoing and harm; in particular I shall have nothing to do with any aphrodisiac treatment, of man or woman, free citizen or slave. When in the exercise of my profession I see or hear that which should not become common knowledge, even if this is overheard in people's company and is not to do with my profession, this I shall keep secret: I shall consider it a secret that is not to be talked of. While I keep this oath and do not break it, then I shall find pleasure in my life and my art, enjoying a good name among men: but if I break this oath, precisely the opposite will befall me.

24. Thomaidi, *supra*, 74 et seq.
25. Gr. Rigatos, *Codes of Medical Ethics*, Epsilon, 1991, 12.

39. Under the rule of the Roman Empire from the second century BC, most of the institutions of the Hellenic city states were preserved, in some cases largely intact, in others somewhat modified. The institution of medical care spread from Greater Hellas, particularly Sicily and the Italian peninsula, to Roman communities. One modification was the abolition of the medical contribution; the service would now be funded from indirect taxation. Another was the renaming of the public doctors as 'itinerant chief medical officers'. These doctors offered their services in the public medical offices in cities and also visited patients in their homes. By a decree of the Emperor Constantine in AD 321, they were obliged to teach medicine. Apart from free State care, non-State collective action still persisted. The guilds and societies employed doctors for their members. The most important of these organizations were the *collegia tenuiorum*, or 'societies of the weak'. As in the case of the troupes and charitable collectives of Hellenic antiquity, these bodies also offered assistance in kind to the families of the deceased, the payment of funeral expenses, and the benefit of the support of fellow members to the unfortunate member or his family.

40. Medicine is rooted in the intellectual and spiritual life of the Hellenes.[26] It is said that a doctor named Arkagathos brought Hellenic medicine to Rome and founded a clinic for wealthy Romans. Later there was Galinos (Galen), who treated ambulant patients in his *taberna medicae*. The best-known doctor of antiquity after Hippocrates, Galinos, codified existing medical theory and knowledge, laying the foundations of medicine down to the seventeenth century. He considered medicine not as a science but as a craft. Indeed, in the Hippocratic view, a human being is not a collection of separate parts but a unified whole entity, while the doctor is merely a kind of servant. The Hippocratic mission is to 'do good, or at least do no harm', perhaps with the help of the Gods. As Plotinus (AD 205–270), the Neoplatonist, wrote, illnesses were not the punishment of Gods but were caused by overtiredness, infection or alterations of state, both internal and external.

II. Byzantine Philanthropy

41. Byzantine Philanthropy[27] was based on the Christian ideals of equality and love and was expressed as assistance to the poor and the suffering. As early as AD 325, at the Synod of Nicaea, the Church called on its bishops to found at least one institution in the seat of their bishopric for the relief of the sick and suffering in their see.

42. Between AD 369 and 372, Basil the Great founded the *Basiliada* in Caesarea in Cappadocia. This was essentially a hospital-cum-residential facility, caring for the poor, aged and orphaned, while there were separate departments for lepers and those suffering from transmissible diseases. Throughout the Byzantine Empire, we find a variety of healthcare institutions. In the fifth century, the Justinian Code

26. W. Scott, *Hermetica*, Vol. A, (I), Oxford at the Clarendon Press, 1924, 114–116, 120, (XII), 250.
27. D.J. Constantelos, *Byzantine Philanthropy and Social Welfare*, Rutgers University Press, 1968.

included legislation on the administration of philanthropic foundations, in which the care of the sick was made the responsibility of the Church. Bishops were authorized to support philanthropic institutions within their sees by the detailing of deacons and deaconesses to work as healthcare personnel. Care was provided in hospitals, leper colonies, guest houses and *katagogia*, without discrimination by the nature of the disease or the age of the sufferer; the aim was that the necessary benefits should be available to all, particularly to the poor.[28]

43. The State, the Church, private enterprise and the Emperor himself were all involved in the founding of hospitals. Their sites were chosen for their natural beauty so that the environment too should contribute to the patient's recovery. In contrast with the hospitals of Europe, those of Byzantium did not discriminate between patients on the basis of wealth. Rich and poor were cared for in the same institution, in accordance with Christian teaching. The very elderly were cared for in homes for the aged, where they were provided with food and shelter, and were treated with respect. Moreover, women were looked after during pregnancy, birth and after. There were maternity hospitals where the mother would normally stay for seven days: on leaving, she received a sum of money as a maternity benefit. According to the historian T. Miller, in 1133, the Emperor Ioannis Comninos II founded the House of the Monastery of the Pantocrator in Constantinople. This was a hospital with departments for separate categories of patients (surgical, infectious, and gynaecological), beds for emergency cases, an outpatients department and a dispensary.[29]

III. Hellenic Communities under the Turkish Occupation

44. During the Ottoman occupation (1453–1821), the actions of the Hellenes were guided by the developing spirit of solidarity and the ideals of freedom and trust. Collective organizations of the subject people continued to pay salaries to doctors to provide free medical care for their members. All such activities developed under a regime of limited freedom, the circumscribed privileges accorded to the subject peoples by the Turkish administration, particularly after the mid-seventeenth century. Thanks to these privileges, the Church and the community elders were able to employ doctors for the care of all the subject peoples in their districts. The necessary funds were collected from all the inhabitants of the district, the contribution per head depending on ability to pay; the indigent and injured were exempt from payment. This form of organized medical care, funded by the insured's contributions, existed in many parts of occupied Hellas. Foreign travellers in Hellas under the Turks have left us their impressions of life in the Hellenic communities, including their measures for public hygiene and health care. Many communities enjoyed a high standard of medical, hospital and pharmaceutical facilities, employing their own doctors whom they had previously sent to study medicine in Europe.

28. N. Photila, *Social Policy*, Typois 'Pyrsou' AE, 1937, 474; Constantelos, *supra*, 76, 152, 181 et seq.; Thomaidi, *supra*, 166 et seq.
29. Constantelos, *supra*, 152 et seq.

45. Doubts have been expressed as to whether nineteenth- and twentieth-century social insurance – the welfare state – should or should not be considered as the lineal descendant of the institution of medical care in antiquity. Social scientists of a historical, radical-left perspective have seen the institution of social insurance as an achievement of German sociopolitical science, dating only from 1881. However, Karl Baas, in 1907, recognized that social insurance has its roots in classical Hellas, in the institution of medical care, which was preserved through Roman and Byzantine times, then in the Hellenic communities through the Turkish occupation, right down through the Hellenic Revolution of 1821; the presence of the institution of public medical care has been attested in the islands of the southern Aegean after the revolution and the establishment of the modern Hellenic State.[30]

46. It is now accepted that the institution of medical care was extended to the West under the Roman Empire, was then preserved by the guilds and later by the trade unions, and contributed to the development of the modern concept of social insurance. Emperor Wilhelm I's Act of 17 November 1881 should be considered as marking the coming of age of social insurance, not its birth, as is evident in the fact that Bismarck was able to take existing schemes for social protection operated by German workers' trade unions, to systematize these, and to extend them to the population in general. An institution such as social insurance could not have appeared overnight, out of nowhere; it was contingent upon many previous centuries of organized action for the protection of health through the provision of medical services.[31]

§2. General Overview of the Hellenic Healthcare System

47. Health services in Hellas developed in tandem with the growth of the new nation-state. In 1827, the Vardakeion and Proion Hospital of Syros was founded, thanks to the contributions of the island's wealthier inhabitants. This idea found imitators as other towns set up their own hospitals. The first and only Governor of modern Hellas, I. Capodistrias, enlisted the community elders in the creation and funding of institutions for social protection and hospitals. In 1836, in the reign of Otho, Athens mayor A. Petrakis founded the Elpis Civilian Hospital. A military hospital was also founded. In 1843, the donations of Hellene benefactors founded the Athens Eye Hospital under the protection of Queen Amalia, while in 1884, the Evangelismos Hospital was established on the initiative of Queen Olga.[32]

30. G. Perrot, *Exploration Archeologic de la Galatie et la Bithynie*, Paris, tom. I., 1872; A. Vercoutre, 'La medicine publique dans l' antiquité grècque', *Révue Archeologique*, Paris, tom. 39, 1880, 99, 231, 309, 348; A. Keramopoullou, *'Amphissaici Epigraphi', Ephimeris Archeologiki*, 1908, 179; A. Kindyni, *Medical Fees Since Ancient Times*, Publication of Iatrikis Proodou, 1907; Thomaidi, *supra*, 201 et seq., T. Koniari, *The Usefulness of Social Welfare Indicators for the Measurement of the Quality of Social Insurances Schemes (in Hellas)*, Editions of the Aristotle University of Thessaloniki, April 1978, 104 et seq.
31. Photila, *supra*, 303 et seq.; Thomaidi, *supra*, 201 et seq.
32. L. Patras, *Social Policy: Introduction*, Sakkoula Br., 2nd publ., 1974, 159.

48. By a Royal Decree (RD) of 1834, the Medical Council was established. This was the supreme advisory body on matters of health and forensic medicine (medical jurisprudence), and was competent to deliberate medical questions arising as well as to set examinations for physicians,[33] pharmacists and midwives. It was replaced by the Higher Medical Council. There followed the setting up of other hospitals, mostly civilian, in Athens and in other urban centres: twelve general hospitals, one maternity hospital and two leper hospitals, apart from the Eye Hospital, were recorded as functioning in 1878.

49. The Ministry of Relief was founded in 1918, basically for the relief of war victims, of those disabled by war, of the families of those in the armed forces, and of the refugees who were beginning to flood into the country. The Refugee Hospital in Athens and the Central in Thessaloniki were set up in 1922 to deal with the refugee population. In the same year, Act 2882/1922 established the Ministry of Health and Social Care. It may be observed that despite the founding of many hospitals by the State, by local government and by private enterprise, the hospitals were not managed professionally, and there remained a lack of suitably trained administrative personnel. On the legal side, Mandatory Act 965/1937 on the organization of public healthcare institutions laid out a basis for standardized administration and operation. Legal Decree 2593/1953 on the organization of medical services referred to services other than those provided in hospitals.

50. By the end of 1961, there were 96 State hospitals, 33 subsidized hospitals operating under private law, and 956 clinics, unevenly distributed between Athens and Thessaloniki. Shortly after that date, Agricultural Medical Centres were established to meet the needs of the rural population. Finally, in 1983, Law 1397/1983 was passed, establishing the National Health Care System (ESY).[34] Annex 1 shows the number of hospitals, beds, doctors, midwives and nurses in the country up to 2015.

51. In accordance with Article 7 of Law 3329/2005, on the National Health Care System and Social Solidarity (ESYKA), hospitals must be legal persons under public law if they are funded in whole or in part by the State. The foundation, closing, amalgamation or moving of a hospital requires a presidential decree (PD) following the consultation with the Central Health Council (KESY). The organization, operation and administration of hospitals are governed by the provisions of Law 2592/1953 since supplemented and amended. University and military hospitals were exempt, but city hospitals have been subject to the provisions of Law 2592/1953 since the coming into force of Law 1397/1983. Law 3868/2010, as well as Law 3329/2005 above, contains the latest revised provisions for their organization,

33. The term ‘physician’ includes also ‘surgeon’.
34. *See also* L. 3329/2005.

operation and administration.[35] All hospitals, of whatever legal form and independent of their affiliation, are subject to inspection by the Ministry of Health and Social Solidarity.[36]

52. University clinics, laboratories and specialized units may be established within hospitals. They are staffed exclusively by university medical and other scientific personnel and are integrated with the relevant department of the hospital, of which they form a sub-department. Their size is limited to forty-five beds, a figure which may, however, be increased or reduced by the decision of the Minister of Health, Social Insurance and Social Solidarity, after consultation with KESY.[37]

53. Besides public hospitals, the large number of private hospitals (clinics) plays an important role in the organization and distribution of care. The Hellenic Orthodox Church does not take part in medical training or in the organization of hospitals or clinics, in contrast with the major role played by the Church in earlier periods of Hellenic history.

54. There are medical representatives on the boards of health service providers and on committees concerned with health matters: the medical profession, however, considers its representation insufficient and lays claim to direct participation in the formation of government policy on health care. Medical associations protested many times against their exclusion from the advisory committees of the competent ministries, which act in isolation.

55. In Hellas, as in other countries, a distinction is made between preventive and curative health care, and the major share of resources goes to curative care. Another distinction is between first-level (primary) health care, second-level and third-level health care that can be provided by public or private entities after special contracts approved by the Minister of Health, Social Insurance and Social Solidarity. According to Article 5 of Law 1397/1983, treatment at the expense of the State and of the insurance organizations and funds is divided into non-hospital (first-level) health care, which is provided by health centres, by their local medical offices and by the outpatient departments of hospitals, hospital (second-level) health care which is provided within hospitals and treatment that is provided by highly specialized physicians and necessary equipment within certain, mainly university, hospitals (third-level) for operations such as chemotherapies, radiotherapies and transplantations.[38]

56. In accordance with Law 4486/2017 on the Reform of the First-level health care (PFY), the term 'first-level health care' refers to the entirety of services provided by the ESY and have the aims of observation, maintenance and improvement of the person's health. These services include promotion of health, prevention of the

35. *See infra* paras 630 et seq.
36. *See also* PD 235/2000, Art. 8, para. 2 of L. 2345/1995, Art. 33, para. 2 of L. 3204/2003 and YA DYid/30536/2005 concerning private hospitals (clinics); *see infra* paras 629 et seq.
37. Article 13 of L. 1397/1983. *See also* Arts 6, 7, 8 and 13 of L. 2889/2001 and Arts 7, 8, 9, 10 and 11 of L. 3329/2005.
38. *See* L. 3235/2004.

disease, diagnosis, treatment and care after the treatment. The term 'first-level' also refers to all healthcare services provided to persons and families. The above structure of the new healthcare system introduces for the first time in Hellas a new first-level that distinguishes itself from the current ambulatory care meaning the specialized healthcare provisions.

57. Article 3 of the above-mentioned Law describes the new structure of the PFY system which further operates on two sub-levels. These sub-levels regulate the 'entry point' of persons into the healthcare system with the provision of PFY services by: (a) Local Healthcare Units, Regional Medical Offices, Local Infirmaries and medical professionals as well as those medical professionals contracted with EOPYY (first sub-level) and (b) health centres that provide ambulatory care (second sub-level).

58. Health centres are decentralized units of the hospitals of the province and are established in each province. Health centres provide ambulatory care and are responsible for the provision of healthcare services to their respective population in accordance with Article 1 of Law 4486/2017. In accordance with Article 4 of the above Law, Health centres perform the following tasks: (a) specialized ambulatory care to those patients that wilfully visit the centres or those that are referred by other PFY units; (b) emergencies; (c) laboratory or visualized controls; (d) dental care for adults and children; (e) care for mothers and children; (f) care for children and adults; (g) specialized prevention; (h) physiotherapy, ergotherapy and logotherapy; (i) occupational medicine; (j) social medicine and public health; (k) promotion of health. Additional competences may be assigned to the health centres after a proposal by the director of the competent Health Care Regional Service and a decision by the Minister of Health, Social Insurance and Social Solidarity.

59. Local Healthcare Units are created in accordance with Article 5 of Law 4486/2017 as decentralized units of health centres and are staffed by a health team.[39] These units are an innovation to the previous healthcare system. They operate as family health providers with a registered population under their responsibility, and their tasks are prevention of disease and promotion of health care of patients having chronic diseases in cooperation with their attending physicians, public health services, home care and home treatment as well as consulting and support services.

60. The above Law also provides for the establishment and operation of Special Care Centres with the aim of systematic meeting of healthcare needs of the population of one or more Local Healthcare Units, Central Diagnostic Laboratories, etc.

61. Personal doctors provide an extensive and continuous care to the patients in the family or community framework in accordance with Law 4931/2022, as a part of the medicine practice and the therapeutic approach in order to contribute to the prevention of the disease and the promotion of health. The new provisions of Law 4931/2022 concerning PFY redefine the role and tasks of the personal doctor who

39. Article 7 of L. 4486/2017.

can either be a physician employed by ESY, a physician that is employed in Local Healthcare Units[40] or a physician contracted to EOPY and having a registered population of responsibility. Law 4931/2022 also defines the specializations of the personal doctor in general/family medicine or internal medicine for the adult population. By the decision of the Minister of Health, ordinary private doctors may be designated as personal physicians, especially when the speciality is associated with monitoring citizens suffering from chronic diseases, and paediatricians for the juvenile population. Paragraph 5 of Article 36 of Law 4931/2022 refers to the registered population of responsibility of the family doctor and sets an analogy of one family doctor per 2,000 registered citizens.

62. Care at the expense of the State or of the insurance funds or of legal persons under private or public law wholly or partly subsidized by the State may be provided in private clinics if there is a special agreement between the State, the Single Institution of Social Security (EFKA) and the private clinic. Such agreements must be approved by the Minister of Health, Social Insurance and Social Solidarity and by the competent minister, with the further approval of KESY.[41]

63. Private group practices and private health centres have been organized in recent years to offer a higher level of medical service and to supplement the socialized provision with preventive and diagnostic services. Doctors of all specializations carry out examinations in modern facilities, and necessary laboratory tests are undertaken. In these private centres, a high level of diagnostic technology (e.g., magnetic tomography) is available.[42]

64. Second-level health care refers to all services and actions that are performed inside a hospital, a private clinic, a mental health unit, rehabilitation centres and chronic diseases treatment centres, including visits for daily treatment.

65. The hospital sector is the most important healthcare service in Hellas, and certain steps taken by the Hellenic Governments in the past years are in the right direction. Nevertheless, it still leaves much to be desired. There is a shortage of beds, mainly in intensive care units, and certain hospitals are overcrowded. Only where there are university hospital beds is the situation more acceptable, and there is a satisfactory teaching environment. Hospitals are subdivided into departments accredited according to published criteria. All hospital departments are accredited for emergency care. Certain special hospitals (dermatological, quarantinable diseases, military) are ready for emergency care, even for twenty-four hours a day. However, after the Memoranda of 2009, a shortage of equipment and consumables in hospitals has been observed mainly due to the cuts in the public sector spending.

40. Article 106 of L. 4461/2017.
41. *See* Art. 2 of L. 3293/2004, which sets up a legal person under private law for the management of health facilities, in the form of a limited company of public benefit and of public character, named 'The Limited Company for Health Units DEMY plc'.
42. L. 2071/1992, PD 235/2000 as supplemented by L. 3918/2011 YA DYd 30536/2005.

66. There is a distinction between general hospitals and special hospitals. General hospitals are those that have departments for more than one specialization. General hospitals are classified as regional or as provincial. Regional general hospitals operate in the principal city of each health region, offering training in all or most medical specializations, and taking part in research. Provincial general hospitals operate in each province, cover the needs principally of the population of that province, offer medical training and take part in the promotion of medical research. Special hospitals are those with a single specialization. They are overseen by the Regional Health Care Administration (DYPE) of the health region in which they are situated and can cover the needs of more than one health region.[43]

67. Mental health care is provided by mental health centres, by the psychiatric departments of general hospitals, and by special psychiatric hospitals. Mental health centres are established by joint decisions of the competent ministers after consultation with KESY, as decentralized units of special psychiatric hospitals or of provincial general hospitals that have a department of psychiatry. The aims of the Mental Health Centre are: psychosocial care, advisory intervention and awareness-raising therapy, rehabilitation and so on. The Centre may include units for part-time (non-residential) or short-term care. Psychiatric departments of general hospitals provide short-term care, in cooperation with a special psychiatric hospital. Mental health centres are staffed by general pathologists, psychologists, social workers and other health professionals and by nurses, administrators and auxiliary personnel.[44]

68. The admission of a patient to a public hospital for mental illness depend on the patient's residence. There are seven psychiatric hospitals in Hellas, and each receives patients from the region it covers. These hospitals have been: the Athens State Hospital for Mental Illness, the Psychiatric Hospital of Leros, the Chania State Hospital (Kriti), the Thessaloniki State Hospital for Mental Illness, the State Hospital for Mental Illness of the Holy Monastery of Petra (on Mount Olympus), the Kerkyra State hospital for Mental Illness and the Tripolis State Hospital for Mental Illness. In recent years, they come under the reorganization schemes integrating new practices in combating mental illness. Efforts have been made to avoid or reverse the institutionalization of hospitalized psychiatric patients: for certain of them, life in homes or apartments in the cities under medical supervision is considered more appropriate (community care).[45]

69. There are in Hellas specific institutions to which the care of the young is entrusted. The National Child Health Institute was established as a legal person under private law by PD 867 of 23 October/7 November 1979, supervised by the Ministry of Health, Social Insurance and Social Solidarity. By Article 51 of Law 3370/2005, the Institute becomes a Special Research Institute. It conducts research on matters pertaining to the bodily health and social protection of the young. Its

43. *See* Ch. B (Arts 7 et seq.) of L. 3329/2005.
44. Articles 91–101 of L. 2071/1992.
45. Articles 21 and 22 of L. 3329/2005.

responsibilities include the application of the results of such research, the specialization and training of doctors and other scientists, cooperation with centres abroad and the organization of conferences. It is based in the Agia Sophia Children's Hospital in Athens. The Institute has six departments: social paediatric, social psychiatric, education, genetics, endogenic metabolic disease and biochemical research, as well as the administration and the administrative committee. The Institute is funded under the National Social Budget and the public expenditure programme as well as by services rendered to third parties. A child's medical history is recorded in its Child's Health Booklet, introduced in 1976, in which entries are made by doctors who examine the child or carry out vaccinations, etc., up to the age of 20.[46]

70. By Law 1036/1980, the State is obliged to disseminate information on genetics and family planning. Now new institutions are implemented in accordance with Law 3305/2005 and PD 10/2016.

71. School health care is preventive in nature and consists of health examinations of all schoolchildren. The whole scheme is now regulated by Article 7 of Law 2519/1997 and certain new Laws.

72. The Council of Health and Safety at Work was founded in 1985 as a new department of the Supreme Council of Labour and as an advisory body to the Ministry of Labour on workers' health and the protection of health and safety at work. Of the fifteen-member board, three are nominated by the trade unions and three by employers' organizations, with one member from each of the Panhellenic Medical Association (PIS) and the Association of Pharmacists. Any employer of fifty workers or more should engage the services of a doctor for his/her employees. An elected workers' committee of health and safety at work acts as an advisory body on health and safety measures and their implementation, on prevention of accidents, etc. In conjunction with the employer, they may ask for the assistance of doctors or other experts on matters pertaining to health and safety at work.[47]

73. Following the opinion of the Council for Health and Safety at Work, training programmes for doctors and other persons involved in health and safety at work may be approved by a joint decision of the Minister of Labour and the competent minister in the case. Other decisions regulate the period of training. Work doctors are employed by the National Health Care and Social Solidarity System (ESYKA) by ministerial decisions (YAs) following consultation with the above Council. However, in Hellas, it is difficult to find qualified personnel, including doctors and nurses, to carry out the protection of workers' health, and so the means to supervise such protection are missing. The National Council of Health and Safety registers the particular dangers of particular sectors of economic activity, and the means and materials needed to confront such health hazards.[48]

46. *See* Presidential Decree 113/2005 on the development of children's departments and units within general and mixed private clinics.
47. *See* especially Arts 4–15 of L. 1568/1985.
48. E. Zimalis, *Occupational and Environmental Medicine*, Titan C.O. Company, 1994.

74. By the National General Collective Labour Agreement for 1991–1992 (of 3 April 1991), the social partners agreed to found the Institute for Health Care and Safety at Work. It was financed by a percentage (0.45%) of the employers' contribution for occupational training. Article 13 of Law 2874/2000 sets in motion the handing over of healthcare and safety services to the private sector, with the operation of External Services for Protection and Prevention.

75. The report of the Special Commission of Experts on the Hellenic Health Services of 1994 found:

(a) significant underdevelopment, improper practices by doctors and nurses, an excessive number of specialized doctors;
(b) first-level services poorly developed to the degree that most of the need is met by hospital outpatients departments;
(c) a level of public dissatisfaction higher than that in any other EU country.[49]

§3. Regulation of the Healthcare System

76. As in other countries, the Hellenic Constitution contains certain obligations for the State to guarantee health services for its citizens. Article 21 states the following:

> (1) The family, being the cornerstone of the preservation and the advancement of the Nation, as well as marriage, motherhood and childhood, shall be under the protection of the State.
> (2) Families with many children, disabled war and peacetime veterans, war victims, widows and orphans, as well as persons suffering from incurable bodily or mental ailments are entitled to the special care of the State.
> (3) The State shall care for the health of citizens and shall adopt special measures for the protection of youth, old age and disability and for the relief of the needy.
> (4) The acquisition of a home by the homeless or those inadequately sheltered shall constitute an object of special State care.
> (5) Planning and implementing a demographic policy, as well as taking of all necessary measures, is an obligation of the State.
> (6) People with disabilities have the right to benefit from measures ensuring their self-sufficiency, professional integration and participation in the social, economic and political life of the Country.

77. Since the healthcare reform of 1983, health care has been the responsibility of the National Health Care and Social Solidarity System (ESYKA). The State is to

49. *Report of the Special Commission of Experts on the Hellenic Health Services*. Ministry of Health and Social Solidarity, 1994.

provide health care and social solidarity for every citizen, regardless of his/her economic, social and/or occupational status, through a unified decentralized national system of health care and social solidarity (ESYKA) as is now defined by Law 3329/2005. The State considers it as part of its mission to exercise a public health policy, not only through regulations and the supervision of their application but also by attending to the organization of hospital care, undertaking almost the whole of such care through the creation and operation of State hospitals. The State also attends to the organization of medical care and has laid it down as its duty to ensure full medical, pharmaceutical and hospital care for the whole population. Furthermore, the State organizes a system of preventive medicine, improving public health standards.[50]

78. A generally accepted list of the most important responsibilities of states in the fields of curative and preventive medicine contains the following:[51]

(1) Organic legislation on healthcare institutions, including hospitals, licensing, etc.
(2) Financing in whole or in part the operating costs of healthcare institutions.
(3) Sickness benefits and disability insurance.
(4) Basic rules for the planning of healthcare institutions including private clinics.
(5) National licensing standards for health care.

The first law on the practice of medicine in modern Hellas was the RD of 14–26 May/27 June 1834 'on those already following, in Hellas, the professions of medicine, surgery, veterinary surgery, pharmacy and midwifery'. A series of laws, decrees and decisions followed: for example, on the establishing of a register of doctors, pharmacists, dentists, veterinary surgeons and midwives (Legislative Decree (LD) 7/15 October 1925); on the code of practice of the medical profession (Compulsory Act 1965/1939); on the exercise of the right to free establishment and provision of services by doctors being citizens of Member States of the EU (PD 84, 12–27 March 1986); decisions on medical specializations by the Ministers of the National Economy, of Health and Social Solidarity and of Social Insurances (A4/1665/28 March–6 April 1990, A4/2557/30 July–7 August 1991).

79. With regard to preventive medicine, the State remains responsible for national prophylactic measures, such as vaccination campaigns. A Regional Health Care Council (SYPE) is established in the administrative centre of each health region.[52] This gives opinions on planning matters, supervises and checks the healthcare system in the region, evaluates the performance of the health system at regional level and follows up the implementation of health planning in accordance with the national plan and the coordination of the KESY. Each Regional Health Council

50. *See also* Ministerial Decision Y4a/24.05.2005 on the nursing or hospital care of insured persons and of the financially disadvantaged.
51. H. Nys, *Medical Law: Belgium*, in: Wolters Kluwer ed., *International Encyclopaedia of Medical Law*, Kluwer, 2017, para. 26.
52. Article 6, para. 4 of L. 3329/2005.

includes representatives of medical associations in the region, one representative of the dental associations, one representative of the pharmaceutical associations, a university teacher of medicine, a representative of the nursing staff associations, and one representative from each local government, the workers' centres, teachers, and the Ministry of Health, Social Insurance and Social Solidarity, as well as two further professional persons.[53]

80. The State had organized the Sanitary and Quarantine Department. Now it is supervised by the National Council of Public Health, which functions as an independent authority as it is provided by the Hellenic Constitution.[54] The Council is dependent on the Minister of Health, Social Insurance and Social Solidarity and has as its aim the supervision of all public health services of the country, the protection of the country from transmissible diseases already present or that may be introduced from abroad by any means of transport, the protection of the environment or the prevention of accidents. The Council is headed by a distinguished scientist in the area of public health. The establishment of a Public Health Functioners Body is also provided by Law 3370/2005 on the Organization and Functioning of Public Health Organizations.[55]

81. The sanitary inspections pertaining to the issue of licences to establish and operate businesses, and the particular conditions for licences to establish and operate food and drink factories and shops, are carried out as stipulated by law. Competent persons for the carrying out of sanitary inspections are public health employees, such as public health doctors, other doctors and sanitary (public health) inspectors. These are supervised by the Regional Public Health Organ of the Ministry of Health, Social Insurance and Social Solidarity or by the Provincial or District Public Health Departments, the Police and the Prefect. Other such competent persons are veterinary surgeons of the veterinary service of the Ministry of Agriculture, employees of the veterinary service of the Ministry of Public Order and chemists employed by the Ministry of Trade. Employees of other services may be co-opted to the task, as the case demands. The public health services of the Ministry of Health, Social Insurance and Social Solidarity are organized under Articles 3 et seq. of Law 3329/2005.[56]

82. The Institute of Social Protection and Solidarity,[57] having a seven-member administrative board, is the new service in place of the old National Council of Social Care of Article 7 of Law 3106/2003. In the law,[58] ESYKA hospitals' social medicine sectors become Sectors of Public Health and a new cooperation, between ESYKA hospitals and public welfare non-profit legal persons under private law, is established.

---

53. *See also* Art. 3 of L. 3329/2005.
54. L. 2071/1992; Art. 5 of L. 3172/2003; Arts 17 et seq. of L. 3370/2005; Art. 101A of the Constitution.
55. Article 22 of L. 3370/2005.
56. *See infra* paras 630 et seq.
57. Article 14 of L. 2920/27.6.2001. *See also* Art. 38 of L. 3370/2005.
58. Articles 21 and 34 of L. 3370/2005.

83. According to the Hellenic Social Budget, there are in Hellas more than 1,500 social care (welfare) institutions. Social care means the protection of individuals or groups who are temporarily or permanently in a state of need (old age, those suffering from incurable disease and unable to work), the protection of family, motherhood and children, the protection of physically and mentally disabled persons, and the housing of lower income groups, refugees and those stricken by an act of God. Institutions have been formed to help the State carry out its task of offering relief to persons in need of social assistance. These include institutions for the care of persons having special needs, and of the elderly (15 institutions which are legal persons under public law and 71 under private law), foundations for the protection and instruction of families and children (1,233 institutions which are legal persons under public law and 73 under private law), institutions of social work and welfare (26, which are legal persons under private law). To a great extent, these are funded by State grants.[59]

84. In accordance with Articles 7 and 8 of Law 1579/1985, the National First Aid Centre (EKAB) was formed as a legal person under public law. It is supervised by the Ministry of Health, Social Insurance and Social Solidarity and has its headquarters in Athens. Its mission is to coordinate the provision of first aid and urgent medical attention in emergency cases, as well as the transport of patients in these cases to healthcare units. EKAB is directed by a board of eight persons,[60] of whom four are appointed by the Ministry of Health, Social Insurance and Social Solidarity, one represents local government, two are EKAB workers' representatives (one physician and one worker) and one represents the medical association. The board serves for three years.[61]

85. The National Organization of Medicines (EOF) was established by Law 1316/1983 as a legal person under public law, based in Athens, with its principle aim of the protection and promotion of public health as well as the furtherance of the public interest in general in the field of pharmaceuticals and other related products (medical aids, filters for kidney machines, etc.), ensuring the availability of high-quality products while promoting research and technical development in the field. EOF controls the issue, withdrawal and renewal of permits of use for pharmaceuticals,[62] blood and blood plasma products,[63] other biological or biologically compatible products produced by advanced biotechnology, radiological equipment, medical aids (instruments, machines), in vitro diagnostic products, sterile materials for single or multiple use, materials for dentistry, sutures, cosmetics,[64] spa waters, medicated animal foodstuffs, detergents, insecticides, fungicides and so on. It also

59. Articles 21 et seq. of L. 3329/2005. *See also* Art. 38 of L. 3370/2005.
60. Article 59, para. 2, L. 4486/2017.
61. PD 376/1988, PD 348/1996, Decision Y4d/8874/1996 and Art. 58 of L. 2519/1997 on new responsibilities of physicians employed by EKAB in ESY. *See also* Ch. 6 (Arts 24–26) of L. 3204/2003, L. 3252/2004 and Ch. 13 of L. 3370/2005.
62. *See* Ministerial Decision 316/2004 on the harmonization of Hellenic legislation with Directives 2003/63/EC and 2001/83/EC.
63. *See* L. 3402/2005.
64. Directives 76/768 EEC, 2004/94 EC and Ministerial Decision DYG/18 Mar. 2005.

inspects and regulates the documentation accompanying pharmaceutical products available in Hellas. EOF was reorganized by PD 142/1989, which laid down its precise responsibilities. Law 1965/1991 amended and supplemented its regulations, while PD 529/1991 promulgated the Organization for Pharmaceutical Research and Technology. Also, Law 2519/1997, in its 9th Chapter (Articles 45–51), regulated topics concerning pharmaceuticals and EOF.[65]

86. In Hellas, the registration of births and deaths is the responsibility of the Ministry of the Interior.[66]

87. Local government has some responsibilities in health care, relating to environmental health and the quality of life of the citizens. In Hellas, PFY and other emergency medical services are no longer a local government responsibility. The institution of town and community doctors, which had operated by custom, was given a legal form in 1923 by the law on the organization of regional health services. This, however, did not function fully in the following years as many towns found themselves unable to revive the institution. In 1952, there were 241 town doctors. The institution was finally abolished by Law 3487/1955, which also established the Agricultural Medical Centres. By Article 22 of Law 2071/1992, 'agricultural physicians' and health centre physicians, etc., are renamed 'rural service physicians'.

88. These days, local government is responsible for the planning, construction, functioning and maintenance of the public water supply, for sanitary and factory inspection, and for taking any necessary measures to guarantee a permanent healthy environment and water supply. The responsible persons or bodies are as follows:

(1) For the water supply of urban areas and communities (villages): the City or Community Council or the delegated water supply organization or company.
(2) For factories, organizations, etc., that have their own water supply: the administration of the organization, etc.
(3) For private water supplies: the owners of the water supply installation.

89. Following a decision of the Ministries of the Interior and of Health and Social Solidarity on 10–14 February 1964, the collection and disposal of garbage are the responsibility of the City or Community. The expense is borne by the owners of property, who pay a charge to the local authority for this purpose.

90. Local government undertakes the functioning of nurseries, youth centres, centres for the aged and other welfare institutions in which the services of physicians are always available.[67]

65. *See infra* para. 660. Ministerial Decision DYG3/89292/2003 on the harmonization of Hellenic legislation with Directive 2001/20/EC.
66. T. Koniaris, *Demography (Courses)*, Publications Service of the Aristotelian University of Thessaloniki, 1978, 55 et seq.
67. *See also* Arts 21, 22, 26 of L. 3329/2005.

§4. Financing of Health Care

91. The years before the economic crisis of 2009 had witnessed a steep increase in health spending in Europe. At the beginning of the 1990s, health spending in Hellas represented 5.20% of the Gross Domestic Product (GDP), compared with an EU average of 7.25%. Expenses for the care of the health of the Hellenic people by healthcare institutions are met by the State Budget. In these expenses are included treatment, payment of personnel, acquisition of property, building construction and improvement, hospital equipment and so on. To these public expenses are added the expenditures by insurance funds: these expenditures appear in the State Budget as an analysis of the provision of health care by each provider of social insurance. Income derives from care charges, subsidies from the public investment programme, income from property and other sources. The State subsidy is taken into account in the budgets of healthcare institutions.

92. By Article 16 of Law 1579/1985, the level of care charges by hospitals and private clinics (private hospitals) was set by a joint decision of the Ministers of Health and Social Solidarity and of Finance. The Minister of Health, Social Insurance and Social Solidarity decides the means of checking and paying out the expenses for the care of persons insured by the State, by the organizations which operate as legal persons under public or private law, or by other insurance services, in healthcare institutions and in health units for first-level treatment and prevention. In the case of programmed agreements for the provision of treatment in accordance with Article 11 of Law 1416/1984, the expenses for which the contracting parties are responsible are deposited in an account which exists for each Province under the name Medical Protection and Insurance, and the sums are then paid out to the beneficiaries. The procedure is regulated by decisions of the Minister of Health, Social Insurance and Social Solidarity.

93. Generally, under a programmed agreement, the insurance fund pays according to the number of its insured persons who are expected to be admitted to hospital, and with the criterion of the particular cost related to the gravity of the illness. The payments under this system fall far short of the real costs of treatment, while it also has the failing of lumping together in the same category illnesses involving little cost with others that are expensive to treat. However, the fee is not absolutely fixed, as doctors and healthcare institutions can specify additional treatments and examinations, thus adding to the cost. For treatment in private clinics, there is a national tariff of fees, to be applied on each occasion. Hospital treatment fees include medical care, paraclinical tests, cardiac pacemakers, transfusions of blood or plasma, surgeons' and anaesthetists' fees, medication given within the institution, and any other kind of material (Article 2 of PD 234/1980). The insurance fund pays for these items in accordance with the national tariff in conjunction with any relevant stipulations of its own regulations. Funds also cover expenses for private nurses, physiotherapists, special medical consultations, intensive care and so on.

94. A 'healthy' fund covers 100% of the expenses for treatment in a State hospital and 80% for a private hospital. If treatment is undertaken abroad, the fund covers 80% of the cost within the EU or 70% outside. As for doctor's visits, the fund pays 70% of the amount written on the receipt up to a maximum defined by law. The maximum number of visits per year is ten for the insured person, eight for dependent persons, and five per family for visits to check the health and development of children. For those insured by the public sector, each visit costs about EUR 10 to EUR 25 as defined by law[68] and the contracted doctors receive their payment after a delay of months.

95. In recent years, the insurance funds have been facing serious financial difficulties in meeting the costs of health care. Moreover, the nation's hospitals had outstanding debts of about EUR 917 million to third parties.[69] Newly proposed policies for dealing with this acute problem are the cutting of expenses for treatment (a reduction in the item in the State Budget for medical services), and the development of a new form of financing for the healthcare institutions, such as the global budgets that are applied in the US and in other EU countries. Under this form of financing, a hospital is financed according to its size, the number of beds, its specialized units and its productivity. Then the total financing is shared out among the departments and clinics of the hospital.[70]

96. According to the PIS, social insurance organizations should not provide medical services. Health services should be integrated by the State into a single system including the private sector while respecting modern medical science and the need for social protection. The contribution of the insured towards treatment expenses is the only way to reduce artificial demand while maintaining access to health services. It is impossible to give everyone everything free of charge, but rather the policy should be 'the greater and graver the need, the greater and better the service'. The contribution of the insured person should be based on the rule 'the greater and graver the need, the smaller the percentage contribution'. This proposal was made because at present many pseudo-scientific fripperies oppress and impoverish the funds. Moreover, the overuse of antibiotics in Hellenic hospitals unnecessarily raises treatment costs as well as leading to the evolution of in-hospital antibiotic-resistant disease strains.[71]

97. As for the precise economic consequences of the over-prescription of medication, it is necessary to collect data on the quantity and value of medication used, the types of cases treated, the precise therapeutic regime and its results, the whole

68. PD 127/2005.
69. In accordance with the State Budget of 2021.
70. L. 2301/2004; Art. 43 of L. 3329/2005; L. 3301/2004.
71. I. Sigalas, *Economic Policy for Antimicrobial Chemotherapy*, Iatriko Vima, January–February 1995, 40–45.

matter of how prescriptions are issued, the organization of the supply of medications to each healthcare institution, and the additional costs incurred by in-hospital diseases.[72] In Hellas, there are at present few checks on the cost of health care when compared with other EU countries.

98. Certain factors have led to the sharp increase in healthcare costs in Hellas in recent years. There is the demographic factor: an ageing population requires more medical care. Then there is the pollution of the environment, the rejection or ignorance of the importance of a healthy lifestyle, the unnecessary recourse to health services and the conviction of each citizen that he/she has the right to enjoy the latest advances in medical and pharmaceutical science.[73]

§5. Health Insurance

99. Social care is a broad field which covers:

(a) care to ensure employment and care of employed people, health care, social insurances, the total of services over and above those offered under health protection and social insurance, housing and dealing with emergencies;
(b) health insurance and complementary social care services, which form the many sectors encompassing social insurance policy;
(c) social protection and assistance of social groups (families, etc.) and individuals permanently or temporarily in a state of need.[74]

100. Health insurance in Hellas pursues two basic objectives: to protect the health of the insured by meeting healthcare costs and to provide an income for those unable to work through sickness or disability. The social insurance funds are responsible for the above benefits. They also offer social services to their insured persons, apart from health insurance. Generally speaking, the whole Hellenic population is insured.

It is worth noting that until 2016 there were 138 social insurance funds in Hellas, supervised by and large by government ministries. Some 119 funds were supervised by the Ministry of Labour and Social Insurances, 11 by the Ministry of National Defence, 6 by the Ministry of the Merchant Navy, 1 by the Ministry of Finance and 1 by the Ministry of Agriculture. There were great differences among the various social insurance agencies, referring to the professional groups involved and the kind of benefits: not all funds provided the same range of benefits. Among those supervised by the Ministry of Labour and Social Insurances, there were thirty-six providing primary insurance, forty-six providing forms of auxiliary insurance, twenty-four healthcare benefits, thirteen sickness insurance benefits. Funds supervised by

72. Sigalas, *supra*, 40.
73. K. Kremalis, *The Right to Health Protection: From Social Insurance Against Disease to a Unified System of Health Services*, Legal Library, 1987.
74. L. 33702005, Art. 22 of L. 3106/2003.

the Ministry of Labour and Social Insurances provided unemployment, military service and family allowances, health protection and leisure services. The many funds were therefore not at all homogeneous in the range of benefits available, nor in the cost of subscription.[75]

101. Law 4387/2016 introduced the EFKA which functioned from 1 January 2017 until 1 March 2020, when it was renamed to e-EFKA by Law 4670/2020. EFKA (hereinafter 'e-EFKA') is the result of the unification of all the above social security funds and is under the auspices of the Ministry of Labour, Social Security and Social Solidarity. In accordance with the justification report of Law 4387/2016, the aim of the major reform, as introduced in Law 4387/2016, was the complete reorganization of the social security system in order to secure decent living standards and social protection characterized by social equality, social justice, social solidarity and redistribution. Although Law 4387/2016 offered a major development in the Greek health insurance system, it was with Law 4670/2020 that the administrative and organizational unification actually took place, as all pension and lump-sum benefits were unified.

102. Article 41 of Law 4387/2016 as amended by Article 37 of Law 4670/2020 sets the percentages of social contributions for the healthcare provision of the insured persons. Article 44 as amended by Article 39 of Law 4670/2020 sets the percentages of social contributions for the healthcare provision of pensioners.

103. Nine pre-existed social security funds having 4.2 million of insured persons and 2.6 million of pensioners were included in e-EFKA. Through e-EFKA, all services and regulations will be unified for all insured persons.

104. E-EFKA is comprised of the ESY for the provision of healthcare services, the National System of Social Solidarity for welfare benefits and the National System of Social Insurances for the insurance provisions.[76] Social insurance, health and social welfare are rights of all citizens and those permanently and legally residing in Hellas. The State is obliged to sustain the Single System of Social Security and for the relevant benefits to all those that comply with the legal preconditions. The National System of Social Insurance operates with single regulations for all the insured persons. Two major developments in the field of social health security are: (1) the abolishment of the stamping of the personal 'health book' of the insured and (2) the creation of an electronic personal account for the insured persons to be aware of their social security situation. Under Article 2 of Law 4387/2016, a National Council of Social Security is established as a consultative organ to the Ministries of Health, Economics and Labour, Social Security and Social Solidarity for the design of national policies concerning the Single System of Social Insurance.

---

75. Social Budget, Ministry of Work and Social Insurances, Hellas. *See also* Art. 63 of Act 2519/1997 on The Solidarity Account of Social Insurances Funds.
76. Article 1, para. 1 of L. 4387/2016. *See also* Law 4670/2020.

105. Along with the above-mentioned major reform, Law 4826/2021 establishes the public body 'Supplementary Capitalization Insurance Fund' (TEKA) which implements a capitalization system of predetermined contributions to the supplementary insurance. Supplementary insurance in Greece is now divided into distributive insurance provided by e-EFKA which will be gradually abolished since all persons insurable for supplementary insurance who enter the labour market after 2022 are compulsorily insured with TEKA and upon request the insured persons in e-EFKA in the subsidiary insurance sector who have been born after 1 January 1987.

106. What is more, researchers in the field maintain that the inequalities in the Hellenic social insurance system are also due to long-term economic depression because of the economic crisis in the country and due to rapid demographic change. The percentage of elderly people in Hellas rose from 8% in 1961 to 13% in 1981, 14% in 1991, 15.17% in 1994, 17% in 2001 and 22.6% in 2021. Since 1920, the administrative and health policy of the country has resulted in a notable reduction in fertility rates. Improvements in the standard of living and progress in medical science brought about radical demographic change, with these results: (a) a dramatic increase in average life expectancy and (b) a dramatic decline in the birth rate in areas such as the Ionian and Aegean islands, mainland Hellas and Evia, where this is now below the population replacement rate (2.1).[77]

107. Hellas has a larger proportion of elderly people than any other Balkan country. As a result, we are heading towards an ageing population that we will be unable to look after. Hellenic society has seen the appearance of an additional social cost imposed by the failure to renew the population. Expenditure on medical and hospital care increases because of the higher rate of sickness among the elderly, while contributions tend to fall because of dependence on immigrant workers employed in the black economy, for whom either no insurance or only lower limit contributions are paid. Demographic change has had a catalytic effect on social insurances as it: (a) increases the cost of treatment, of which a large part (more than 40%) is expended on the elderly; (b) increases the number of pensioners, as people live longer, and so increases expenditure on pensions to a point where it can no longer be met by the income of the funds; and (c) constantly changes for the worse the ratio between pensioners and insured workers, who can no longer bear the cost of the pensions (there is already one pensioner for every two working insured persons).

---

77. *See also* T. Dardavessi, *Analysis of Demographic Characteristics of Hellene Elderly People*, Iatriko Vima, March 1993, 53–57.

Chapter 3. Definitions and Notions

108. Social legislation in Hellas comprises labour law and social security law. Social security law covers unemployment, social insurance, health, social assistance or welfare aid. Health (care) law is related directly only to the care for health and the application of constitutional, civil, criminal, economic, administrative and international law designed to provide healthy conditions.[78]

109. Under the meaning of *Sanitary Legislation* there are laws, decrees, decisions, etc., which refer and are applicable to the Administration of Hygiene (e.g., to the national health board, the national health system, blood transfusion services), to the provision of health services (e.g., to hospitals, health centres, public health offices, psychiatric units, private clinics and laboratories, private residential homes and services for the elderly and those with special needs, child protection agencies, and healthcare fees), to the Public Hygiene examination of those entering the country, to General Hygienic measures (inspection of foodstuffs, of water, of holiday resorts, of drains, of the collection of wastes, radiological protection, family planning), to the Pension and Insurance Funds for public health employees, to pharmacies, to the trade of pharmaceuticals, to the misuse of drugs/narcotics, to international health treaties, to the combating of specific diseases (such as STDs, diphtheria, malaria, smallpox, cancer, tuberculosis and poliomyelitis), to the health professions (e.g., the exercise of the profession of doctor, medical specializations, medical associations, medical fees, dentists, midwives, masseurs, nurses, aestheticians/beauticians and psychologists).[79]

110. Medicine is that science and art that has as its aim the maintenance of health and cure or relief of the sufferer. Medicine has its origins in prehistory when the diagnosis of disease was unachieved, and the aim of medicine was the cure of the sufferer by chiefs, kings or priests. According to a contemporary scientist, Hans Georg Gadamir, medicine as a Science is concerned with living subjects, though it tends to ignore this in the name of objectivity. Medicine must become again an art because art is always a kind of individual practical experience rather than a mechanical implementation of a rule. Scientific medicine studies the stable and objective characteristics of a disease and ignores the great differentiations and varieties of clinical expression of that pathology.[80]

111. Hygiene is the physical and mental well-being of man.

112. Constitutional law plays a supplementary role with its stipulations regarding the protection of every citizen's right to health, the social insurance of all workers (Article 21), the protection of genetic identity (Article 5) or of the environment

78. Medical law is a part of health law, as quoted below in paras 122 et seq.
79. P. Raptarchi (special cooperation N. Katsini), *Continuous Code of Legislation*, Vols. 34, 34A, 34B, Autonomous Department of Administrative Codifications, 1938.
80. M. Arvaniti-Sotiropoulou, *Medicine as Political Act at Hippocratic Writings*, Iatriko Vima, March 1993, 34–37.

(Article 24), the protection of personal data from electronic processing (Article 9A) or of medical information on the basis of the protection of human dignity (paragraph 2 of Article 7), professional secrecy and the code of ethics. The *Civil Code* (CC) is, of course, of relevance when, for example, defining the civil liability of healthcare personnel, while the *Criminal Code* defines their criminal liability. *Financial (economic) law* influences, for instance, the development of the relation between health institution and healthcare personnel, and the setting of the levels of fees and commissions. *Administrative Law* provides regulations which apply, for example, to the administration of hospitals and their personnel, to the relation between the healthcare worker and the State as a whole, and to the definition of specializations and of the profession of medicine, which constitute *jus cogens*, as well as regulations applying to medical ethics with reference to the doctor-patient relationship or to instances of misconduct, which regulations constitute *jus dispositivum. International Public Law* protects intellectual property rights, health information, international telecommunications on health matters, and matters of international criminal liability, while *International Private Law* assists in the free international mobility of workers in the health profession.

113. Medical associations are associations of a compulsory character (not syndicalistic associations) to which all those who exercise the profession of medicine must belong. In Hellas, they were established by the Orders of 17 October 1923 and 13 November 1925: an association functions in each city or judicial district.

114. Forensic medicine or medical jurisprudence is the science that employs medical knowledge to assist in the pursuit of justice. One of its main tasks is the examination of the dead (autopsies and inquests).

115. Death is the cessation of the phenomena associated with life, which surcease is not seen as instantaneous but rather as a process in which there is no clear-cut line between life and death.

116. Medication, as defined in the law establishing the National Pharmaceutical Organization (NPO), is a substance or combination of substances or a compound that is supposed to have therapeutic or preventive properties for human or animal diseases, or a substance or combination of substances or compound that may be administered to a human or animal following a medical diagnosis to improve, restore or replace a natural function in a human or animal. A substance, for the purposes of the above, is any material, independent of its origin, which may be human, animal, vegetable or chemical.

117. A *medical product*, as defined by Law 1316/1983, is the product of the mass, standardized production of a pharmaceutical, which is put in circulation, defined as an 'unbranded composition' (a generic pharmaceutical product), when its manufacture and name are officially recognized, and as a 'branded pharmaceutical composition' when the pharmaceutical produced as above is circulated in a particular packaging under a particular name (brand name), which must not be misleading, and which must be recognized by the competent authorities as belonging to the manufacturer, who thus has the sole right to its use.[81]

118. A *beauty product* is any substance or composition intended to come into contact only with the surface of the body or with the teeth and the mucous membrane of the oral cavity, having as its sole or principle purpose the cleansing, perfuming and/or protection of the above in order to maintain them in good condition, to modify their surface, or to prevent body odour.[82]

119. A *profession* involves lifelong dedication to work performance such as that of a doctor: it contrasts with the concept of job, which has to do with the idea of possible changes of workplace and occupation.

120. A *Nuclear Medicine Laboratory (facility)* is a laboratory that uses, as a diagnostic measure, a radioactive source of any kind, whether for in vivo or for in vitro diagnostic studies.[83]

121. A *Physical Medicine and Rehabilitation Facility* is the place where, with the assistance of trained personnel, particular services in physical medicine or rehabilitation (physiotherapy) are provided.[84]

122. A *Medical Centre* is a unit that provides health services, including at least three different clinical medical specializations, without being equipped with in-patient beds. A *Dental Health Centre* has at least three dentists, including at least one with a specialization within dentistry.

81. *See also* in vitro diagnostic medical product YA DY8/2001 and Directive 98/79/EC.
82. *See also* YA DYG/2005 and Directive 76/768/EEC as revised.
83. *See also* YA DY8/2001.
84. *See also* Art. 33, para. 2 of L. 3329/2005 and sources there cited.

Chapter 4. Medical Law

§1. Definition and Functions of Medical Law

123. According to one definition, medical law is the sum of rules (legal measures and established institutions) that determine the rights and duties of doctors who have been enrolled to serve the medical function, considered as the highest of the sciences, dedicated to the health of the whole community.[85] Medical law does not form one of the well-established divisions of legal science, such as criminal law, family law or public law: rather, it cuts across many subjects, and must be regarded as a subject in its own right. Medical law in Hellas displays this cross-disciplinary nature, extending over the fields of constitutional, administrative, criminal, civil and financial laws as well as proper professional medical conduct (medical deontology). This extension of medical law across the various divisions leads some theorists to consider it as a branch of public law, principally of administrative law, with provisions from obligatory law and the law of contract.[86]

124. From another perspective, medical law is considered part of healthcare law and studies the juridical relations to which the doctor is a party.[87] Within healthcare law, there are other juridical relations to which the doctor is not party.

125. Then again, medical law or law of medicine (in the US) is the sum of those laws made by society and in the name of society and that refer to the medical profession. It is also the determination of the rights and duties of doctors. By this definition, the important data on which we draw are:

(a) professional malpractice and bioethics;
(b) forensic medicine;
(c) proof of medical facts;
(d) interactions between physicians, physicians and patients, physicians and other factors in healthcare performance;
(e) medical fees and other economic issues pertaining to doctors.

Key issues from this perspective are respect for autonomy, consent, truth, secrecy, respect for mankind and for individuals, respect for dignity and justice,[88] and professional conduct.

126. These days it is increasingly difficult to draw the line between the liberty of science and medical responsibility. A doctor may make grave errors so cannot go unchecked, but doctors would be able neither to advance science nor to carry out their work if their every action carried the threat of legal action or sanction.[89] It is

85. P. Epivatianos, *Medical Law, Deontology and Problematics*, U.S.P., 1984, 11.
86. A. Alexiadis, *Introduction to Medical Law*, Publ. M. Dimopoulou, 1996, 16.
87. Nys, *supra*, para. 44 and sources there cited.
88. Nys, *supra*, paras 42 et seq. and sources there cited.
89. Epivatianos, *supra*, 11.

a fact that medical science is constantly opening new perspectives, challenging society and culture. It is the task of medical law to orient the application of advances towards the greatest benefit of the people, building on the principles and guidelines of proper medical practice and medical ethics.

127. Proper medical practice (or medical deontology) is the code of behaviour for the profession of doctor, which was accepted voluntarily and was not usually imposed by laws of the State, though this is no longer the case. From the point of view of justice, the code of proper practice is a code of behaviour applicable to all, not an internal code limited to the medical profession. The Hippocratic Oath is considered the first such code: another, much later, is the Code of Geneva. Since 1955 Hellas has had a code of medical deontology imposed by law.[90] Since 28 November 2005, Hellas has a new code of medical deontology.

128. *Medical ethics* is another significant term which has to do with matters that coincide with those with which medical law is concerned; however, it is not a synonym for medical law and must be distinguished from this. The doctor is charged not only with the preservation and prolongation of life but also with its amelioration. The meeting of these requirements necessitates careful consideration and the detailed examination of the logic of the positions which are brought to bear on any problem that has to be confronted in the exercise of the medical profession. The doctor needs to take carefully considered decisions with a clear mind. In his/her choices, a doctor must take a serious view of the human significance of death and illness. At this point, we may note the view of Plato (Republic: 410a) that sufferers from incurable bodily illness should be abandoned, while sufferers from incurable mental illness should be put to death.[91] A code of medical ethics represents the whole of the rules, regulations and guidelines that have to do with the medical ethic that is at the disposal of doctors when they need to make difficult decisions.[92]

129. Ethics as a science examines the bases of action of humans as social beings, and describes the rules by which they live. As there is a variety of ethical systems, each of which states the ethical problem in a different way, it is not possible to give a general definition of its object. So, according to a definition of the ethic of duty, the fundamental principle is that a person must act in such a way that from his/her actions, one may deduce a general law of humanity (without there necessarily being any such legal form).

130. In Hellas, legislation in the field of medical law cannot be considered strict. This may be the result of a new scientific thinking, in relation to the problem of appropriate methodology. Medical law, as a new scientific field, overpasses classical, neoclassical or Marxist-dialectic methodologies and needs a new methodology,

---

90. Epivatianos, *supra*, 37. L. 3418/2005 on the Code of Medical Deontology as supplemented by Presidential Decree 25/2015.
91. N. Papanikolaou, *Plato and We the Doctors*, Iatriko Vima, March–April 1995, 62.
92. Epivatianos, *supra*, 57. D. Gritzalis, et al., *Study: Safeguarding Medical Secrecy at Information Systems of ESY*, TEI of Athens, Computer Department, 1990, 152 et seq. *See also* Art. 3 of L. 3418/2005.

the methodology of control or continuous control. Certain important scientific problems which earlier methodologies are unable to solve can be successfully confronted by the methodology of continuous control.[93]

§2. Sources of Medical Law

I. International Sources

131. The internationalization of medical activity through private or public international organizations, such as the EU, the Council of Europe and the WHO, has been reflected in Hellenic medical legislation. LD No. 436 of 21–30 October 1947 approved the International Health Treaties signed in New York on 22 July 1947, which were amended many times by decisions of the Ministers of Foreign Affairs, of Health and Social Solidarity, and of Social Insurances (e.g., *see* Decision 4–17 September 1990). Also, in 1947, the Protocol on the International Office of Public Health was approved by LD No. 437 of 21–30 October 1947.

132. Other international sources of medical law are the European Convention for the Protection of Human Rights and Fundamental Freedoms of 4 November 1950, and the International Covenant on Civil and Political Rights of the United Nations (UN), 19 December 1966. The revised International Health Regulation (Code), as adopted by the Twenty-Second World Health Conference in January 1971, was approved by RD No. 383 of 10–22 June 1972. The revised Regulation (Code) was approved in Hellas by PD No. 16 of 11–26 January 1980 and further revisions by PD No. 1383 of 19–31 December 1981. Hellas has also signed many cross-border treaties on the prevention and elimination of transmissible diseases and in the field of public health in general.[94]

133. Bodies belonging to international intergovernmental organizations, such as the Health Ministers of European Countries, adopt resolutions (e.g., on the transplantation of human organs) and general ethical principles (Paris, November 1987). The Committee of Ministers and the Parliamentary Assembly of the Council of Europe approve resolutions and recommendations (e.g., on bioethical questions, Strasbourg, 1989). Hellas also signed the Convention on Human Rights and Biomedicine of 1996 in Oviedo (Spain) on 4 April 1997. Law 3305 (27 January 2005) refers to methods of medically assisted conception and the ways in which these may be applied while fully securing personal integrity and maintaining respect for individual freedom.

93. T. Koniaris, *Social Policy and Social Administration, Book 1, Introduction*, Aristotelian University Publishing Service, 1991, 181 et seq.

94. L. 3313/2005 on the ratification of the agreement between the Hellenic Republic and the Republic of Albania on cooperation in the health sector. L. 3347/2005 on the ratification of the agreement between the Hellenic Republic and the Republic of Georgia on cooperation in the health sector.

134. Hellas, as a member of the EU, is obliged to accept measures which have a direct or binding effect on the citizens of member countries. Accordingly, with regard to the principle of the free movement of persons, PD No. 84 of 12–27 March 1986 refers to the exercise of the right to free establishment and provision of services by doctors being citizens of Member States of the EU, as well as making certain other adjustments, in compliance with the Directives of the Council of European Communities Nos 75/362, 75/363 of 16 June 1975, 81/1057 of 14 December 1981, and 82/76 of 26 January 1982. These Directives defined the primary qualifications (basic medical knowledge) of a doctor and defined the Fully Registered Medical Practitioner. In paragraph 2 of Article 8, the above decree set out the official medical specializations accepted in the EU.

135. By a Decision of the Ministers of National Economy, of Health and Social Solidarity, and of Social Insurances (A4/1665/28 March–6 April 1990), new specializations were added. By another Decision of the above ministers (A4/econ. 3277 of 21–27 June 1990), the particular qualifications for the practice of general medicine were defined in order to bring Hellenic legislation into compliance with EU Decision 86/457.[95] Now, specializations are defined by Articles 5 and 7 of Council Directive 93/16/EEC as modified by Council Directive 97/50/EEC, Articles 10, 11 and paragraph 9 of Article 14 of Council Directive 2001/19 EC, and Article 7 of PD 38/2004.

136. The international forums of medical associations regularly call upon governments, health authorities and others making health policy to recognize the substantive advisory role of such forums and associations. Declarations and decisions of such forums become a source of the description of the ethical duties and obligations of doctors, though not of legislation. The international non-governmental bodies of importance from a Hellenic perspective are the World Medical Association (WMA) and the European Forum of International Medical Associations. Some first declarations of importance for the medical field are the Declaration of Geneva (1948, modified 1968) and the Declaration of Helsinki (1964, modified Tokyo 1975), both drawn up and adopted by the WMA.

II. National Sources

137. The National Constitution of Hellas, passed by vote of the 5th Revisionary Parliament in June 1975, revised and transcribed into modern Hellenic by the 6th Revisionary Parliament on 6 March 1986, and again revised by the parliamentary resolution of 6 April 2001 of the 7th Revisionary Parliament, and the resolution of 27 May 2008 is a source of medical law. The most recent revision is of 2019 when it was revised by the resolution of 25 November 2019 of the 9th Revisionary Parliament.

95. *See also* Art. 20 of L. 2519/1997.

138. It follows the same general line as most liberal constitutions, being based on ideological pluralism and on humanistic values. The Constitution takes precedence over the other laws of the land. Certain provisions refer to human rights and values and define the area for the implementation of individual and social rights. Article 25 affects medical law as regards the processing of personal medical data. Paragraph 2 of Article 5 protects personal freedom and freedom of expression, which may be endangered or redefined by biotechnology and genetic technology. It reads in paragraph 5: '*All persons have the right to the protection of their health and of their genetic identity. Matters relating to the protection of every person against biomedical interventions shall be specified by law.*' Recently, Law 3305/2005 has allowed for the creation and operation of artificial insemination facilities.

139. Other Articles of the Constitution of importance to medical law are paragraph 2 of Article 4, on the equality of rights and obligations of all Hellenes, paragraph 2 of Article 7, on the protection of human dignity. Articles 21, 22 and 24, already mentioned, oblige the State to protect the health of its citizens, with special reference to families, the young and the elderly,[96] to attend to social insurances for working people,[97] and to supervise environmental and land use planning to ensure 'the best possible living conditions'.[98]

140. It should be mentioned that the revised 2001 Constitution introduced, among other things, new individual rights (e.g., protection of genetic identity, protection of personal data from electronic processing); it introduced new rules of transparency in political and economic life and reinforced decentralization. Today, Hellas possesses a Constitution of political and historical legitimacy, which is modern, adapted to international developments and provides the institutional framework for Hellas in the twenty-first century.

141. Certain Articles of the Penal Code (PC)[99] concern the medical profession. Article 302 refers to the death of a person by the fault of a doctor. Article 314 refers to doctors' liability in the case of injury or damage to the health of patients. Article 371 regulates the processing of medical data. Article 8 of Law 2251/1994, as amended by Article 10 of Law 3587/2007, defines the civil liability of a person offering services *(see also* the proposed EU Directive under this same title): this also applies to doctors' liability.

142. By Article 13 of Law 3418/2005 on the Code of Medical Deontology Profession, doctors are legally (not merely ethically) obliged to maintain medical secrecy. In accordance with the above law, RD 25 May–6 June 1955 on the Code of Medical Deontology (proper medical practice) had imposed definite obligations on doctors in Hellas.

96. Article 21 of the Constitution.
97. Article 22, para. 5 of the Constitution.
98. Article 24 of the Constitution.
99. PD 283/1985.

143. Law 2071/1992 allowed for a PD to introduce a new code of medical deontology. More recently, Law 3418/2005 is the new Law which regulates medical deontology in Hellas. There is also the law establishing the ESY, Law 1397/1983, as amended many times and the new Laws on ESYKA, which are main sources of Hellenic medical law.[100]

144. Jurisprudence, in the sense of the decisions of courts, forms and contributes to the development of law, providing new interpretations and safeguarding rights. To a certain extent, these decisions may be considered another source of national law.

100. *See also* L. 2519/1997.

Part I. The Medical Profession

Chapter 1. Access to the Medical Profession

§1. Medical Education

I. Historical Note

145. The history of medical education in Hellas is not like that in most Western European countries. To the end of the Turkish occupation (1453–1821), medical practice was exercised by physicians trained at a university in Italy, Germany, Austria, Eastern Europe or Russia, and competent in internal medicine, by surgeons, also respected and trained mainly by practice, and by itinerant practical doctors. Anyone was free to practise medicine, but there was supervision by the 'elders' in the national Communes. The situation changed after the liberation, in the Hellas of that period, and very soon the Athenian University was organized, including its medical department. In 1843, the first Hellene physician graduated from the Athenian University. After the liberation of other Hellenic territories, Thessaloniki became a new centre of cultural and scientific progress. Its Aristotelian University was founded in 1925 and organized its medical school shortly after 1927. Very soon, Hellas was capable of creating a satisfactory number of physicians, midwives, nurses and paramedical personnel. Law 463/1912 created a new situation, distinguishing physicians from other paramedical personnel. It also restricted the simultaneous practice of medicine, surgery, obstetrics and pharmacy. Article 1 of the above act underlined that no one may practise medicine unless he abides by Article 20 of Law 3823, on the organization of the national university, which required a leaving certificate from high school or practical lyceum for candidates to the medical school taking entrance examinations. Various laws created the legal status of physician, defined the terms of pharmacy as a separate profession, and organized dentistry. Law 4069/1929 founded the National School of Public Health, which functions, basically, in accordance with the provisions of Article 3 of Law 2194/1994.

146. After 1983, a Committee on Education and Post education[101] was created in order to help the Central Board of Health (KESY) to:

101. *See* Art. 4, para. 4 of L. 1278/1982.

(a) instigate the establishment, separation, merging or abolition of medical and dental specializations;
(b) conduct needs analyses and opine on the number of doctors needed in each specialization;
(c) set up programmes for the training of medical specialists, and establish the criteria for the designation of units offering training for the acquisition of specializations, the duration of such training, and the number of doctors to receive such training;
(d) set up an integrated programme of continuing education for doctors, medical scientists, nursing personnel and other professionals in the field; this programme is applied at the level of the health region by the regional education committee of each hospital;
(e) approve proposals for the functioning of compulsory or optional educational programmes and to control, observe, coordinate and evaluate their execution and performance.

147. The qualifying conditions, means, and procedure for the acquisition of a medical specialization were defined in accordance with a PD issued under paragraph 2 of Article 31 of Law 1397/1983, on the proposal of the Minister of Health, Social Insurance and Social Solidarity, following the opinion of the KESY. For those who had met the qualifying conditions for the acquisition of such a title before the issue of the above PD, the previously valid conditions are applicable.

II. Constitutional Competence

148. According to paragraph 5 of Article 16 of the Constitution of 1975 as amended on March 1986, April 2001, June 2008 and November 2019:

> Education at university level shall be provided exclusively by institutions which are fully self-governed public law legal persons. These institutions shall operate under the supervision of the State and are entitled to financial assistance from it; they shall operate on the basis of statutorily enacted by-laws. Merging or splitting of university level institutions may take place notwithstanding any contrary provisions, as a law shall provide.

Paragraph 8b makes it clear that the establishment of university-level institutions by private persons is prohibited.[102] Paragraph 3 of the same Article stipulates that the duration of compulsory education should be no fewer than nine years. The minimum conditions for the granting of degrees are foreseen in the internal codes of the said institutions. In Hellas, there is no communitarization of educational policy. The 2019 revision of the National Constitution (under schedule) should have renewed our nineteenth-century educational system, including medical education and the

102. Note: the phrase 'higher tertiary' reflects the Hellenic distinction within tertiary education between *anotatos* and *anoteros:* the latter might be just 'tertiary' by contrast.

academic title of physician. Already the PIS has asked the provincial medical associations to be the principle competent bodies setting the number of candidates accepted at the medical schools, and the number of employed specialized doctors in the district of their responsibility.[103]

III. Undergraduate Medical Education

149. The normal course of medical studies lasts six years. Two cycles of studies are proposed by law, and university departments and faculties are solely responsible for introducing them. After the courses of the first two years of studies, some clinical and practical training in a university hospital is simultaneously offered in parallel to courses. There are presently seven medical schools or departments of sciences of health: of Athens, Thessaloniki, Larissa, Patra, Ioannina, Alexandroupolis and Heraklion. They offer training and practice in their university hospitals.

150. For admission to a medical school, all candidates should hold a high school leaving certificate to participate in the entrance examinations according to the national system of Panhellenic examinations. Candidates are usually aged 18. Enrolments are not open. Only candidates-applicants who have passed the entrance examinations are admitted. Anyone possessing a secondary school matriculation diploma has the right to participate in the open entrance examinations for all faculties, medicine and dentistry included. According to the existing system (which is under revision), each faculty accepts a certain number of students. The level of the students' marks determines their right of entrance to one of the faculties of their choice. There is a limit on the number of students each faculty may admit each year.

151. The pursuit of medical studies is not limited by failures in successive examinations. Actually, there is a negligible attrition rate. A student may have passed examinations on courses belonging to subsequent years and may have left courses from earlier years, which he/she has someday to pass in order to graduate. There are candidate physicians who have succeeded in all different branches of medical study, apart from a course, e.g., from their first year. They still need to pass it if they wish to acquire their degree.

152. Medical schools, being self-governed institutions of the universities, have autonomy in programming the different branches and courses and may add other studies leading to graduation.

153. According to informed opinion, undergraduate medical education in Hellas does not greatly differ from the European Community proposals, but it needs a certain degree of revision and reorganization and a drastic lessening of the number of candidate doctors in medical faculties. The current practices of transferring medical students from universities abroad and of carrying forward courses that failed to the

103. *Iatriko Vima*, March–April 1997.

subsequent year of studies should both be abolished, and it should also be possible to expel students who repeatedly fail examinations: ten times or more is not unheard of.

IV. Graduate Medical Education

154. There is no special exam for the academic title of physician. The candidate doctor has to pass all the various subjects spread over six years of studies. From the third year, practical clinical work must be attended at the university clinics. This is a variety of the internship served in European hospitals. All medical schools follow a programme approved by the Ministry.

V. Postgraduate Medical Education

155. The postgraduate medical education of physicians has been influenced by the autonomy in programming which medical faculties enjoy in Hellas. Medical departments of Hellenic universities, or Departments of Sciences of Health, institute postgraduate training for physicians with or without speciality or practised in medicine and other scientists holding a degree from a university school.[104]

156. With respect to the autonomy of the Medical Faculties, the EU has also influenced the postgraduate medical education of physicians, while promoting equivalence (of training, etc., and qualifications) and quality.

157. Training leading to a formal qualification in postgraduate medical education in Member Countries to the EU has to meet certain minimum requirements, including those laid down in Council Directives (*see* below).

§2. Licensing of General Practitioners and Medical Specialists

158. No legal obligation for specialization or continuing education exists.[105] Physicians are entitled to practise medicine during their total professional career.[106] However, the payment of higher fees to specialists promotes specialization. More than that, specialization becomes necessary because vacancies in the Social Insurances Schemes, the National Health Service or in other medical services are almost always open to physicians who have obtained a certificate of specialization. Education for specialization was organized by Decision No. DY 13/19338/1995 as completed by DY 13 c/econ 51948/1996.[107]

---

104. *Oikonomikos Taxydromos*, of 16 Mar. 1995, and personal research. According to Art. 18, para. 4 of L. 3232/2004, Hellene physicians and postgraduate students may be insured by TSAY.
105. But there are moral obligations according to Art. 10 of L. 3418/2005.
106. L. 1397/1983, L. 1579/1985, Art. 82 of L. 2071/1992, L. 2194/1994, Art. 10 of L. 3418/2005.
107. *See also* LD 3366/1955 and L. 2519/1997.

159. Articles 21 and 22 of Law 3418/2005, on medical deontology, stipulate that in the case when specialists are called in by a patient's physician for assistance, they are obliged to provide in writing the result of their examination. They should not have any other medical relation with the patient, and particularly on matters irrelevant to their specialization. Physicians are forbidden to claim competences not acquired by them through specialization. The use of a specialization by a non-specialist physician also has disciplinary consequences according to Article 319 of Law 4512/2018. The courts considering medical responsibility always take into account the specialization practised by a physician.[108]

160. Medical education for specific specializing training of physicians follows Council Directives of the European Communities. In the beginning, Council Directive No. 86/457 EEC of 15 September 1986 on specific training in general medical practice and now PD 38/2004 introducing Council Directives 2001/19, 1999/46, 1998/63, 1998/21 EC and 1993/16 EC oblige the Member States to institute the training, meeting at least the following minimum requirements:

(a) Entry shall be conditional upon the successful completion of at least six years' study of undergraduate and graduate medical training.
(b) It has to be a full-time course lasting at least three years, supervised by competent authorities or bodies. However, without prejudice to this principle of full-time training, Member States may authorize specific part-time training in general practice when the conditions mentioned in Article 5 (of the Directive) are fulfilled.
(c) It shall be practically rather than theoretically based. This practical instruction shall be given in licensed hospitals and licensed general medical practices or healthcare centres.
(d) There shall be a requirement of the personal participation of the trainee, who must have obtained the diploma of physician, in the professional activities and responsibilities of the persons with whom the candidate works.[109]

Council Directive No. 86/457 on specific training in general medical practice had been implemented after a proposition placed by KESY[110] which led to the introduction of PD 415/1994 and later of PD 38/2004.

Furthermore, YA 64843/2018 (Greek Official Gazette 4138/B/2018) increased the time of the specific training in general medical practice from four to five years, the scope of which now covers the following:

- The pathological cycle (sixteen months), i.e., ten months in pathology (emphasis on patients with multi-disease and chronic diseases such as hypertension, diabetes, coronary heart disease, chronic obstructive pulmonary disease, heart failure, renal failure, thyroid, gastrointestinal and musculoskeletal and gastrointestinal

108. *See also* Arts 83 and 84 of L. 2071/1992.
109. *See also* Art. 5 of PD 67/2000.
110. *See* L. 1278/1982 and Art. 13 of L. 2519/1997.

diseases of infectious diseases), six months of basic theoretical and clinical training in the management of common health conditions, acute and chronic diseases, problems related to other diseases of the Pathological Sector, in respective clinics, outpatient clinics and the Department of Emergency, Cardiovascular, skin (Dermatological), central and peripheral nervous system (Neurological), as well as in Physical Medicine and Rehabilitation.

- The surgical cycle (eight months), i.e., three months in General Surgery (basic theoretical and clinical training in the clinic, outpatient clinics and the Emergency Department in the management of routine surgical cases, in the basic principles of asepsis and antiseptic, the technique of suturing small fractures and performing small surgeries at the practice level) and five months of theoretical and clinical training in clinics, outpatient clinics and the Emergency Department related to the management of common acute and chronic diseases, problems and health conditions of sensory organs (ENT, Ophthalmology), urological, urological (M) system (Orthopaedic).
- The mother and child circle (four months), i.e., three months in paediatrics (basic theoretical and clinical training in the clinic, outpatient clinics and the Emergency Department in the management of common health conditions and diseases of childhood and adolescence, including developmental monitoring, nutritional problems and diseases of the cardiovascular, respiratory, digestive, urinary, musculoskeletal, infectious and febrile diseases, allergic and parasitic diseases) and one month in Obstetrics-Gynaecology (basic theoretical and clinical training in the clinic, in the outpatient clinics, in the delivery room and in the Emergency Department of the most common acute and chronic gynaecological diseases, including the basic principles of antenatal care, follow-up and obstetric emergencies, including childbirth and eclampsia as well as preventive medicine services and in particular the prevention of cervical and breast cancer).
- The mental health sector (three months), i.e., training in the Mental Health Department takes place in Psychiatric Clinics, mental health units and other community care structures for patients with mental disorders (basic theoretical and clinical training in outpatient clinics and the Emergency Department), as well as in emergency care services, chronic psychiatric illnesses and health conditions, including depression, generalized anxiety disorder, psychosis and dementia syndromes, treatments and prevention of psychosocial syndromes (in particular, alcoholism and psychoactive substance use, and their social rehabilitation).
- Laboratory Sector (two months), i.e., basic theoretical and clinical training in subjects of Biopathology and Medical Diagnostic Imaging.
- Primary Healthcare Cycle (twenty-seven months), i.e., one-month seminar of Introduction to Primary Health Care and General Medicine first year of speciality, one month of basic theoretical and clinical training in Emergency Pre-Hospital Medicine in collaboration with EKAB-first year of speciality, one (1) month Public Health seminar – fourth year of speciality.
- Final twenty-four months in training period in a health centre.

161. 161 Council Directive No. 75/363/EEC of 16 June 1975, concerning the coordination of provisions laid down by law, regulation or administrative action in respect of activities of physicians, regulated certain medical specializations. Also,

Council Directive 93/16/EEC, modified by Council Directive 97/50/EEC, influenced the preconditions and the form of medical practice for acquiring medical specializations in Hellas.

Twenty-four years after the entry into force of PD 415/1994, YA 64843/2018 brought an actual institutional change in the legal framework concerning medical specialization in Greece. In Circular No 72404/2018 by the Ministry of Health, Social Insurance and Social Solidarity (explaining provisions of YA 64843/2018), it is mentioned that doctors not listed will continue to practise accordingly with the provisions of PD 415/1994, which means that provisions of PD 415/1994 are still in force.

162. Those having already started specialization before YA 64843/2018 might follow the old regime. Their training leading to a qualification in specialized medicine should meet the following requirements at least:

(a) successful completion of six years' study within the framework of undergraduate and graduate training;
(b) comprising both theoretical and practical training;
(c) full-time course supervised by the competent authorities or bodies;
(d) in a university centre, in a teaching hospital or, where appropriate, in a health establishment approved for the purpose by the competent authorities or bodies;
(e) personal participation of the physician training to be a specialist in the activity and in the responsibility of the establishment concerned.

163. It is not allowed for a physician to use more than one specialization.[111] For acquiring any medical specialization, a period of practice, of at least six months, is spent at Rural (Agricultural) health centres and their dependent sub-centres. Physicians posted at rural health centres and their sub-centres are exempt from compulsory rural service.[112] The period of practice for each speciality at these centres or their sub-centres, the procedure for their posting and all details are being changed and are to be laid down by PDs.

Article 166 of Law 4600/2019 as specialized by YA 38377/2021 abolished the specialization committees and established a new system of national examinations in Greece for obtaining a speciality, organized by the PIS.

164. 164 The speciality of Work Medicine is now awarded according to PD 213/1986 and PD 415/1994.[113] Physicians with other specialities may no longer practise it. By YA 64833/2018, the speciality is renamed as Work and Environmental Medicine.

165. Special provisions for dentists and their specializations in gnathoplasty (gnathosurgery) and orthodontics are found in paragraphs 8, 9 and 10 of Article 20

111. Article 12, para. 1 of LD 3366/1955; Art. 2 of L. 1579/1985.
112. Article 4 of L. 1579/1985.
113. Article 20, para. 6 of L. 2519/1997. *See also* Art. 2, para. 6 of L. 3418/2005.

of Law 2519/1997 by which provisions of paragraph 2 of Article 5 of Law 2256/1994 are replaced and provisions of paragraph 8 of Article 38 of Law 1397/1983 are also applied to foreign dentists.[114]

166. Hence, general conditions for training and licensing of medical specialists and other details are found in acts, PDs and YAs.[115]

167. To be eligible for specialization, a physician has to submit an application. The placement of the physician for practice is by decision of the Ministers of Health and Social Solidarity and Finance. Placement is by order of priority according to a list to be drawn up in accordance with the relevant provisions.[116]

168. Military doctors may specialize in intensive care specializations at ESY hospitals.[117]

§3. Manpower Planning: Freedom of Establishment

169. Access to undergraduate medical education is subject to entrance examinations, and the competition is very high. One candidate with a certificate of higher education out of four or five candidates succeeds in entrance examinations to one of the medicine departments of Hellenic universities. Access to postgraduate education is also limited and only a small number of graduates with the highest degrees shall be admitted for receiving a postgraduate diploma or a doctoral degree. Nevertheless, the number of physicians having acquired a specialization is very high in Hellas.

170. The overproduction of medical scientists continues in greater numbers each year. To the provincial medical association of Thessaloniki, there belong more than 6,000 physicians, a ratio to population 1:130, whereas the ideal ratio proposed by WHO is 1:400 for all specializations. Since about 1980, a large number of specialized physicians have not been fully employed though they are spread all over the country, and medical fees are higher now.[118] But, according to the EU's proposed ideal ratio, the large number of Hellene physicians is appropriate for a population of 40,000,000 and not of 10,000,000.[119]

171. In Athens, a large number of physicians are receiving unemployment benefits, while at the Medical Association of Athens in 1995, 716 physicians had

114. *See also* Council Directives 78/686/EEC and 78/687/EEC.
115. For example, LD 3366/1955, PD 415/1994 and PD 379/1995.
116. Article 3 of L. 1579/1985.
117. Article 20, para. 4d of L. 2519/1997.
118. PD 127/2005.
119. G. Petropoulou, *Medical Population*, Iatrikos Typos, t. b', February 1995, 6; Iatriko Vima, May 1992.

declared themselves as unemployed.[120] The situation became worse. Annex 2 shows the ratio of inhabitants per doctor and available beds, as well as the average duration of treatment per patient.

172. About 1,800 Hellene physicians graduate from medical schools in Hellas and abroad yearly and are added to the number of physicians in Hellas. At the same time, about 600 physicians retire from practice, leaving each year a new surplus of 1,200 physicians. We should also mention that from 1984 to 2001, the population of Hellas increased by 9%, while the number of physicians increased by 144%.[121]

173. In accordance with Law 1975/1991, there exists no legal restriction regarding freedom of establishment. The Hellenic Government, in order to abide by the Directives of the European Community, issued PD 84/1986, by which Council Directives 75/362, 75/363 of June 1975, 81/1057 of 14 December 1981, and 82/76 of 26 January 1982 on the right of establishment in Hellas of physicians citizens of EU Member States had been incorporated into Hellenic legislation. At present, Council Directive 93/16/EEC (already modified by Council Directive 97/50/EEC) provides that physicians being citizens of the EU may practise medicine in Hellas after having received the special licence (visa) according to Hellenic legislation. Among the preconditions for acquiring the licence are:[122]

(a) a recognized medical document, described by Article 5, on the titles of degrees and attestations in the Member States, and Article 7, on the names of degrees and certificates of specializations in the EU Member States, which are recognized in Hellas;
(b) interested parties should indicate:
  - the least preconditions provided by Council Directives;
  - ethical preconditions and honourable behaviour for entering medical science and its practice according to the legislation of the Member States of origin;
  - not to be incompetent in practising medicine and their specialization;
  - acceptance of the responsibility to know the Hellenic language by signing a document according to Law 1599/1988.
(c) certificate of nationality.

174. The Hellenic Government may stop issuing or recall the licence of medical practice in the case that the parties do not prove to be of ethical or honourable behaviour by providing documents issued by their respective countries. Licences to

120. *Iatrikos Typos*, t. b', November 1995.
121. NSSG, CSYG 2009, pp. 34, 94 and personal research.
122. *See also* Council Directives 93/16/EEC, 97/50/EEC and paras 13, 14 of Art. 14 of Council Directive 2001/19 EC.

nationals who graduated abroad are awarded after passing examinations at the Hellenic National Academic Recognition Information Centre (DOATAP) in certain medical courses out of sixty-two courses included in the teaching programmes of Hellenic medical faculties.[123]

175. The competent authority for giving certificates or accepting diplomas or certificates of EU physicians, or to certify preconditions for the licence for practising medicine, is the prefecture of the occupational residence of the physician or of the area where the physician is to reside.[124]

123. *To Vima* of 26 May 1996 and personal research.
124. Article 22 of PD 84/1986.

Chapter 2. Practice of Medicine

§1. Legal Conditions for the Practice of Medicine

I. Historical Note on Healing Arts and Medicine

176. The first law of modern Hellas regulating the practice of medicine is the RD of 14–26 May/27 June 1834 concerning those persons in Hellas who were already practising medicine, surgery, dentistry, veterinary, pharmacy and obstetrics. The law was complemented by Law 241 of 7 December 1852/19 August 1853 on the creation of provincial doctors. After 1882, following the incorporation of newly liberated territories into Hellas, laws regulated the practice of medicine in the new lands, headed by Law 122 of 22–25 June 1882.

177. Important laws which changed, completed or annulled Articles of the law on the practice of medicine are: Law 463 of 18–20 February 1912 on the practice of medicine in Hellas; LD of 7–15 October 1925 on the compilation of a register including all doctors, pharmacists, dentists, veterinaries and midwives who practise throughout the land.; Compulsory Degree (CD) 1565 of 11–14 January 1939 on the code of practising the medical profession; LD 3366 of 20–23 September 1955 on the practice of the medical profession and medical specializations, and other provisions; LD 67 of 16–20 December 1968 on measures for the hygienic needs of the rural areas LD 1175 of 3–19 June 1972 on the turns of duty of physicians during Sundays and holidays as amended; Law 1397/1983 on the national health system as amended; PD 84 of 12–27 March 1986 and the Decision A4/1665/28 March–6 April 1990 by the Ministers of National Economy, Health and Social Insurances, on the freedom of establishment of physicians from EU Member States and the recognition of specializations according to EU Directives; Decision A4/econ. 3277 of 21–27 June 1990 by the Ministers of National Economy, Health and Social Insurances on the harmonization of Hellenic legislation with the provisions of Directive 86/457/EEC on special education for the specialization of general medicine; the Laws on the National Health System, headed by Law 1397/1983.[125]

178. There is a distinction between healing arts and medicine. Healing arts has a wider meaning as it comprises medicine, in which dentistry is included, when practised on human beings, as well as curative or preventive pharmacy.

II. Legal Monopoly of Physicians

179. According to Article 1 of Law 463 of 18–20 February 1912, no person may practise medicine in Hellas unless he/she holds a degree of Doctor of Medicine of the national university or equivalent. No person may practise dentistry unless that person abides by Article 7 of Law 463. The above means that physicians (of all

125. *See also* L. 2519/1997 and L. 3329/2005.

kinds) have a legal monopoly for the practice of medicine, being the only competent persons to practise every activity that is considered by law or jurisprudence as belonging to medicine.[126]

180. The monopoly of physicians accepts an exception concerning midwives. According to LD No. 2593 of 17–18 September 1953, on the practice of the occupation of midwife and the education of midwives, any person holding the diploma of midwife, awarded in accordance with Article 1 of the above LD, was authorized to practise normal (i.e., unproblematic) deliveries and other activities belonging to medicine, as they are laid down respectively in Article 11 of the above LD 2593/1953. New PD 262 of 12 December 2004 modified PD 266/2003 according to Council Directives 89/594, 89/595, 90/658 and 2001/19 EC.

181. The second exception concerns the practice of dentistry. Law 3038 of 17–25 August 1922 on the practice of the profession of dentist in Hellas, in Article 1, reads that the practice of dentistry is allowed only to holders of a degree of the School of Dentistry of the national University or to those persons who have been awarded, in accordance with the provisions promulgated by previous laws, the permission to licentiate in dental science. Holders of a diploma of dentistry issued by a foreign university may practise dentistry in Hellas, following the provisions of law. However, activities considered as belonging to dentistry may be practised by medical doctors if in that area there should be no dentist.[127]

182. The monopoly of physicians implies that every physician is competent to practise from the most simple to the most sophisticated medical activity. But differentiation and specialization are a necessity imposed by the great progress made by medicine in our days and the health system or the legislation which demands it.[128]

III. Legal Conditions for the Practice of Medicine

A. Legal Degree (Diploma)

183. The possession of the legal degree of doctor of medicine is the necessary requirement for the practice of medicine in Hellas. The legal degree of doctor of medicine is obtained on the award of academic degrees following the syllabi for university examinations according to law (unless one has been exempted therefrom or unless one has been assimilated with the holder of such a legal degree).[129]

126. *See also* Mandatory Act 1565/1939 and L. 1026/1980.
127. *See also* L. 1026/1980, Ch. 12 (Arts 38 and 39) of L. 3418/2005 and PD 235/1988.
128. *See also* Art. 10 of L. 3418/2005.
129. L. 1975/1991, ‘Part A’ of MA 1565/1939, Art. 12 of PD 84/1986 and Council Directive 2001/19 EC.

184. In Hellas, this requirement of a legal degree is found in Article 1 of Law 463 of 18–20 February 1912. Before this law, RD of 14–26 May/27 June 1834 had given the guidelines for those persons already practising medicine, surgery, dentistry, veterinary, pharmacy and obstetrics in Hellas. No legal provision prohibited at that time the practice of medicine without a degree. But since 1912, a physician, generally, a midwife, a nurse, a masseur and a disinfection worker have had to acquire a licence after registering their occupation with authorities. The prefecture and the local authorities had to register all persons practising medicine, or paramedics, in their territory.

1. Exemption from the National Legal Degree

185. For practising medicine in Hellas, a person must graduate from a medical school of a Hellenic university. According to Law 4512/2018, possessors of a degree in medicine of a medical school abroad are exempted and may participate in the legal procedure for obtaining the licence for practising medicine.[130]

186. If a person holds no degree at all, he/she is practising medicine illegally. Certain exemptions for humanitarian or scientific reasons were made by DOATAP.[131]

2. Assimilation Based on Mutual Recognition

187. PD 38/2010 implements into Greek legislation Directive 2005/36/EC on the recognition of professional qualifications and enables the free movement of professionals such as practitioners of medical profession. According to Article 21 of PD 38/2010, regarding the principle of mutual recognition, Greece recognizes evidence of formal qualifications as doctor giving access to the professional activities of doctor with basic training and specialized doctor, as nurse responsible for general care, as dental practitioner, as specialized dental practitioner, as veterinary surgeon and as pharmacist, listed in the Annex of the above-mentioned PD and should satisfy the minimum training conditions referred to in this PD respectively, and shall, for the purposes of access to and pursuit of the professional activities, give such evidence the same effect on its territory as the evidence of formal qualifications which it itself issues.

188. According to Article 24 of PD 38/2010, admission to basic medical training requires possession of a diploma or certificate providing access, for the studies in question, to universities. Furthermore, basic medical training shall comprise a total of at least six years of study or 5,500 hours of theoretical and practical training provided by or under the supervision of a university. The foreign degree, certificate or any other medical document has to be one of those mentioned in PD 38/2010.

130. *See also* L. 1975/1991.
131. Article 19 of L. 3328/2005 which replaced DIKATSA with DOATAP.

B. Licence (Permit, Visa)

189. According to Law 4512/2018, no one is allowed to use the title of doctor (*iatros*) for practising medicine, unless he/she has received a licence according to law. More precisely, according to Article 339 of Law 4512/2018, usurping the title of doctor is punished with imprisonment of up to one year and a fine of up to EUR 20,000. This licence was awarded by the Minister of Health and is now awarded by the PIS according to Article 271 of Law 4512/2018. The law is announced to the health centre and the provincial medical board which has under its jurisdiction the area in which the doctor intends to practise. It is also announced to the interested physician, and a protocol is signed verifying this announcement.

190. According to the above basic law, a physician, in order to receive the licence, has to submit certain qualification documents prescribed by the law, and the PIS has to verify and approve these qualifications.

1. Exemption from the Licence

191. Mandatory Act 1565/1939 in Article 3, paragraph 2b, determines that there is no obligation to obtain a licence by a doctor of foreign nationality who legally practises medicine abroad, in the case that he/she comes to visit a patient in Hellas. These physicians cannot visit a second patient, unless in council with another Hellene physician, who asks, for the particular case, permission from the relevant provincial medical board or the order of physicians. The same procedure is followed by a foreign doctor on holiday in Hellas.

192. A national of a Member State of EU may temporarily practise medicine, without the obligation to obtain a licence. That person has to inform the relevant authorities in advance, or afterwards in case of emergency.

2. Withdrawal of the Licence

193. According to Article 114 of Law 4600/2019, the validity of the licence is withdrawn in the following cases:

(a) if the doctor or dentist enters into guardianship or automatic permanent deprivation of his or her civil rights;
(b) after the opinion of the Supreme Disciplinary Council of Doctors or the Supreme Disciplinary Council of Dentists, if the certificate or the licence to practise the medical or dental profession has been granted by mistake;
(c) after the opinion of the Supreme Disciplinary Council of Doctors or the Supreme Disciplinary Council of Dentists, if for a continuous five years the doctor or dentist does not exercise the medical profession nor is he engaged in medical science;

(d) if the doctor or dentist has lost the ability to properly practise the medical profession due to physical or mental injury or illness or due to exhaustion of his physical or mental strength;
(e) if the doctor or dentist is irrevocably convicted of theft, fraud, embezzlement, forgery, counterfeiting, forgery, intentional homicide, child murder, crimes against sexual freedom, criminal exploitation for profiteering, for bribery, for kidnapping, as well as for the offences of Articles 221, paragraph 1 (issuance of false medical certification); 304 A (harm to a foetus or newborn); 304, paragraph (report) P.C.

194. The withdrawal of the licence in the above cases is preceded by an affirmative opinion of the Supreme Disciplinary Board.[132]

195. The physician under question may appeal to the secondary disciplinary board, and this shall stay the implementation of the decision. All decisions are to be communicated to the implicated parties and authorities. The attribution of the licence, being an administrative measure, is subject to the final judgment of the Supreme Administrative Court of Hellas.

196. When a decision to withdraw a licence has become definitive, the physician concerned is no longer legally competent to practise medicine. According to Law 4512/2018, the decision is immediately to be reported to the competent provincial medical association of the Order of Physicians, which must then erase the name of the physician concerned from the list of physicians practising medicine in its territory.

3. Restricted Licence

197. A disciplinary medical board may subject the maintenance of the licence to the acceptance of restrictions which it imposes if it is found that a physician is (disciplined as) unfit to practise for a period. This restricted licence limits the competence to practise.

C. Inscription on the List of the Order of Physicians

198. It is an offence for anyone to practise medicine or use the title of physician without being inscribed on the list of the Order of Physicians.[133]

---

132. *See also* Art. 36 of L. 3418/2005.
133. Article 35 of L. 3418/2005.

§2. Illegal Practice of Medicine

I. Legal Definition of the Offence

199. No one can carry out the practice of medicine in Hellas without holding the required diploma of doctor of the medical school of the national university or of equivalent or without being legally exempted from holding such.[134] Also, it is an offence if any person practises medicine without having obtained the practical permission of practising medicine in Hellas, or undertakes the therapy of pathologic illnesses or surgery without obtaining a licence of the medical board or without being inscribed on the list of the Order of Physicians.[135]

200. Medical students assisting a doctor or undertaking the activities of an assistant doctor, or who are directed by a doctor attending a patient, are excluded from the above obligation.

201. Law[136] defines the illegal practice of medicine and the activities belonging or not to the practice of medicine, as well as the unauthorized person.

II. Medical Activities

A. *General Remarks*

202. Article 7 of Law 463/1912 referred to the illegal practice of medicine by any person without a licence and, in order to describe the activities of that person, used the term 'undertaking the healing of pathologic or surgical illnesses' (or practising dentistry or midwifery activities) without giving a definition of these as a whole. Moreover, Article 9 reads that whosoever practises medicine illegally or misappropriates the title of doctor is liable to penalty.

203. There is a variety of laws which determine acts as belonging to the field of medicine, whenever this act has the purpose or the purported purpose in respect of a human being:[137]

(a) examination of a human being;
(b) detection of diseases and disabilities;
(c) establishment of a diagnosis;
(d) introduction or administration of any treatment or therapy of a pathological illness or condition, whether physical or mental, real or supposed;
(e) vaccination;

134. Article 1 of L. 463/1912, Part A of MA 1565/1939.
135. Article 7 of L. 463/1912; para. 6 of Art. 4 of MA 1565/1939.
136. Article 15 of MA 1565/1939.
137. Article 1 of L. 3418/2005.

(f) supervision of pregnancy, childbirth and puerperium, as well as any related procedure;
(g) the selection of the kind of dressings, bandages or bands and its scientific application;
(h) the publishing of cases and other medical opinions in the medical press; the name of the patient is not to be mentioned.

204. Paragraph 1 of Article 112 of Mandatory Act 1565/1939 determined the meaning of illegal practice of medicine. Whosoever does not meet the legal preconditions but who undertakes, even in the presence of a doctor, examination or therapy of patients, through personal activities or by oral or written advice, or by any kind of publication, this person was considered as practising medicine illegally and shall be punished by Article 111 of the same Act. Paragraph 2 considers as a therapeutic operation any act implemented for aesthetic reasons and during which a surgical appliance (truss) or mechanical apparatus is used which through physical or chemical elements may lead to the establishment of a diagnosis or exercise a physiological influence. According to Article 339 of Law 4512/2018 which abolished Mandatory Act 1565/1939, whosoever practises medicine illegally is liable to penalty by Article 339 of Law 4512/2018.

205. Several legal dispositions bestow certain activities upon physicians, regarding them as medical activities:

(a) the treatment of sexually transmissible diseases is considered a competence of physicians;
(b) the removal or transplantation of an organ can only be practised by a physician;
(c) the interruption of a pregnancy.

206. Certain medical acts in exceptional circumstances may be carried out by persons who are not legally authorized to practise medicine. These acts are:

(a) intravenous injections and venipunctures;
(b) the removal of any therapeutic substance of human origin such as blood cells, plasma and the like, which, however, has to be carried out by or under the direction of a physician.

B. Specific Medical Activities

1. Preventive Medicine

207. Certain acts are classed as preventive medicine. For example, RD of 3–12 May 1921 on the measures for the prevention of the spread of transmissible diseases, in Article 2, mentions among the medical activities of the physician, who is called upon to detect the disease and undertake the necessary research, those preventive medical and police measures intended to stop the spread of the disease.[138] In Hellenic legislation, healing acts comprise medicine in both its curative and preventive aspects.

208. In certain cases, for the administration of a treatment, preventive medical activities are not necessary, but for the examination of the state of health, the detection of diseases or the establishment of a diagnosis, preventive activities can be practised.[139] Hence for activities mentioned in the law as medical activities, preventive medicine belongs to the legal monopoly of physicians.

2. Self-Care

209. Self-care or self-help is not considered as illegal practice of medicine by anyone since the activities of self-help are practised by the person itself. Furthermore, relatives and neighbours who undertake care of a calming and simple nature, which does not require any special medical knowledge, are welcomed and not condemned. However, this general opinion has no legal foundation. Law does not make distinctions on the basis of the complexity of the activities nor on the practices of professionals, hence leaving this matter rather unclear.

210. On 27 February 1997, the European organizations of physicians headed by the Standing Committee of European Doctors (CPME) decided on the implementation of responsible and restricted self-medication. It permits the use of non-prescription medications by the patients themselves on their own initiative and responsibility. It enables the prevention and therapy of symptoms and trivial illnesses which do not require medical education. Of course, the right of diagnosis belongs solely to physicians and medications prescribable by physicians are described by EU Directive 92/26/EEC (Article 3.1). Self-medication is for the symptoms and has nothing to do with medical diagnosis; its duration should not be more than seven days.

211. We should mention here a natural and risk-free method of self-care which neither makes diagnoses nor heals illnesses: Reflexology. This liberates therapeutic strengths of the body which help in the relaxation of the human organism, and its restoration, giving the body the opportunity to harmonize its functioning.

3. Taking of Blood: Venipunctures

212. The blood donation system is organized in accordance with the provisions of Law 3402/2005.[140] The first Article of this Law stipulates voluntary blood

138. Article 13, para. 3 of L. 3418/2005.
139. YA No. C2 b 3312/1974 (para. 5a of Art. 2).
140. As completed and amended by L. 3527/2007, L. 3868/2010 and L. 4274/2014.

donation. Articles 2 to 8 describe the new body, the National Blood Donation Centre (EKEA), and define its aims, resources and organization. Article 10a deals with Blood Centres: blood donation services supervised by EKEA, while Article 10b deals with hospital-based donation services. Article 12 lists the conditions for the preservation of blood in private clinics, while Article 13 states the penalties to which offenders are liable. Article 14 refers to the Blood Donation Advisory Council, which is to assist the EKEA. The analysis of blood is an examination coming under the legal monopoly of physicians, but the taking of blood has been disputed. All Hellenic laws on organizing blood donation services consider it necessary that a physician should judge the suitability of blood donors. But the implementation of taking of the blood is delegated to health visiting nurses and paramedics, or a physician may delegate the implementation to specially trained technicians.[141]

213. LD No. 683 of 1–7 May 1948 on nurses, prescribing the list of services that may be carried out by nurses, the manner in which these services are to be carried out and the qualifications required for servicing in nursing care, in paragraph 2 of Article 3, forbids the implementation of any therapy by a nurse without a physician's delegation, except, among other services, the application of cupping vessels.

214. However, venipunctures as technical services in nursing care may be practised by nurses on the request of a physician. The courts have taken this point of view in Hellas, as in other European countries. A special case is the taking of blood samples for the purpose of determining the alcohol level, which is always to be performed by a physician.[142]

4. Radiographies

215. Radiography is a purely technical procedure, and the courts consider it as not belonging to the practice of medicine. The radiographer, though, may not use it for establishing a diagnosis, which as a practice of medicine is reserved to physicians.[143]

5. Blood Pressure Measurement and the Use of Other Simple Measuring Apparatus

216. The use of the sphygmomanometer and other simple apparatus to measure, for instance, heartbeat and pulsation in the context of self-examination and self-care cannot be considered as (illegal) practice of medicine: but if the apparatus is used

141. Article 11 of L. 1820/1988, Art. 53 of L. 2519/1997 and L. 3402/2005.
142. *See also* L. 3252/2004.
143. YA DYG3/2003, Art. 19 of L. 3293/2004.

to examine the state of health of another person, this can be considered as an act of medicine reserved to physicians.

6. Eye-Examination and the Measurement of Eye-Deviation

217. An optician may measure deviations of the eye following the subjective method. Different opinions have been recorded from the courts as to whether an optician may use described objective methods that involve apparatus such as an ophthalmometer, a scianscope, etc. The optician should not establish a diagnosis, consider or interpret causes, and so on, as this is an act of medicine reserved to physicians.

7. Psychoanalysis and Psychotherapy

218. There are diverging opinions on the question of whether psychoanalysis and psychotherapy are acts of medicine. It is questionable whether the use of verbal and non-verbal forms of communication is a treatment, as well as whether psychoanalysis and psychotherapy are directed towards a pathological state. Positive legal answers are not available yet. There is the opinion that a psychoanalyst does not perform acts of medicine but behaves as a friend or spiritual advisor. But there is also the opinion that relaxation and hypnosis sessions are to be considered as acts of medicine when they aim at influencing the mental state of the persons concerned so that their self-confidence grows stronger.

8. Group Therapy

219. Group therapy was not considered as belonging to the field of medicine because of its technique, which was a group-oriented approach. Nowadays, this consideration is out of date, and a group-oriented approach may be of therapeutic value for an individual patient. Therefore, group-oriented diagnostic or therapeutic procedures are also included in the field of medicine.

9. Written and Oral Advice and Recommendations

220. Written and oral advice and recommendation concerning diseases and their treatment are not considered as acts of medicine. However, if these acts concern one specific disease, are directed towards a defined group of patients and contain very detailed prescriptions, all these elements together might constitute (illegal) practice of medicine.[144]

144. Article 1, paras 2 and 3 of L. 3418/2005.

10. Non-conventional Medicine and Medical Techniques

221. Acupuncture is a well-known type of non-conventional medicine and a medical technique. The field of non-conventional or alternative medicine includes chiropractic, homeopathy, homosophic medicine, traditional Chinese medicine including acupuncture-shiatsu, therapy by natural means such as electro-acupuncture, osteopathy, and others. Medical associations have decided to oppose future recognition of non-conventional medicine. In Hellas, certain physicians, as well as the member of the European Parliament and physician professor Dr A. Trakatellis, consider that cooperation between physicians and practical doctors (alternative practitioners) should begin following the responsible organization of all sectors of non-conventional medicine, as the existence of these is a de facto reality. Moreover, it may answer the question of the climate of a legal toleration which exists towards those techniques and other sectors of non-conventional medicine in European countries.[145]

222. In Hellas, there is a climate of toleration, but a practical doctor officially recognized in another Member State will have difficulties in practising medicine. In 1996, the Hellenic society of acupuncturists had about 230 members, all physicians (including 40 dentists). All these Hellene physicians accept the diagnostic methods of modern medicine and consider acupuncture a medical act practised only by physicians, independent of their specialization. There is also a small number of persons who practise acupuncture without being physicians.

III. An Unauthorized Person

223. The description of the conditions for the practice of medicine as prescribed by law may help the court to decide who is an unauthorized person.[146]

IV. Illegality

224. Article 7 of Law 463/1912 on the practice of the medical profession in Hellas and more recent laws consider as illegal practice of medicine any case when a person without a licence undertakes the therapy of a pathologic illness or conducts surgery. These acts are an offence and do not have to concern different patients. Medical acts are not required by law to be performed in a professional way.

225. Law considers it as a repetition of the act when a person has already been convicted of the same act or for an act of the same character. Moreover, the law considers it as an illegal practice of medicine when a person illegally assumes the title of physician (any title or specialization legally protected) in order to make people

145. A. Ahang et al., *Are the Clinical Effects of Homeopathy Placebo Effects?*, Lancet, 366, 2005, 726–732. *The End of Homeopathy*, Lancet, 366, 2005, 690.
146. Article 111 of MA 1565/1939.

believe that the person is a competent physician. The misappropriation of the title constitutes the element of the offence of illegal practice.

V. Sanctions

226. Article 36 of Law 3418/2005 provides for a penalty from fifteen days at least to six months' confinement and/or a fine from EUR 50,000 to EUR 200,000 by a YA after an opinion given by the National Board of Medical Ethics and Deontology. The same law refers also to the illegal practice of dentistry and provides similar penalties and fines.[147]

147. *See also* Arts 111 et seq. of MA 1565/1939, paras 1 and 3 (new) of Art. 52 of L. 1026/1980 and paras 10 and 11 of Art. 38 of L. 3418/2005.

Chapter 3. Control over the Practice of Medicine

§1. The Order of Physicians

227. The Order of Physicians was established by LD of 17–29 October 1923. This decree as well as two others, of 1923 and 1925, were abolished by Article 57 of PD of 5–7 March 1934. Another basic law was LD of 13–19 November 1925 on the establishment of the Order of Physicians. It was amended frequently up to 1943. In 1943, Law 767/43 amended Article 77 of Mandatory Act 1565/1939 and especially Article 25 of LD 698/1941. CD 1843 of 14–19 June 1951 amended and complemented provisions of CD 1565/39 on the code of practice of the medical profession.

228. Other basic laws have been: RD of 11 October/7 November 1957, which complemented and codified provisions on the Councils of Physicians; LD 3895 of 10–11 November 1958 on codifying provisions on the Councils of Physicians; LD 4111 of 9 October 1960 on amending and complementing provisions concerning the order of physicians, medical and paramedical professions, social insurance of medical personnel, pharmaceuticals and other provisions for public hygiene.

229. Law 727 of 6–13 October 1977 on amending certain provisions concerning legislation on the Panhellenic Order of Physicians and provincial medical associations has been amended especially by Law 1425/1984, but still includes the main provisions on the PIS and the Supreme Disciplinary Council in Hellas.[148] The PIS is finally regulated by Law 4512/2018 which abolished MA 1565/1939.

I. Registration on the List of the Order

A. Obligation to Register on the List

230. Law 463 of 18–20 February 1912 in Article 4 already provided that each doctor, dentist and midwife within a month of taking up residence in a city or village is obliged to declare their identity to the local authorities. Article 5 of the same law provided that each year the prefectural or local authorities keep a register in which names, surnames, place of residence, year and issuing body of the certificate or the doctor's degree are recorded.

231. A little later, LD of 7–15 October 1925, on the keeping of State registers of physicians, pharmacists, dentists, veterinary surgeons and midwives, provides for the compulsory registration of all persons who legally practise the medical profession (and midwifery) in each prefecture where they reside, and their registration with the Ministry of Health, Social Insurance and Social Solidarity.

148. Article 85 of L. 1026/1980 and Art. 20 of L. 2071/1992.

232. The Order of Physicians shall include all doctors in medicine, surgery and obstetrics who are permanently resident in Hellas and who are obliged to enter on the register of their province. All doctors in each province legally residing and practising medicine, or having acquired a position for which the medical degree is a precondition (e.g., physicians, professors, members of the Faculty of Medicine), are obliged to be on the register of their province and constitute the Provincial Medical Order.[149]

233. According to paragraph 2 of Article 2 of RD of 11 October/7 November 1957, provincial medical orders are legal persons of public law, not free associations but compulsory organizations; there is one such order established in the same location as each health centre. In accordance with paragraph 3 of the aforementioned RD, the medical orders take their name from the city where it is established.

B. *Exceptions*

1. Non-nationals of EU Member States

234. Physicians of a foreign nationality who legally practise medicine in their respective countries, but who are not nationals of EU countries, may visit a patient in Hellas, and may do so without registering on the list of the Order, and no licence is required. They may not visit a second patient except in conference with a Hellene physician and after an application by the Hellene doctor to the competent authorities of the provincial order (in urgent cases, the application should be made as soon as possible after the services rendered). The same procedure shall be followed by any physician residing for any reason in Hellas. Visiting foreign physicians are not registered on the list of the Order, but they are subject to the jurisdiction of the Order for their activities and conduct on Hellenic territory.[150]

2. Nationals of EU Member States

235. Nationals of a Member State who work as physicians in their respective countries may freely reside and provide medical services in Hellas after receiving a licence for practising medicine according to Hellenic legislation. Preconditions for acquiring the licence are: application by the interested physician, degree or any other certificate according to the law (titles of degrees and other certificates issued by Member States of EU and names of titles and certificates of medical specializations recognized in Hellas) on practising medicine, having acquired a specialization or not.[151]

---

149. Article 2, para. 1 of RD of 11 Oct./7 Nov. 1957; Art. 145 of L. 2071/1992; *see also* StE 3826/2009, StE 3827/2009 on the constitutionality of the provision.
150. Article 3 of MA 1565/1939 and L. 1975/1991.
151. PD 84/1986 and PD 38/2004, PD 38/2004 was abolished by PD 38/2010, which harmonized the Hellenic legislation to: (a) Directive 2005/36/EC of the European Parliament and the Council of 7

236. The interested physicians shall have at least the minimum preconditions found in Directive 93/16/EEC, as modified by Directives 97/50/EEC and 2001/19/EC, on acquiring degrees, certificates or other medical specializations. They shall also have preconditions of ethics and honesty as prescribed by the country's legislation for entering and practising medicine (or any other certificate issued by the Member State to testify the above). They shall not be under a court bar or injunction. They shall have the necessary knowledge of the Hellenic language for practising medicine and/or their medical specialization. They must produce a certificate of proving their nationality.

3. Military Doctors

237. Military physicians are obliged to enter on the list of the Order if they practise medicine outside their military duties. Article 6 of LD 67/1968 refers to physicians who are undertaking their obligatory military service. Until their discharge from their service, they may serve temporarily at Agricultural Medical Centres, hygienic stations or medical institutions.[152]

C. The Obligation to Register and the Freedom of Association

238. According to Hellenic law, all physicians practising medicine are obliged to register on the list of the Order. This obligation has nothing to do with the freedom of association which is a voluntary free decision taken by the physician to become or not a member of a trade organization. This freedom of association is protected especially by Articles 12 and 23 of Hellenic National Constitution and other Hellenic laws (e.g., Law 1264/1982), as well as European legislation (e.g., paragraph 1 of Article 11 of the European Convention on Human Rights). The obligatory Hellenic Order of Physicians is a legal person under public law, founded by the legislature to serve public order. It is a public law institution integrated within the structures of the State in promoting national health policies. The European Forum of National Medical Associations (NMAs) and WHO, meeting in London 23–24 March 1995, reaffirmed the duty and obligation of NMAs to give considered advice to those responsible for the formulation of health policies in their countries as key partners in the provision of advice on health policy.[153]

Sep. 2005 on the recognition of professional qualifications which sets the rules regulating the undertaking and the execution of a legally regulated profession, the qualifications that have been obtained in one or more Member States (thereof Member States of origin) and provide to the holder the right to execute this profession; (b) Directive 2006/100/EC of the Council of 20 Nov. 2006 on adapting certain Directives on the field of free movement of persons, be reason of the accession of Bulgaria and Romania for the part that this Directive amends Directive 2005/36/EC; (c) Directive 2013/25/EU of the Council of 13 May 2013 on adapting certain directives in the field of right of establishment and freedom to provide services, by reason of the accession of the Republic of Croatia for the part that this Directive amends Directive 2005/36/EC.

152. Article 23, para. 4 of L. 2071/1992.

153. *Iatriko Vima*, March–April 1995, 20, Arts 3 and 35 of L. 3418/2005.

239. The Order of Physicians and/or the provincial medical associations and/or lately (Law 3252/2004) the Union of Care Personnel of Hellas, like Bars of Lawyers, Chambers of Commerce, etc., are not free trade organizations but compulsory institutions pursuing an aim of general public interest. Hence, the Order (as with the Bars of Lawyers or the Chambers of Industry, etc.) cannot be considered as a free organization protected by legislation safeguarding the freedom of association. However, a recent amendment in Law 4512/2018, Article 271, introduced the phrase '*of a trade union character*' that may attribute to the Greek Order of Physicians (or PIS) a double character, both of a trade union and a compulsory institution. For that reason, when we refer to the Order of Physicians, we use the term 'association' (*syllogos*) contrary to the term 'council' (as in the case of the British Medical Council).

240. Physicians may become members of their free trade organizations, formed to protect their professional interests, as lawyers or mechanics are free to become or not become members to their respective trade organizations. However, registration with their respective Bar or Order or Chamber is obligatory, and they are subject to the authority of their disciplinary organs. There is a clear distinction between the obligation (registration with the Order) and the right (membership of a free-formed association, e.g., the Association of Hospital Physicians of Athens and Pireas, EINAP). At a European level, the CPME is a trade-free organization having acquired its rulebook at the meeting of the national delegations in Athens on 10–12 April 1997.

D. Competent Provincial Medical Association

241. According to Article 293 of Law 4512/2018, physicians who practise the medical profession in Greece are required to be registered as a member of a medical association. In particular, physicians who are professionally established in public health services, i.e., the doctors of the National Health Service, hospital or primary health care, the doctors of the field services, the university doctors, the military doctors, the doctors of its fixed structures or insurance organizations, are required to register with the Medical Association where they practise their profession and their service is located. Physicians cannot practise medicine if they do not have the status of a member of a Medical Association or if they are not registered in the special registers. Physicians may practise their medical activities in another city or village if they obtain the relevant permission from their Medical Association, and they register at the relevant list of the Medical Association they wish to practise their activities and pay special fees.

242. In accordance with paragraph 3 of Article 293 of Law 4518/2018, occupational doctors are allowed to offer medical services in provinces different to the one that they are member of without a permit from the provincial medical association of the place of the offer under conditions.[154]

154. *See infra* para. 271.

E. Refusal or Delay of Registration

243. In accordance with Article 293 of Law 4518/2018, membership of a provincial association is obligatory for all physicians permanently residing in the respective territory and practising the medical profession. Permanent political or military staff being physicians, who are not allowed by law to practise medicine in private, should be members of the provincial association, but have no right to vote or be voted into office in its organs. Foreign physicians who practise in Hellas are obligatory members of a provincial association.[155] *Homogenis* (foreign citizens considered as Hellenes by right of descent) have this right.[156] Physicians who are EU citizens have all the rights of a member, but they may not stand for the administration of the Council.

244. The physician has to register on the list of the provincial association within a period of two months from publication of the licence (visa) according to paragraph 3 Article 295 of Law 4518/2018. Before their registration, physicians are not permitted to practise medicine.[157]

245. The provincial association may refuse or defer entry on the register if the physician applying has been guilty of crimes or serious misconduct damaging to reputation or dignity according to law. Appeal against such a decision of a provincial association may be heard by the appeal council and/or the Supreme Administrative Court in Athens.

246. In accordance with Article 145 of Law 2071/1992, physicians who practise medicine within the area of a provincial association under any kind of labour relation or occupy a position requiring a medical degree are obliged to register on the list of the respective and only provincial association within a month of their arrival at that place. Their refusal to enter the list is considered a disciplinary offence and is punished according to law.

F. Re-registration after Removal from the Register

247. According to Article 63 of RD of 11 October/7 November 1957, in each provincial association, a disciplinary council is organized for disciplinary activities, at a first-level, and the Supreme Medical Disciplinary Council (APSI) in Athens, mostly at a second-level, without forgetting the Supreme Administrative Court of

155. *See* PD 84/1986. They have no right to be voted into office.
156. Article 3, para. 1 of L. 1425/1984.
157. Article 5, para. 3 of RD of 11 Oct./7 Nov. 1957.

Athens for final appeals. The disciplinary council may decide on the temporary suspension from the practice of a physician from one month to three years.[158] A problematic request for registration has to be decided upon by the competent provincial disciplinary council.

G. Removal from the List

248. Hellenic law allows the removal of the names of physicians from the list and the annulment of their licence if that they have permanently lost their political rights by a court decision or they have been put under a court bar or injunction. These are the cases when the physician no longer fulfils the conditions for practising medicine for reasons of physical or mental disability and the provincial medical association has so decided and notified this decision to the Order. Furthermore, the resignation of a physician from practising medicine is a cause for removing his/her name from the list, at his/her own request, after a YA notified to the respective administrative office and the respective provincial medical association of the Order of Physicians.[159]

249. There are also cases where the licence is recalled after a decision of the Minister of Health, Social Insurance and Social Solidarity published in the State Gazette:

(a) when the licence was issued by mistake concerning the existing preconditions for issuing it;
(b) when the physicians have not practised medicine for a continuous period of five years and they have been absent from scientific practice for the same period;
(c) when the physician because of loss or weakness of physical or mental fitness has lost the medical ability and does not give necessary guarantees that he/she is able to continue to practise the profession;
(d) when the physician is convicted in case of relapse of a misdemeanour that entails the loss of his political rights or for the breach of Compulsory Act 1075/1938.

In the above cases (b) and (c), the request for a new registration is admissible after a previous affirmative opinion is given by the APSI.[160]

250. According to Article 8 of the above law, the right to practise medicine or to be registered after being struck off the register in the cases of annulment or recall of the licence, the right is re-established by a new licence, when the reasons which led to annulment or removal no longer exist.

---

158. During the period of temporary suspension, the physician has no right to vote or be voted into office. *See* Art. 23 of the above RD of 1957 and L. 1425/1984.
159. Article 5 of MA 1565/1939 and Art. 10 of the above RD.
160. Article 7 of MA 1565/1939 and Art. 6 of the above RD of 1957.

251. The names of physicians can be removed ex officio when they have died or have definitely left Hellas without asking for their names to be removed. It is also accepted that a provincial association remains competent to discipline physicians whose names have been removed at their own request for misconduct committed before the removal.[161]

H. Maintenance of Registration Subject to Restrictions

252. In the case that a provincial medical board has made and notified a decision that it is necessary to place restrictions on the practice of medicine by physicians for reasons of their physical or mental disability or, because of the exhaustion of their physical or mental powers, they are not able to practise and do not give the necessary guarantees for practising medicine, the competent medical association makes the maintenance of their names on the list subject to observance of the restrictions ordered. In the above cases, the request for re-registration on the list of the competent provincial association requires the previous positive opinion of the APSI.[162]

II. Disciplinary Competence of the Order of Physicians

A. Control over the Observance of the Rules of Professional Conduct

1. General Description of the Disciplinary Competence

253. An important function of the provincial medical associations of the Order of Physicians is to ensure observance of the duties and obligations imposed upon their medical members. Any misconduct in or in connection with the above duties and obligations committed by physicians is considered disciplinary misconduct to be judged and punished by the respective disciplinary board of the provincial association by a disciplinary penalty, independent of any other liability or consequence according to the law.[163]

254. Among the general duties of a physician, law[164] defines:

> A doctor is called upon to be the very example of an honest and blameless person in every manifestation of his/her private and public life, practicing medicine conscientiously and in accordance with the law and behaving in a manner that reinforces the worth and trust that the medical profession should inspire. The doctor's behaviour, appearance, language, work and exemplary mode of

161. Article 10 of the above RD of 1957.
162. *See also* Arts 7–9 of the above RD of 1957.
163. Article 57 of the above RD.
164. Articles 13–22 of MA 1565/1939; L. 2071/1992, *see also* StE 3697/1986, Armenopoulos 1987, 334 and Art. 2 of L. 3418/2005.

life should attract respect for his/her honour and worth as a person and for the honour and worth of the medical profession as a whole. Any act or omission in relation to the above duty shall be censured in accordance with the gravity of the misconduct and with the relevant provisions of code of medical practice. The correct interpretation of the above disposition is that any misconduct outside or inside the realm of professional activity of physicians (the seriousness of which shall be judged by the disciplinary council) which has acquired a certain level of publicity, for instance in the media, may be taken as a disciplinary offence. Even in the case that only the personal honour or dignity of the physician is damaged, and not the reputation or dignity of the profession, it may be professional misconduct which needs to be disciplined.[165]

255. Article 1 of the Code of Medical Deontology solves a difficulty in the difference between misconduct in or in connection with the practice of the profession and misconduct committed outside professional activity. Serious misconduct is not required for a sanction to be imposed if the behaviour of physicians or their appearance or their acts or their way of life is not considered a respectable conduct. Of course, it is a matter of discretion for the disciplinary councils to avoid legally imposing a disciplinary sanction, as an act which may have been assessed as possible misconduct may, in fact, be an activity coming under the constitutional freedom of physicians, more specifically freedom of opinion.

2. Rules of Professional Conduct and Standards of Discretion, Probity and Dignity

256. The organs of the provincial medical associations of the Order of Physicians, and concerning appeals, the appeals council, base their disciplinary decisions on legal structures, and especially on the regulations of RD of 11 October/7 November 1957, of Law 4512/2018 which abolished MA 1565/1939, the Code of Medical Deontology, regulations of certain medical laws, of the Internal Code of the respective provincial association and the decisions of the disciplinary councils, of the Supreme Administrative Court in Athens, on the regulations of the European Code of Medical Deontology and of other legal acts. The above comprise the main sources for medical disciplinary regulations and procedures.

a. The Code of Medical Deontology

257. The Hippocratic Oath is the original guide to medical deontology in Hellas. Its principles have been implemented continuously for about twenty-five centuries. Hellene candidate doctors take it as a part of their graduation. In modern Hellas, PD of 1–19 March 1926 introduced the temporary Code of Deontology for the medical profession. It was abolished by RD of 25 March/6 July 1955 on the Code of Medical Deontology. CD 1565/1939 on the Code of Practicing the Medical

165. *See also* Art. 6 of L. 2194/1994 and Art. 9 of L. 2345/1995.

Profession in Article 27 imposed on the PIS the establishment of a code of deontology on the professional duties and obligations of physicians and other stipulations for safeguarding the honour and dignity of the medical profession. The Association responded by presenting a code of deontology which became the above RD of 1955, having stipulations obligatory to all physicians practising medicine in Hellas. In 1988, the PIS prescribed a draft of a new code of deontology, but this proposal had not been declared binding by law. A little later, Article 62 of Law 2071/1992 provided for a PD that would order the drawing up of a new code of deontology, but nothing followed, leaving the Code of Deontology of 1955 to suffice up to the year 2005.

258. The Code of 1955 contained the rules concerning the duties of physicians towards their patients and their relations with colleagues, dentists, pharmacists and allied health professionals. The Code formulated the bases on which the social obligations of physicians were built. It determined which acts of advertising or clauses were not compatible with the therapeutic freedom of physicians. The old Code of Medical Deontology of 1955 was composed of six titles and forty-seven Articles: Title one contained some general dispositions regarding general obligations and duties (Article 1), prohibitions on cooperations (Article 2), advertisements (Articles 3 and 5),[166] malpractice of the occupation (Article 6). Title two related the physician with the service of the patients and concerned the physician-patient relationship (Articles 7, 8, 9 and 10),[167] the organizing of a medical association (Article 11), the right of the patient to replace the physician (Article 12), the right of the physician to deny services to the patient under certain circumstances (Article 13), the obligation not to interfere in family or religious matters (Article 14), the duty to medical secrecy (Article 15). Title three dealt with the physician at the service of the community, medical cooperation with authorities for the protection of public health, and contained the social and economic responsibilities of the physician (Articles 16 and 17), and the strict observance of medical secrecy (Article 18).

259. Title four treated relations between physicians and dealt with collegiality and relations based on dignity (Articles 19 and 20), or socializing (Articles 21 and 22), prohibitions on the practice of medicine by a replacing physician (a *locum tenens*) (Articles 23, 24, 25 and 26), the organization of a medical consulting body (Articles 27, 28, 28, 30 and 31), or the treating of a second physician (Articles 32 and 33), prohibition of practising pharmacy or dentistry by a physician (Article 25). Title five related to the medical fee, and dealt with the proper fee and relations with pharmacists, dentists, veterinarians, midwives, nurses, paramedical professionals, etc. (Article 36), the denial of receiving a fee from colleagues or their dependent relatives (Article 37), the determination of equitable wages from different patients (Articles 38, 39, 40, 41, 42 and 43) to different physicians (Articles 44 and 45).1 Title six, finally, related the physicians to their provincial medical association of which the physicians were members, and dealt with their duties and obligations towards the association with which they were registered (Article 46), which duties

166. *See also* Art. 41 of L. 1379/1983.
167. *See also* Art. 5 of L. 2345/1995.

the physicians had to obey and how they had to serve the good functioning of their medical associations and their disciplinary councils (Article 47).

260. After fifty years, Law 3418/2005 is the law which introduced the present Code of Medical Deontology in Hellas. Law 3418 of 28 November 2005 on the Code of Medical Deontology contains forty-six Articles grouped into twelve chapters. Chapter 1 covers meanings, definitions, and the field of application of the Code (Article 1). Chapter 2 lays down the general rules for the practice of the medical profession, referring to this as function (Article 2), and refers to the ethical and scientific independence of the physician (Article 3), to ensuring the quality, safety and effectiveness of medical practice (Article 4), to the reliability of medical certification and opinion (Article 5) as amended by paragraph 2 of Article 6 of Law 3627/2007, to the impediments and conflicts of the medical profession and to its place of practice (Article 7).

261. By paragraph 1 of Article 29 of Law 3996/2011, paragraph 5 was added to Article 7 of the aforementioned law which allows the offer of medical services from occupational doctors to different provinces without the permit of the respective provincial associations. Chapter 3 covers the relationship between physician and patient, attaching great importance to behaviour such as will place medicine in a position of trust and respect (Article 8). Article 9 deals with the obligations of the physicians towards the patient, which obligations have to do with continuing professional and scientific education, awareness of other branches of science, and professional cooperation (Article 10), the necessity of informed consent by patients (Article 12), the maintenance of medical secrecy (Article 13) and medical records (Article 14), always maintaining respect for human life and the patient's dignity (Article 15). Chapter 4 records the relations between physician and community, referring to his/her social function (Article 16), the avoidance of any form of advertising or of imprudent appearance in the mass media (Article 17), as complemented by Law 3599/2007, or on the internet (Article 18). Medical fees or rewards are referred to (Article 19), as is the practice of medicine within the framework of social insurance (Article 20), as complemented by paragraph 3 of Article 29 of Law 3996/2011. Chapter 5 defines the correct relations of the physician with his/her colleagues and refers to the relations of the physician with other personnel (Article 21) as well as with colleagues sitting on medical associations (Article 22). Chapter 6 is dedicated to education and training and defines the role of the physician in the educational process (Article 23). Scientific research is covered in Chapter 7; research using human subjects is permitted under certain preconditions (Article 24), while clinical study of new pharmaceuticals, diagnostic methods and therapeutic methods is permitted only in accordance with those limiting terms that the law may determine (Article 25). Non-therapeutic biomedical research is permitted under conditions (Article 26), as is the publication of findings (Article 27).

262. Chapter 8 defines the role of the physician in mental health care (Article 28). Chapter 9 covers various specific issues, such as the decision that the patient's life has ended (Article 29), the decisions that a physician must take in case of incurable illness (Article 30), the artificial interruption of pregnancy (Article 31), the transplantation of tissues or organs (Article 32), blood donation (Article 33) and the protection accorded to genetic identity (Article 34). Chapter 10 describes the duties of a physician towards the medical association and defines his/her relationship with the same (Article 35). Chapter 11 deals with penalties for breaches of the Code (Article 36) and makes reference to the expiration of the validity of the previous, 1955, Code (Article 37). Finally, Chapter 12 contains provisions to do with dentists (Articles 38 and 39), with the improvement of the income of the Organization for the Care of State-sector Insured Persons (Article 40), with situations that concern only certain physicians (Article 41) and with physicians in certain specific circumstances (Article 42). This chapter also covers the amendment of articles in previous legislation (Articles 43, 44 and 45). The final Article, 46, covers the coming into force of the Code, with its publication in the State Gazette (28 November 2005).

b. The Code of Practice of the Medical Profession: CD 1565 of 11–14 January 1939

263. The Decree of 1939 on the practice of medicine contains certain obligations, the compliance with which has been made a disciplinary matter by the legislator. This is the case of the obligation to practise their duties with dignity (Article 13), not itinerantly (Article 14), not other than from their established place of practice (Article 15). Physicians are not allowed to practise while on vacation (Article 16), at two medical residencies (Article 17) or at a pharmacist's or from commercial premises (Article 18). Physicians shall not be allowed to practise other occupations limiting their medical practice or dignity (Article 19) or to use a public health office where they serve for their own purposes (Article 20). Physicians shall give the public authorities any assistance, information and certificates about their observations concerning persons asking for public help and insurances (Article 21). Physicians are not permitted to issue certificates or medical prescriptions, without mentioning the purpose, the names, etc., or to advertise their practice (Article 22).[168] Physicians shall keep medical secrecy (Article 23), serve with dignity (Article 24), any time of day and night as law prescribes (Article 25), without advertising their practice (Article 26).[169]

MA 1565/1939 was abolished by Article 341 of Law 4512/2018 which is still in force as amended by Law 4565/2018, Law 4633/2019, Law 4690/2020 and Law 4771/2021.

168. *See also* Art. 122 of L. 2071/1992.

169. *See also* Art. 6 of L. 2194/1994 and Art. 2 of L. 2256/1994 as it was complemented by Art. 9 of L. 2345/1995.

c. RD of 11 October–7 November 1957 on Amending, Complementing and Codifying Provisions of MA 1565/1939, Concerning Medical and Disciplinary Councils

264. Legally determined rules of professional conduct are found in Articles 57 et seq. of the above RD. They refer to disciplinary councils, their functioning, define the disciplinary offence, describe procedural topics and refer to the organization and functioning of the APSI in Athens.

d. Other Rules of Professional Conduct

265. According to paragraph 8 of Article 37 of Law 2519/1997, the Councils for the assessment and selection of ESYKA physicians will also consider their professional conduct, in accordance with the internal code of the hospital.

e. Stipulations of the Internal Codes of the Provincial Associations

266. Stipulations of the internal codes of the provincial medical associations are rules of professional conduct and standards of discretion, probity and dignity, besides those found in the Code of Professional Conduct or in jurisprudence.

f. The Precedent Authority of Disciplinary Decisions

267. The judgments of the different provincial associations are crucial because they play the most important role in the elaboration of rules concerning professional conduct and standards of discretion, probity and dignity. Certain rules of professional deontology will need to follow changes in society and incorporate new standards and improvements in medical science. In 1988, the PIS announced the drawing up of a draft code on medical deontology after many discussions influenced by the experience accruing from decisions of the disciplinary councils. Although the draft code proposed alterations on many topics, it did not receive acceptance, and the whole work was set aside. By Article 62 of Law 2071/1992, a PD charged the responsible Hellenic Medical Association with the preparation of a new code (the process initiated by Article 62 was materialized in 2005 as Law 3418/2005).

g. Supervision of Decisions by the Minister of Health, Social Insurance and Social Solidarity

268. According to Articles 54–56 of RD of 11 October/7 November 1957, the Minister of Health, in his duty of supervision of all provincial medical associations and the national association, may bring proceedings against, after his personal decision and a call for pleading, independent of any disciplinary proceedings, any member of the provincial associations and Panhellenic association who does not abide by the provisions of this law or of any other legal act, decision, circular, etc. The Minister may suspend members of the boards of medical associations or the whole board of a medical association for serious reasons according to his judgment and impose upon a directive committee the handling of running matters and the organizing of the elections for a new board within six months.

h. The European Code of Medical Deontology

269. The NMAs of EU approved the European Code of Medical Deontology at their meeting on 6 January 1987. The European Code defines the professional conduct of physicians among themselves with their patients and towards the general public. The Code is applicable in parallel to existing national codes and other legislation. The European Code of Medical Deontology is composed of thirty-three articles.

270. A physician's function is to protect the bodily and mental health of people and to relieve pain with respect to life, human dignity, without any discrimination by colour, religion, nationality, social status, political ideology or other such criteria during times of peace or of war (Article 1). There are some general obligations and duties of physicians towards patients (Articles 2 and 3) about notifying patients and their consent (Article 4). The following Articles deal with professional ethics and self-independence (Articles 5 and 6), medical secrecy (Articles 7 and 8), medical specialization (Articles 9, 10 and 11), assistance to patients in terminal illnesses (Article 12), replantation of organs (Articles 13, 14 and 15), reproduction and contraception (Articles 16 and 17), experiments on human beings (Articles 18–21), tortures and other inhuman acts (Articles 22 and 23), the physician and society (Articles 24–27), collegiality (Articles 28, 29 and 30), publication of findings (Articles 31 and 32) and the duration of treatment (Article 33).

3. Limitations on the Disciplinary Power of the Provincial Councils

a. Non-interference in Fundamental Freedoms

271. According to Article 3 of Law 3415/2005, the doctor, while practising medicine, acts with complete freedom, within the framework of the generally accepted rules and methods of medical science, as formed on the basis of the results of the applied modern scientific research. MA 1565/1939 defined in Article 96 (it is Article 64 of the Codified RD 11 October/7 November 1957) that whatever misconduct having to do with the duty and obligation of physicians imposed by the above law and the Code of Medical Deontology constitutes a disciplinary offence. The above-mentioned RD in Article 2 underlines that physicians may not sacrifice their scientific and professional independence, which shall always be guarded intact as the physician's most precious possession. Article 7 of the above law stipulates that physicians shall show to all patients equal care, diligence and devotion, shall not be motivated by the economic status, social position and the gravity of the illness of the patients, paying no regard to their personal feelings towards them. There is also Article 1 of the European Code of Medical Deontology, which states that a physician shall not be motivated by racial, religious or other prejudices. Any interference in the above matters is prohibited. Decision No. 1064/1964 of the Supreme Administrative Court of Athens judges that a disciplinary decision violates the fundamental freedom of the physician when the physician is obliged to abide by the decision (of the provincial association deciding abstention from duty) and not by the law.

272. Medical associations, established as legal persons under public law and constituting a special kind of administration, may, in the exercise of the power accorded to them, take decisions that, insofar as they refer to the ethically correct practice of medicine by their own members, are to be considered as legal decisions binding upon their own members. However, decisions taken by such associations in their other capacity, that of professional organizations that collectively pursue clear professional interests, are regarded as falling outside the field of the general public interest; this means that, in accordance with the rule of law, such decisions do not have the quality of acts of public law, much less the quality of executive legal decisions with regard to their members, who are therefore in no sense legally bound or obliged by such decisions. Decisions referring to relief from duty clearly fall into the second category, as they conflict with the basic obligations of a physician as imposed by the provisions of domestic law. Non-compliance by physicians with such decisions does not constitute a basis for disciplinary action.

273. On the other hand, any act of misconduct by a physician in relation to the duties and obligations imposed on them by law or the Code of Deontology is a disciplinary offence. The Supreme Administrative Court in Athens judged in its Decision No. 2659/1989 that advertising on the part of a physician is not permitted because law does not allow it, and this is not a restriction of the physician's basic personal freedoms.[170] There are also the cases when physicians express freely their opinions: but in expressing their opinions, they are to observe the standards of discretion, probity and dignity of the members of the Order; otherwise, they shall be disciplined.

b. Duty to Support Decisions

274. The publication of a judgment against a physician subject to disciplinary investigation may be made only after the examination of the matter at the second-level by the APSI. Only then may names be made public, which of itself constitutes a sanction. The President of the medical association executes the decisions of the APSI,[171] and judgments are, of course, subject to appeal to the Council of State. The Minister of Health, Social Insurance and Social Solidarity supervises the correct application of the law, in the process of arriving at reasoned disciplinary decisions. Articles regulating the organization and functioning of the disciplinary councils are found in the above-mentioned laws.

170. *See also* Art. 6 of L. 2194/1994, Art. 15 of PD 84/2001.
171. Article 319 of L. 4512/2018.

4. Disciplinary Sanctions

a. Possible Disciplinary Sanctions

275. According to Articles 321 and 322 of Law 4512/2018, the sanctions which may be imposed by the provincial disciplinary councils, and also if appropriate, by the presidents of the provincial medical associations (light sanctions) or the appeals council are: censure, fines and temporary suspension of the right to practise medicine for a period of one month to three years. The provincial disciplinary councils and the appeals council shall respect the adage *nulla poena sine lege* in the sense that they cannot impose a sanction not provided for in Article 322. The sanction to be imposed in a given case is determined by the disciplinary councils.[172]

276. The final decisions of all disciplinary bodies are subject to appeal to the Supreme Administrative Court of Athens. The legitimacy of disciplinary measures is not questioned as a degrading or inhuman sanction forbidden by Article 3 of the European Convention. On the contrary, it is intended to penalize a doctor 'whose misconduct has shown that he no longer satisfies the required conditions for exercising the medical profession'.[173]

b. Consequences of a Disciplinary Sanction

i. Regarding the Right to Vote and to Be Elected

277. Physicians who have been sanctioned can no longer be elected as members of any of the organs of their associations. A suspended physician loses the right to vote for the elections of the organs of the provincial medical associations as long as the suspension lasts.

ii. Regarding the Right to Practise Medicine

278. The temporary suspension of the right to practise medicine means that the physician concerned is no longer authorized to practise medicine, which would constitute an offence.

5. Disciplinary Procedure

a. The Applicability of Article 6 of the European Convention in Disciplinary Proceedings

279. In disciplinary proceedings of medical tribunals, there are guarantees, e.g., of personal impartiality of the members of the disciplinary provincial councils or the appeals council of Athens, which satisfy the requirements of paragraph 1 of Article 6. Disciplinary proceedings do not normally lead to contention over 'civil rights and obligations in the sense of Article 6 of the European Convention'.[174]

---

172. Article 321 of L. 4512/2018.
173. Nys, *supra*, para. 148.
174. Nys, *supra*, para. 148 and sources there cited.

b. Public Character of Disciplinary Proceedings

280. In accordance with Article 325, paragraph 1 of Law 4512/2018, the disciplinary council always meets in full session and decides by absolute majority. During the deliberations, minutes are kept, which remain secret. The President of the Council may be a non-voting participant in the deliberations. Hence, the hearings and judgments of the provincial disciplinary councils are never open to the public.

c. Hearing Within a Reasonable Time

281. In accordance with Article 325, paragraph 2 of Law 4512/2018, the disciplinary power is practised by the relevant disciplinary council on its own initiative or on a written or oral report or communication by the public authority or on the application of any interested party. Article 327 of the above Law states that from the initiation of the disciplinary hearing or within six to eight months of the report, the disciplinary council must complete its enquiry and issue its final decision. Hence, the provincial and appeals councils are to decide within a reasonable time. After an accusation directed to the provincial council against a physician or the discovery of any misconduct, the President of the Council makes it known to the first meeting of the board, which in reasonable time issues a reasoned decision to continue or discontinue the procedure. The same procedure is followed by the Supreme Medical Council of Athens. Should the Council decide to continue the procedure, it sends the case to the disciplinary council, which orders an assessor to start calling witnesses to examine under oath. The accused physician has to be called for a hearing or to testify after having been informed of the accusation, not less than fifteen days after having been properly summoned in writing. The physician is summoned five days before the date of the hearing, and he/she may appear alone or accompanied by a lawyer.[175] During that day, the Council may examine witnesses or hear the defence of the accused, and, in the case of his/her non-appearance, although legally summoned, the Council may nevertheless come to a decision, which is to be published within eight days. Any party involved may lodge an appeal within ten days.

d. Right to Challenge Members of Councils

282. In accordance with Article 330, paragraph 6 of Law 4512/2018, the right of the physicians concerned to challenge the members of the organ hearing their case follows the rules of Civil Procedure of Hellas.[176] The application is presented to the President of the disciplinary council.

e. Implementation of Disciplinary Procedure

283. The disciplinary procedure for slight misconduct begins before the President of the Provincial Medical Council, who may call any physician and, after hearing him, impose the sanctions of reprimand or low financial penalty. More serious

175. Article 327, para. 3 of L. 4512/2018.
176. Article 335 of L. 4512/2018.

disciplinary procedures take place before the provincial disciplinary councils and the appeals council of Athens. For physicians working with the ESY, there are parallel disciplinary organs for any misconduct of physicians in the sphere of the ESY. Moreover, there are parallel disciplinary organs for physicians serving their obligatory period in rural medical services.

284. In accordance with Article 321 of Law 4512/2018, the Provincial Medical Board of the Provincial Council may decide to start disciplinary proceedings and pass the file to the disciplinary council. The disciplinary procedure begins before the Provincial Disciplinary Council which acts through one of its members, appointed to act as assessor, who undertakes any necessary examination by calling witnesses to testify under oath.

285. The procedure may continue before the APSI, which judges at the second level. In accordance with Article 332 of Law 4512/2018, the accused physician, or the provincial medical association or the interested party (e.g., a patient) may appeal within ten days. The period for practising the right to appeal or an appeal itself has a suspensive effect.[177] Final decisions are executed by the Supreme Medical Council.

286. Final decisions of the provincial disciplinary councils or the appeals council may be referred to the Supreme Administrative Court by the interested parties (e.g., the Minister, the physician concerned). The Supreme Administrative Court does not have jurisdiction to rectify factual errors on the part of the appeals council or to examine whether the sanction is proportionate to the fault.

287. According to paragraph 2 of Article 328, the disciplinary council appoints each time an assessor outside its members for any necessary examination. The assessor shall call and examine witnesses under oath. The physician concerned is called and informed as soon as possible of the opening of the enquiry and the accusation as framed and of the documents of the case against him. The procedure provides for time limits and formalities, allowing the accused physician time and facilities for his/her defence. After the end of the hearing and the examination of the accused physician, the President of the disciplinary council defines the date of the meeting of the Council to decide. The accused is called to be present five to ten days before this hearing. The physician may appear in person or may be assisted by a counsel.[178]

288. The physician concerned must be promptly informed of the decision, which must be taken in a period of eight days from the meeting of the Council and must be notified to the accused in another eight-day period. They are reasoned decisions taken by a simple majority, do not refer to minority votes, and are signed by the President and the Secretary of the disciplinary council.

177. Article 332, para. 3 of L. 4512/2018.
178. Article 327, para. 3 of L. 4512/2018.

289. Appeals may be lodged by any interested party with the Secretary of the Council which delivered the decision, and a written document is signed by the Secretary and the person lodging the appeal. Within a period of ten days, the Secretary sends all documents to the Secretariat of the administrative board of the PIS.[179] Disciplinary decisions which have become final are acted upon by the President of the Provincial Medical Association and notified to the accused.

B. Preventive Control

290. In accordance with Article 292 of Law 4512/2018, the provincial associations have authority and jurisdiction over the physicians registered on their list. Any failure on the part of a physician to conform to a decision of the provincial association is a disciplinary offence (paragraph 3). Paragraph 2 also explains that the provincial associations ensure observance of the rules and laws of professional conduct having to do with the rights and obligations of physicians.

291. Nevertheless, the above competence to ensure observance of the best scientific education, safeguarding dignity, or the creation of a spirit of brotherhood, etc., is not merely a repressive function. The associations may act in a preventive way in order to implement, e.g., professional deontology. The above preventive competence of the provincial medical associations is explicitly provided for in Article 292 of the above Law as the main object of the associations. Though preventive competence is different from disciplinary competence, a preventive measure of a provincial association is open to appeal to the Council or to the Supreme Administrative Court.

III. Organs of the Order of Physicians

A. Provincial Medical Associations

292. In accordance with Article 291 of Law 4512/2018, physicians legally practising medicine in the area of a Health Region of Hellas constitute the provincial medical association of the area. They are legal persons under public law, and their seat is the city where the Hygienic Centre is situated. Each medical association takes its name from that city. The administrative organs of the provincial association are the Assembly and the administrative board.[180]

293. Article 301 of Law 4512/2018 defines the Assembly and its functions. Apart from the functions already discussed above (keeping the register of the Order, ensuring observance of the rules of professional conduct, etc.), the following competences belong to the Assembly:

179. Article 332, para. 2 of L. 4512/2018.
180. Articles 300–304 of L. 4512/2018.

(a) Election of the members of the administrative board and its control.
(b) Election of the members of the disciplinary council.
(c) Election of the examining committee for examining the budget and approving, or not, its economical administration.
(d) Decisions on any matter arising and having to do with the objects of the association.
(e) Approval or amendment of the internal Code of Functioning of the Assembly or the administrative board.

294. The administrative board of the medical associations consists of the President, the vice president, the secretary, the treasurer and one member when the number of physician-members of the association does not exceed 50, three members when that number is not higher than 150, five members when the number does not exceed 250 registered physicians, seven when the physicians do not exceed 1,000, nine members for up to 3,000 physicians, eleven members for up to 10,000 registered, and thirteen members when the number of registered physicians on the list of the provincial medical association is 10,001 or more.[181]

295. According to Article 306 of the above Law, the election of the members of the administrative board, of the disciplinary council and of the examining committee is by secret ballot and the simple proportional system.

B. Disciplinary Medical Councils

296. The disciplinary council[182] is composed of the President and four members (with their replacements) if the registered physicians are no more than hundred, and six members if the association has more than hundred registered members.[183] For the positions of President, vice president and members of the disciplinary council, physicians having practised for at least twenty years are eligible.

C. PIS and Appeals Council

297. In accordance with Articles 271–342 of Law 4512/2018, the PIS is the central coordinating and supervising body of all physicians and provincial medical associations of Hellas. It is a legal person under public law situated in Athens. Its administrative organs are the Assembly and the administrative board. The Assembly is composed of the representatives elected by the Assemblies of all provincial associations, in accordance with the number of their registered members, and also of the presidents of the provincial associations.[184] The Assembly of PIS elects its fifteen-member administrative board and the APSI of Athens.

181. Article 304 of L. 4512/2018.
182. Article 321 of L. 4512/2018.
183. Article 324 of L. 4512/2018.
184. Article 276 of L. 4512/2018.

298. According to Article 71 of RD of 1957, the APSI of Athens, judging at a second instance tribunal, may order a new hearing, may call the accused and may annul or amend the decision of the first-level disciplinary council. The APSI is situated in Athens. It consists of five persons, who are the President (or his/her substitute), one judge, or his/her substitute, of a second instance court appointed by the President of the Appeals Court of Athens,[185] and three physicians as ordinary members (with their physician-substitutes). All physician-members are elected by physicians with more than twenty years of practice. The Secretary of the Council is the Secretary of the PIS. Their period of office is three years, and all members may be re-elected.[186] Certain modifications of the provisions on APSI were made by Article 21 of Law 1076/1980 and paragraph 3 of Article 5 of Law 1425/1984.

§2. Professional Liability

I. Introduction

299. Professional liability is considered to be the responsibility in general of the physician as a person having all the qualities and qualifications needed for the practice of this profession. In addition to general disciplinary misconduct, professional liability embraces obligations enjoined by civil and criminal law. Parts of the professional liability of physicians are governed by specific laws. Both civil liability and criminal liability of physicians for the damage or injury caused by improper performance of their duties during their professional activities and functions are governed by the general rules as to professional liability, but there are also specific laws and/or articles entailed in the discharge of their medical functions.

300. The law on professional liability of physicians has undergone an unprecedented growth, and the number of cases reported in law journals has increased steadily. Though there is no register of all the cases, it should be mentioned that from the beginning of the twentieth century, there are found in medical journals and Hellenic medical bibliography about hundred decisions of second-level courts and of the Supreme Court on serious cases where physicians were accused of mistakes of diagnosis or of therapy of patients. Up to 1960, there were about ten serious cases. During the 1970s, there were three to four reported serious cases, while since 1990 we have already seen fourteen serious cases. In fact, the reported court cases are three or four times more frequent, but there are difficulties with accurate designation. It is also a fact that it is very difficult to prove a connection between physician's mistakes, especially those occurring during therapy, and the damage or injury caused by their improper performance. In case of medical error, the patient or his/her family may seek disciplinary action against the physician, and/or may also instigate an action under criminal law, or seek damages through the civil jurisdiction.

185. *See also* Art. 10 of L. 727/1977.
186. Article 73 of RD of 11 Oct./7 Nov. 1957.

301. Information on the number and type of patient claims against physicians is very limited either in Hellas or in other European countries. The insurance companies covering professional liability do not disclose information on the number of cases resolved or of patient claims. At the same time, social insurances pay the medical costs, and usually no other compensation is given through other sources. Generally speaking, there is no medical malpractice crisis in Hellas. However, the President of a physicians' association declared before a national conference that over 7,000 persons die annually as a result of medical error and calculated that approximately 200 patients a day suffer serious damage to their health.[187]

302. There is an established opinion that the significance of the court cases reported is debatable because most of the cases are from lower courts and have little significance for legal practice or for influencing legal principles. Furthermore, when after many years, the final court decision is out, medical knowledge and techniques have evolved, and a few lessons may be drawn from most reported cases.[188]

II. Civil Liability

A. *Classification of the Physician's Liability*

303. The EU Directive of 9 November 1990 constituted a first attempt at the regulation of questions of medical liability. The Directive of 12 May 1992 followed. Finally, the matter reached a favourable issue when Law 2251/1994 on consumer protection was passed as part of the harmonization of Hellenic law with Directive 93/131 of 5 April 1993. In Article 8 of Law 2251/1994,[189] the liabilities of service providers, including physicians, are regulated for the first time; 'false *(nothos)* objective liability' is established for whosoever causes damage to a consumer through provision of defective services.[190]

304. The new provisions of the above act suffice, though they avoid (conflicting with) the relevant provisions of the Hellenic CC concerning contractual liability (Article 33 of CC) or tort (Article 914 of CC). Any matters not so far regulated fall under existing Hellenic law. The new regulations strengthen the position of the patient. In particular, the new provisions of Article 8 of the above law are incomplete and defective, failing to solve problems, while even creating new ones, as equity in the domain of medical liability is not followed, and the jurisprudential principle of equal treatment of litigants in cases of civil liability is not respected.[191]

187. As reported in the newspaper *Adesmeftos Typos*, 25 Apr. 2005.
188. Decision of The Supreme Civil Court, *Areios Pagos*, on damages, July 1997.
189. As amended by Art. 10 of L. 3587/2007.
190. *See also:* E. Alexandridou, *Law 2251/94 on Consumer Protection: Similarities to and Differences from Law 1961/91: Relationship to Law 146/1914*, Armenopoulos, 1996, 3, 289–298.
191. I. Karakosta, *The Civil Liability of the Physician in Community Law*, Armenopoulos, 1994, 1, 15, 22.

305. In accordance with Article 8 of Law 2251/1994 as amended by Law 3587/2007 and Law 4512/2018, entitled 'liability of service providers':

(a) the provider of services is responsible for every moral or property damage that has illegally caused by fault with an action or an omission during the provision of these services to the consumer. The provider of services is every person who under the framework of his professional activities provides services in an independent manner;[192]
(b) a provision which has as its immediate and exclusive aim the manufacturing of a product, or the transfer of actual or intellectual property rights, is not a service within the meaning of this article;
(c) the aggrieved party (plaintiff) must prove the fault and the necessary causal connection between the provision of the service and the damage;
(d) the service provider bears the burden of proof of the absence of culpability. In the assessment of the absence of culpability, reasonable expectations in safety standards and the particular conditions as a whole will be taken into account and in particular:
   - the nature and the object of the service, especially in relation to the degree of danger involved;
   - the presentation and the manner of the provision of the service;
   - the time of the service;
   - the value of the service;
   - the freedom of action allowed to the aggrieved party within the service;
   - whether the aggrieved party belongs to a category of disadvantaged or vulnerable persons;
   - whether the service provided was a voluntary service on the part of the provider.
(e) the existence or the possibility for a better service provided during the time of the specific service or on a subsequent time does not constitute, without any other reason, a liability;
(f) the provisions of paragraphs 10–12 of Article 6 concerning joint liability, the reduction or nullification of liability, and the inadmissibility of exemption clauses, are also applicable to the liability of a service provider.

306. Civil liability of a physician arises when provisions of civil law, such as those of Article 8 above, are violated by act or by omission. The physician is liable for compensation to the person who suffered as a result of the misconduct. However, it is not necessary that the unfortunate outcome be ascribed to medical error, that is to say to an action diverging from established medical practice, such as has always constituted a cause of liability at law, nor to any other medical act or omission, as it may be ascribed to the nature of the illness, to the necessary limitation on the power of medical science, which is unable to make human beings immortal, or to the fact that the patient is a biological organism that will not always react in a

192. Article 10, para. 1 of L. 3587/2007.

precise and predictable manner.[193] This is why the patient/plaintiff, in order to seek compensation, must prove the damage and the causal connection between the service provided and the damage (paragraph 3 of Article 8). The party who provided medical services will be absolved if able to show that the service provided was entirely in accordance with the principles of medical science, that is, that he/she acted accordingly with established obligations in respect of welfare and safety. This form of establishment of the concept of objective liability is of practical importance in the case of the compensation being due to a patient because of tort on the part of the doctor. It constitutes a conflict with the regulation by the CC of liability as tort, according to which the patient also needs to prove the culpability of the physician.[194]

307. According to paragraph 3 of Article 8, the patient (or the surviving relatives) may be in a position to receive compensation after proving (apart from the damage) merely a causal connection between the medical service provided and the undesired result: this places the party providing services on dangerous ground and adds to her/his liabilities. As far as the damage is concerned, the patient (or the relatives or heirs of the deceased) will be obliged to prove the direct damage that stems from the harm to her/his health or bodily integrity and/or the material/financial damage caused by the aforementioned direct damage.[195]

308. Hence, an obligation to compensate may be incurred in two ways:

(1) by a breach of contract for the provision of medical services between a physician together with a clinic or hospital, and a patient; or
(2) by a tort.

1. Contractual Liability

309. The relation between a physician and the patient is contractual. A breach of professional obligations leads to liability of a contractual character. In the case of contractual liability, the physicians are obliged to offer services to their patients, and they should not stop the therapy without a reasonable cause; otherwise, they are obliged to compensate for not executing or improper execution of the contract. According to the law,[196] there are also cases where the patient or a person in the responsibility of the patient is also responsible, when the responsibility of the physician may be lessened or nullified.[197] The contract is as a rule a contract for the

193. C. Politi, *Distribution of the Burden of Proof in Actions Concerning Medical Liability*, Diki, 1987, 19, 75 et seq.
194. A. Georgiadis, in C.C. Georgiadou-Stathopoulou, *Introductory Observations on Articles 914–938*, Editions Sakkoulas, Athens, 2006, 6.
195. Karakosta, *supra*, 4.
196. L. 2251/1994.
197. The same as Art. 300 of the C.C., which thereby acquires complementary validity.

provision of services, but on occasions may be a contract of work, when, for instance, it is a matter of the manufacture and supply of a prosthesis: the case of dental prostheses is ambiguous here.

2. Tortious Liability

310. Non-contractual or tortious liability usually arises when damage to a third party occurs or services are rendered without the consent of the patient. According to Article 8 of Law 2251/1994 as amended by Law 3587/2007 and Law 4512/2018, in the case where obligation for compensation originates from tort, whosoever against the law or by his/her own fault causes damage to another person shall be liable for the damage. Hence, the services of a physician or of any professional person (even a legal person), by their very nature, repel a legally binding civil contract. The physician should abide by the fundamental principles of medical services provided by Article 2 of Law 3418/2005.

311. Between contractual or tortious liability, there is little difference in practice. The identification of an error by the physician – medical professional error – is a precondition of medical liability. As regards the consequences, a physician injuring a person through malpractice breaks the contract and also commits a tort.

B. Contents of the Physician's Duty

312. The content of the contractual obligation of physicians is the implementation by the physician of a therapeutic treatment and not the achievement of a specific result (result obligation). The contractual obligation has the meaning that the physician is not obliged to cure or bring any positive result concerning the patient but to offer him a consistent medical help and care conscientiously and diligently (effort obligation), using all current data and advances of medical science in order to attempt to bring about a cure, without this obligation necessarily extending to the actual achievement of the desired result. A physician does not guarantee the results of treatment.[198]

313. Physicians' principle obligations are to offer in full their scientific assistance in diagnosis and therapy and in informing the patients about their state of ill health as well as any potential dangers of the treatment or operation; they are also obliged to ensure that the patient consents and that the administering of the treatment is properly organized. There are also secondary obligations: the keeping of medical records, the protection of the patient's files from unauthorized access by third persons[199] and the provision of data on discoveries.[200]

198. A. Koutselini & M. Michalodimitraki, *Medical Liability*, Gutenberg, 1984, 35.
199. Article 14 of L. 3418/2005.
200. Article 27 of L. 3418/2005.

314. The duty of diagnosis, more specifically, involves finding out the family background of the patient, as well as describing the type, the nature and the severity of each presenting symptom, then comparing these symptoms with the symptoms of every known illness in clinical writing as well as with the results of laboratory tests to which the physician has recourse in order to verify his/her clinical diagnosis.[201]

315. The physician cannot guarantee that cure will follow because this has to do with unpredictable human nature. It has to do with the human body or the human mind which does not function in accordance with fixed rules. Hence the physician may not guarantee a result, but his/her duty to use reasonable care and skill, in certain cases, leads to an obligation to do certain things, e.g., have encephalography carried out or visit a patient at home. In the case that this is not done, the physician bears the duty to prove that the failure is not attributed to him.

316. The physician exercises care of a professional standard. A fault in the practice of medicine shall be considered any deviation from that model standard of the prudent and competent physician. Physicians should not deviate from this objective standard. Any deviation means negligence, regardless of the opinion of the physician about this standard. In accordance with paragraph 4 of Article 8 of Law 2251/94, as it is replaced by paragraph 3 of Article 10 of Law 3857/2007, the standard of care should take into account expectations in safety standards and the particular conditions as a whole under which medical services are rendered, and the competent physician should be judged under these conditions. There is, however, the problem of whether this 'objective' standard should be defined by the practice of the profession by certain exceptional, respected physicians, by the practices of the bulk of poorly paid physicians working in inadequate conditions, or by the standards of reasonable care demanded by law. Judges find themselves in great difficulty when they try to follow a normative application of the criterion of *bonus medicus*, which means the legally determined standards, while the public or the medical community think differently and ask for a factual application of the criterion.[202]

C. The Basis of Liability and Burden of Proof

1. Fault

317. As mentioned below,[203] a fault is any act or omission of the physician by which the recognized rules of professional behaviour in the said part of medical science are breached.[204] It may be the illegal behaviour of the physician towards the patient which is against written provisions of law, as well as against general rules of the legal order or against the idea of justice and of social needs. The breach of these

201. Karakosta, *supra*, 20.
202. *See also* Nys, *supra*, para. 178.
203. *See infra* para. 319.
204. *See* Art. 24 of CD 1565/1938.

obligations, which are reciprocal obligations to promote care (welfare), constitutes erroneous behaviour when the physician does not practise due diligence, objectively determinable by the level of knowledge and the facts in the particular field of medicine as pertaining to the time of the medical attendance.[205] In case of breach of the obligation to due diligence, both contractual and tortious liabilities arise, which are normally limited to compensation to the patient for the damage suffered. Satisfaction for moral damage will probably occur only in cases of tortious liability. Any deviation from professional standards is to be considered as a fault.

2. Damages

318. A patient suffers damage when he/she suffers immediate damages to his/her person and possibly material or monetary damage accruing from the damage to health, to personal freedom, etc. The patient who actually suffered damage may recover damages in respect of negligent medical treatment. All damages suffered have to be compensated. One kind of damage is the loss of a chance of a better medical outcome.

319. The system of responsibility which is introduced by Law 2251/1994 and the nature of professional services rendered justify shorter periods within which a civil action must be lodged. These shorter periods take precedence over those of the CC which are in general use. Civil action is possible only during a period of five years from the day the physician offered his/her medical services. This period shall be interrupted by the bringing of a judicial, administrative or disciplinary action against the physician. Furthermore, the right of the patient to compensation lapses three years from the day the injury was noticed by the patient. The Court shall accept a civil action, e.g., for causation of physical harm (which might be also a criminal act) more than five years after the incident but not more than three years from the day the injury was noticed by the patient.

3. Causation

320. The plaintiff must prove the damage and the causal connection between the supply of the medical services and the damage. He/she shall not prove the negligence of the physician but that because of some negligence, he/she has sustained the damage. The factor that has necessarily contributed to the existence of damage has to be considered as *sine qua non* cause of the damage.[206] The service provider bears the burden of proof that he/she was not responsible for (i.e., did not cause) the damage suffered by the patient.[207]

205. Karakosta, *supra*, 21; S. Kotsianou, *Medical Liability, Civil and Penal*, Digital Repository of Historical and Cultural Archives of S. Kotsianos, 1977, 63, 189.
206. Article 8, para. 3 of L. 2251/1994.
207. Article 8, para. 4 of L. 2251/1994, as replaced by Art. 10, para. 3 of L. 3857/2007.

D. *Aspects of Vicarious Liability*

1. Liability of Hospitals for the Acts of Their Medical Staff

321. The liability of physicians in hospitals, of the hospitals themselves and of auxiliary staff are judged aspects of vicarious liability in most cases of professional medical liability. Any person who provides services making use of a representative or a legal dependent or any other intermediary is still to be considered a service provider. His/her liability is not diminished when the damage was caused by his/her error in conjunction with the intervention of a third person, e.g., a colleague, an assistant or a nurse.[208] According to Nys,[209] a lot of malpractice cases relate to medical apparatus, mostly to defective equipment or to inexpert use of available apparatus and/or lack of supervision of the auxiliary staff using this apparatus, or the failure to use apparatus even though it was available. The patient's stay in hospital for at least one night before and one night after treatment is a frequent source of malpractice action; the in-patient, who may even be unconscious, is in the hands of a variety of personnel, not only of the physician.

322. The contractual liability of the physician exists up to the point of choosing the appropriate form of medical assistance. A wrong diagnosis does not necessarily prove the physician's negligence. Negligence exists when the physician is led to a wrong diagnosis because he/she failed to apply the rules of medical science, art and deontology (e.g., he/she showed indifference for the patient, he/she did not act as the conscientious specialized physician using all the means at his/her disposal during the examination of the patient). The physician must act like a scientist, bearing in mind the law of probabilities. Moreover, civil liability extends not only to physical persons, but also to legal persons, e.g., the hospital. Hence, the question is against which person the malpractice suit will be issued: whether the malpractice suit for compensation will be brought against the physician, the auxiliary staff or the medical institution (hospital, private clinic, medical enterprise, etc.). The kind of work relation of the physician with the institution is not relevant, but the kind of institution, if it is a legal person under private or public law, is important.[210]

323. Hellenic jurisprudence and law consider the person of physician responsible in whole with (as also) the legal person of the medical institution, which has the right to turn against the physician or the person who is the one actually responsible for the malpractice. For physicians who are civil servants or who are assimilated with the latter by law, law rules that civil servants are responsible to the State for any positive loss they cause by fraud or gross negligence during the execution

208. Paragraphs 1 (as replaced by Art. 10, para. 1 of L. 3857/2007) and 6 of Art. 8 of L. 2251/1994; Karakosta, *supra*, 17. *See also* equal treatment by the provisions of Arts 330, 334 (para. 1) and 922 C.C.
209. Nys, *supra*, para. 184.
210. C. Politis, *Does or Doesn't Medical Error Attract a Penalty?*, To Vima, 1996, A42 (66).

of their services and for any compensation the State pays to a third party because of negligent acts or omissions during the practice of their duties which were also committed with fraud or gross negligence.[211]

324. In the case where the patient contracts with a private physician, in a case of malpractice, the patient may act against the physician. The private medical institution where the malpractice took place may respond by refusing to pay any compensation on the grounds that the case belongs to the freedom of the physician with no right on its behalf to interfere.[212] But in cases where the patient contracts with the private clinic, and the physician is employed (under any kind of contract) by the clinic, then the clinic is responsible for compensation. The physician may be held liable for medical examination and treatment. The clinic that has been held liable may recover from its physician-employee in the case of gross negligence or fraud on his/her part. Anyway, if more than one person (e.g., the clinic and the physician) are responsible for the same malpractice, each one of them is responsible, as previous Hellenic legal provisions also ruled. These provisions, of Articles 334, 480 et seq., 922, 926, 927 of the CC, now have complementary implementation.[213]

325. In accordance with Article 6 of Law 2251/1994 (as replaced by Article 7 of Law 3587/2007), the provider of medical services cannot diminish or be exempted from the responsibility against the victim of its malpractice. Any provision that discharges from responsibility the bearer of medical services in cases of medical professional faults in the field of contractual or tortious activities shall be null and void.

326. According to some authors, discharge from responsibility is not allowed because provisions for the profession of physicians are of a public order, and private contracts cannot alter them. Other authors maintain that the malpractices of physicians act against life and health, that is against the patient's personality, which is protected by the law[214] and the Constitution.[215]

2. Physician's Liability for Medical Activity of Other Persons

327. A physician who employs others (e.g., assistants, nurses) to help him/her performing his/her medical duties shall be liable for their malpractices; hence, he/she has the right to control their work. Of course, the physician may prove that it was not his/her staff but the hospital staff, in which case the hospital is liable. Anaesthesiologists are always physicians and liable for their own medical activities.

---

211. Alexiadis, *supra*, 21, in accordance with Art. 85 of PD 611/1977.
212. Alexiadis, *supra*, 22.
213. AP 1429/2012, AP 1683/2014, AP 181/2011 and Court of First Instance of Larisa 191/2012.
214. *See* Arts 178, 179, 288 and 57 of the CC.
215. *See* Art. 7, para. 2 of the Constitution.

III. Criminal Liability

328. A fault of a physician may cause bodily harm to the patient and for this reason may be qualified as a criminal act. Criminal liability is the liability of physicians when by act or omission they are in breach of one or more of those provisions of the law for which a penalty is applied under the PC and other penal laws. It is possible that in the course of his/her duties, a physician may commit crimes of two categories: premeditated crime or crime by negligence. Premeditated crimes include abortion (Article 304 of the PC), wilful homicide (Article 299 of the PC), intentional bodily harm (Articles 308 et seq. of the PC) and assisted suicide (Article 300 of the PC). Crimes by negligence include involuntary homicide (Article 302 PC) and involuntary personal injury (Article 314 of the PC). The physician is responsible both for grave and for trivial negligence.[216] Other specific cases of criminal liability concern the refusal to offer medical services (Article 441 of the PC) and breach of medical secrecy (Article 371 of the PC).

329. Law 4509/2017 establishes new provisions concerning criminal liability of psychiatrists, psychologists and social workers. In accordance with Article 40 of Law 4509/2017, the aforementioned categories that are employed in public Children's Psychiatric Hospitals and are under a judicial or social enquiry concerning child abuse are not prosecuted for opinions that they establish during the exercise of their duties unless they acted wilfully or infringed the confidentiality of the information that they received. The scope of this provision is to ensure protection of both professionals and children and especially the professionals that could be sued with the aim of intimidation.

330. The civil fault and the fault under the PC are identical, and the criterion of the reasonable, careful physician applies in judging both the civil and the criminal liability of physicians.

§3. Quality Assurance

331. By 1990, all European Community Member States should have built effective mechanisms for ensuring the quality of patient care within their healthcare systems.[217] Prior to the economic crisis of 2010, Article 9 of Law 2519/1997 introduced a new institution, the National Centre of Health Research, and required that the quality of health services, the statistical analysis and economic evaluation of all medical acts and services, the control ensuring the quality of health services, the certification of the quality of the medical activity in a hospital, the cooperation with international organizations, the issuing of reports for medical services, all be evaluated.

216. A. Vougiouka, *The Physician's Professional Liability*, 1993, 87 et seq.; Alexiadis, *supra*, 19.
217. Target 31 of the 'Strategy for Health for All by the Year 2000', Regional Committee for Europe of the WHO.

332. Complementing the above, by paragraph 1 of Article 9 of Law 2519/1997, an Institute for Quality Research and Control of Health Services was provided to undertake the difficult task described above. Also, the National Centre of Health Research, introduced by paragraph 3 of Article 9 of Law 1579/1985, provided for the functioning of the above institute, planned to deal with total quality management and continuous quality improvement in the health sector in Hellas.[218] However, in accordance with Law 3895/2010, these Institutions were abolished, and their competences were transferred to relevant Units of the Ministry of Health. As regards quality assurance of physicians working in hospitals, provisions of Law 2519/1997 promoted it, and already the research which has been undertaken to evaluate occupational stress, professional burn-out and generally the psychological pressure physicians, and especially specializing physicians, suffer in public hospitals, had been systematized.[219] By paragraph 6 of Article 2 of Law 3418/2005, if the judgment of a physician was likely to be affected by a medical condition from which the physician himself/herself suffers, whether the physician has symptoms or whether she/he is the carrier of a transmissible disease, the physician must seek the advice of the work physician or of a suitably qualified colleague as regards the necessity of, or any possible modification of, his/her provision of services. In such cases, the physician must not be left to his/her own devices in the assessment of any possible risk.

333. Under Article 1, paragraph 1z of Law 3895/2010, all the above legal persons were abolished, and the objectives of the National Centre of Health Research, as evident by Article 9, paragraph 2 of Law 1579/1985, as well as those of the Quality Research and Control of Health Services, as evident by Article 9, paragraph 1 of Law 2519/1997, are met by departments of the Ministry of Health, Social Insurance and Social Solidarity with similar competencies.

§4. National Council of Medical Ethics and Deontology

334. The WMA had stated that the design and performance of biomedical research involving human subjects should be formulated clearly in a protocol which should be the object of consideration, comment and guidance by specially appointed independent committees. The solid legal base for such a committee in Hellas was Article 2 of Law 2519/1997 by which the National Committee of Bioethics and Deontology was established, by renaming the national council of medical ethics and deontology (ESIHD), as provided for by paragraph 1 of Article 61 of Law 2071/1992. After a decision of the Minister of Health, Social Insurance and Social Solidarity, preceded by an opinion of KESY and an introductory report of the National Committee of Bioethics and Deontology, special rules and preconditions for the implementation of new experimental methods and clinical research were defined,

218. Article 9, para. 2 of L. 2519/1997, referred to the temporary organization of these institutions.
219. The research is being undertaken in the first place by Prof. Gary Cooper of UMIST, UK; *see also To Vima* of 15 Jun. 1997, A49 – Art. 8, para. 6 of L. 3418/2005.

and the general rules for the operation of this National Committee were established.[220] Nevertheless, by Article 40 of Law 3204/2003, the National Committee for Bioethics and Deontology is renamed as the ESIHD. It is competent to investigate, from the point of view of medical ethics and deontology, both facts and actions of great importance, according to public opinion, and to carry out preliminary administrative investigations that may lead to disciplinary procedures.

§5. Other Disciplinary Organs

335. The Manager of a hospital acting as a disciplinary supervisor of all staff, including that of regional medical offices and health centres within his/her area of competency, may impose on any staff member and on practised in medicine (not specialists) doctors the penalty of a reprimand or a financial penalty up to half of a monthly salary. The President of a community care facility holds the same right. The Administrative Council of a hospital or a community care centre, a collective disciplinary body, may impose on any staff member, apart from a specialist physician, a reprimand or a financial penalty of up to one month's earnings. The Head of a DYPE may also impose a reprimand or a financial penalty of up to half-monthly earnings, and may also instigate a preliminary investigation and an Administrative Investigation under Oath against administrators, and forward the findings to the Minister of Health and Social Solidarity. Appeals against the above disciplinary decisions may be lodged with the Primary Service Council, which as a disciplinary body judges in the first instance or as a secondary instance tribunal. Appeals to the second instance against final judgments in the first instance are allowed.[221]

336. The Manager of a hospital and the President of the Administrative Council of a community care facility may impose on ESYKA medical personnel (not included those practised in medicine) the penalty of a reprimand or a financial penalty of up to half-monthly earnings. The Administrative Councils of hospitals or community care facilities may impose on physicians (specialists) the penalty of a reprimand or a financial penalty of up to one monthly salary. The Head of the DYPE may also impose on medical personnel a reprimand or a financial penalty of up to half-monthly earnings. The disciplinary authority which is exercised over ESYKA physicians is provided for in the stipulations of Laws 1397/1983, 2071/1992, 2519/1997 and 2889/2001. The provisions of the disciplinary code for civil servants are also applicable, under Law 2683/1999.[222] By decision of the Minister of Health, Social Insurance and Social Solidarity, in each DYPE, a five-member disciplinary council of the first and second instances is set up to deal with disciplinary matters concerning physicians (practised in medicine not included). As a first instance tribunal, it may impose penalties as in Article 39 of Law 2519/1997 (first to third points). Acting in the second instance, it may bring a plea against the Manager of a

220. *See also* Regulation 536/2014 of the European Parliament and of the Council of 16 Apr. 2014 on clinical trials on medicinal products for human use, and repealing Directive 2001/20/EC.
221. Article 163 of L. 2683/1999; *see* L. 3528/2007.
222. *See* L. 3528/2007.

hospital, the Administrative Council of a hospital, or the DYPE itself. Accused parties may not sit on the disciplinary council.

337. Appeal to the Central Disciplinary Council may be made in cases where the First Instance Disciplinary Council has imposed a penalty of loss of four months' earnings or greater, or the penalty of disbarment from candidacy for promotion. The Central Disciplinary Council acts as a first instance tribunal in cases in which the penalty may include the withdrawal of the right to practice, and as a tribunal of appeal against first instance decisions where financial penalties of the loss of four months' earnings or more were imposed, up to disbarment from candidacy for promotion to a higher grade. Appeal to the Administrative Court may be made against final decisions of the First Instance Disciplinary Council and against definitive decisions of the Central Disciplinary Council within thirty days. The disciplinary supervisor of DYPE Heads and of Managers of hospitals and community care centres is the Minister of Health, Social Insurance and Social Solidarity.[223]

223. Article 11 of L. 3329/2005, as amended by Art. 3, para. 27 of L. 3527/2007.

Part II. The Physician-Patient Relationship

Chapter 1. General Description

§1. Duties of Physicians and Patients: Rights of Patients

I. Introductory Remarks

338. In Hellas, the relation between patients and physicians has been regulated by provisions in various legal acts and not by specific legislation. These acts include rules on the rights of patients[224] and the duties of physicians. In particular, CD 1565/1939 on the Code of the Practice of the Medical Profession contains, in Articles 23 to 25, certain obligations of physicians regarding their patients. But more explicitly and in detail, RD of 25 May/6 July 1955 on the Code of Medical Deontology contained, in Articles 7–15, the obligations of physicians to their patients. Now, Articles 8–15 of Law 3418/2005 on the Code of Medical Deontology have replaced those regulations of RD of 1955 with new ones. Already, recent laws concerning medical activities, e.g., in the new area of organ transplantations[225] or in new methodologies,[226] are of relevance to certain patient rights. Last but not least, the Hellenic PC contains general provisions which also apply to physicians, such as Articles 28 (due care) or 302 (the felony of homicide, duty to go to rescue) or Article 304A on bodily harm of foetus or newborn, or Article 371 on professional secrecy or Article 458 on wilful breach of administration rules, etc.

II. Duty of Care

339. Professional help is what the patient seeks when he/she contacts a physician. The duty of care of the physician is the first issue when the rights and duties of physicians and patients are to be analysed. Physicians' duty of care can be based upon the contract normally undertaken between physician and patient. A considerable risk that the gift of human life may be taken away is associated with the practice of medicine. The provider of medical services must, therefore, take measures to

224. *See* Art. 47 of L. 2071/1992 on the rights of hospitalized patients.
225. L. 3984/2011.
226. L. 3305/2005, as amended and complemented by L. 4272/2014.

reduce the risk. The greater the risk, the greater the diligence which must be displayed by the responsible person in order to fulfil the duty of care. Physicians' reciprocal obligations towards welfare (the well-being of persons) are not only laid down or codified in provisions of the Constitution, of the PC, and of civil law, in specific articles which refer to physicians or to the medical profession, but also to be found in the general principles of law. Any failure to follow the principles known as 'duty of care' (for the life, health and bodily integrity of persons) constitutes a clear breach of contractual obligations and also gives a foundation for considering acts as illegal under Article 914 of the CC, and as culpable behaviour on the part of one bound to the duty of care. Physicians' reciprocal obligations define their expected behaviour as that which is displayed by the typical representative of the milieu or profession, taking into account the state of scientific knowledge in the field at the time of the behaviour under consideration. The basic duties towards the well-being of persons, as found in the current legal order, may be summarized as follows:

(a) the duty of diagnosis, therapy and possible intervention;
(b) the duty to inform and to ensure consent;
(c) the duty to keep records;
(d) the duty of secrecy.

340. These duties shape both the tortious and the contractual liability of physicians, being complemented by further particular duties or responsibilities arising from the nature of medical services and from autonomous free will, as well as from specific legal provisions.[227] In certain circumstances, this duty can be based on specific legal provisions, as in the following articles.

A. *Mandatory Act 1565/1939 on the Code of the Practice of the Medical Profession*

341. Although Mandatory Act 1565/1939 was abolished by Law 4512/2018 as amended and currently in force, the basic principles remain the same. The physician is obliged to carry out his/her medical attendance with zeal, diligence and devotion, in accordance with the founding principles of medical science and with the experience acquired, for the care of the sick and the protection of the healthy.[228] Non-compliance with these principles in the execution of his/her task is to be considered as a breach of law, and the physician incurs an obligation to compensate the aggrieved party. Medical scientists accept that no physician may knowingly, without legitimate reason, and on his/her own authority, discontinue a course of treatment unless he/she has previously made all the necessary arrangements for it to be continued by another physician. The associations of the Order of Physicians are to ensure that this obligation is observed.[229]

227. Karakosta, *supra*, 19–20. MA 1565/1939 on the Code of the Practice of the Medical Profession, Act 3418/2005 on the Code of Medical Deontology.
228. Former Art. 24 of L. 1565/1939 and currently Art. 2 of L. 3418/2005.
229. Nys, *supra*, para. 219.

342. In accordance with CD 67 of 16/20 December 1968 on taking measures for covering hygienic needs of rural areas and Law 2071/1992 on reorganizing the health system, all graduating physicians from the universities of Hellas, as well as those having their degree from abroad recognized in Hellas, are obliged to serve at rural health units, health stations and health centres and mobile health units for a period from six to twenty-four months.[230] Physicians who are civil servants or fall into certain other categories are exempt; there are reasons for the derogation of the fulfilment of this obligation by pregnant physicians, university assistants or those receiving scholarships, and there are certain provisions for physicians during their obligatory military service or serving in the ESY. Salaries and lodging are provided to physicians under the provisions of this law. There are also provisions for physicians of ESY, who serve as rural doctors.[231]

343. According to paragraphs 2 and 3 of Article 4 of LD 127 of 29 October/4 November 1974, in the case that fulfilment of the obligation of rural service is not undertaken, the physician is subject to sanctions, both administrative (withdrawal of licence) and penal (Article 458 PC). A decision of the Minister of Health No. 10391 of 27 March/30 April 1991, on the placing of physicians in rural clinics, dependent clinics, hygiene stations and health centres for the completion of their compulsory rural service, lays down the procedure for the fair selection of doctors and their placement on the basis of a points system. Now, paragraph 3 of Article 26 of Law 2519/1997 incorporates this service into ESY and underlines its future termination.

344. The obligations of physicians to be on call for night duty, etc., have a particular character. Physicians of the ESY, specialists, and physicians attached to universities are obliged to be on call according to a duty roster, and, when called, to offer their services without further remuneration beyond that provided for by Article 86 of Law 2071/1992. The physician who is on call is obliged to remain in the vicinity, so that when called he/she may turn up for service with suitable promptness.[232]

345. Physicians in full-time exclusive employment, in full-time employment, specialists (civil or military), university physicians, ESY physicians and tenured physicians in State posts are all liable to be on call. The times that they may be on call are determined according to their category, for between six and twelve days per month, for sixteen hours on working days or for twenty-four hours on Saturdays, Sundays and national holidays. Remuneration is calculated, for ESY physicians, for instance, in accordance with paragraph 5 of Article 28 of Law 1579/1985, Article 7 of Law 1810/1988, and Decision No. 4556/27 July 1991 of the Ministry of Finance.

230. *See also* L. 1579/1985, Art. 2, para. 7 of L. 1821/1988, L. 2071/1992 and Art. 12 of L. 2256/1994.
231. Article 26 of L. 2519/1997. Rural physicians and physicians of medical country centres are renamed as rural service physicians.
232. *See also* LD 1173/1972. A new system of a duty roster for physicians on hospitals is under way.

They may be on call to departments of care institutions under Law 2592/ 1953, hospitals, Institute of Social Insurance for Employees (IKA) health centres and therapeutic units, university workshops, and EKAB, as well as to in-patient care institutions under private law.[233]

346. Article 1 of LD 1175/1972 obliged physicians practising in administrative capitals of prefectures or in towns of more than 20,000 inhabitants to participate in duty rosters covering Sundays and holidays. Those so obliged were mostly those specializing in pathology, general medicine, paediatrics, cardiology, obstetrics and surgery, as well as non-specialized physicians for a period of five years.[234]

347. PD 479/14–21 May 1981, amended by Official Journal of the Government (FEK) 135A of 26 May 1981 by which paragraph 1 of Article 3 of RD of 15 August/ 15 September 1947 was replaced, instituted a system of turns of duty for pharmacists in all municipalities and communes. Pharmacies that are on duty may remain open during the midday break (lunchtime); if they close, they must display a notice giving the name, home address and telephone number of the duty pharmacist.

348. The night-duty pharmacy must remain open from the time of evening closing until 22:00 or 23:00, then, if closed, must display clearly, until the time of morning opening, the name, etc., of the night-duty pharmacist.

349. On Sundays and other holidays, day- and night-duty pharmacies function as above. The Prefect may decree, for reasons of social need, the continuous (twenty-four) opening of duty pharmacies, etc. Any breach of the above provisions is judged and sanctioned in accordance with the provisions of Article 24 of the PD of 8–14 March 1930 on the codification of laws concerning Sunday as a day of rest.[235]

350. By Article 4 of Law 3601/1928 on the establishment of pharmaceutical associations, all pharmacists permanently resident and legally practising in an area are obliged to belong to such an association. By Article 5, any pharmacist who takes up residence in an area in order to practise her/his profession is obliged to declare this in writing within fifteen days to the State hygiene authority and to the local pharmaceutical association, enclosing all relevant documents. The pharmacist who fails to do so will be practising her/his profession illegally, and as such is subject to disciplinary and penal sanctions. Pharmacists are obliged to follow the duty roster and opening hours as established; failure to do so is subject to sanctions by the authorities and by the associations of the order of pharmacists.

233. ESY physicians come under Art. 57, para. 3 of L. 1539/1985, tenured physicians in the state sector come under Art. 1, para. 3 of L. 1579/1985, while physicians in full-time employment come under Art. 4 of L. 2194/1994.

234. Decision of the Minister of Health No. 17/3807, 4/14 Aug. 1972. This institution no longer exists. By a new Ministerial Decision, a new system of daily duty rosters for all hospitals in Attica is established for the coordination and distribution of empty beds.

235. *See also* Art. 51 of L. 2519/1997.

351. In Hellas, physicians and pharmacists must be members of their respective boards and must respect their decisions, such as those concerning the duty roster and any changes to it. There are also dispositions providing for the permanent availability of physicians in hospitals. All hospitals participate in a system of turns of duty so as to ensure the regular provision of health care to the population.

B. Articles of Hellenic PC

1. Penal Code

a. Applicability to Physicians

352. Article 441, which replaced Article 25 of MA 1565/1939 on the Code of Practice of the Medical Profession, was included in the Hellenic PC of 1951, making punishable some cases of minor offences of refusal of services and omission, concerning doctors and midwives. The above Article 441 stated that physicians and midwives who refuse without sufficient reason to carry out their work, or who in the execution of that work are guilty of any negligence that might place others in danger, may be punished by a fine or by up to three months' imprisonment if the act is not subject to graver punishment under another legal provision. This article was abolished by Law 4619/2019 along with a series of other articles of the Greek PC concerning minor offences, and such omissions are now covered by the General Provisions of the PC on omission (Articles 288 and 307) in combination with Article 319 of Law 4512/2018 on disciplinary offences.

353. After the entry into force of Law 4619/2019, only serious offences are punishable by the Greek PC, leaving minor omissions, such as provisions of former Article 441, to be processed at an administrable level, in this case by the PIS.

354. Problems arise when physicians on duty are called to leave their posts. In doing so, they might have deprived potential emergency cases of their services. But a real and accurate danger always has a priority over a potential danger. Punishment that may be imposed is determined by articles of the PC on bodily harm (Article 308) and on homicide by negligence (Article 302). ESY physicians are obliged to offer their medical assistance on request and without remuneration.

2. Emergency Medical Care

355. For emergency medical care, physicians should respond (e.g., to the instruction of a competent authority) to attend a situation which requires immediate care, due to an accident or illness. Non-compliance with this obligation can be punished with criminal sanctions. Refusal may be justified by more urgent professional duties, another exceptional situation or in the case that help may be offered by a physician who is more conveniently nearby.[236] This article is applicable to physicians who are to evaluate the urgency of the exceptional situation.

III. Respect for the Privacy of the Patient

356. The obligation to informational privacy of the patient and the obligation of physicians to respect this aspect of the patient's privacy (the obligation to medical secrecy is dealt with elsewhere) is found in Hellenic legislation. The most important pieces of legislation are MA 1565/1939 on the code of practice of the medical profession, Act 1599/1986 on the State/citizen relationship, the establishing of a new national identity card, Law 1805/1988 on the updating of the criminal record, the modification of penal provisions and the adjustment of other related matters, Law 2400/1996 which recognized Protocol 11 of the Convention on Human Rights and Basic Freedoms and acts mentioned below and Law 4624/2019 which implemented Regulation (EU) 2016/679.

357. Many authorities asseverate that the above legislation gave inadequate protection to personal medical information; a precise table of rights of access should be drawn up, by class of information and by type of employment/profession, in order to provide proper protection for the citizen against the (mis)processing of personal data. Recently, new legislation has given adequate answers as regards respect for the privacy of the citizen (e.g., Law 3089/2002, Law 3305/2005 and Law 3418/2005).

358. It is accepted that rules of medical secrecy alone cannot face all the problems raised by automatic or manual processing of medical personal data, which also involve a number of non-physicians. Moreover, the privacy of a patient is at stake because medical personal data can be collected and stored in a short period of time and on a large scale. Moreover, medical secrecy (Article 23 of CD 1565/1939) may not protect the individual against negligence of the physicians, who are punished under criminal law (Article 371 PC) when they knowingly and willingly expose confidential data.[237]

359. In 2001, the revised Hellenic Constitution introduced a new individual right in Article 9A which reads:

> All persons have the right to be protected from the collection, processing and use, especially by electronic means, of their personal data as specified by law.

236. Articles 441 and 473 of the C.C.; *see also* Art. 25 of the PC (state of emergency).
237. *See also* Art. 13 of L. 3418/2005.

The protection of personal data is to be ensured by an independent authority, which is constituted and operating as specified by law.

A. *Prohibition of Processing of Medical Data*

360. In accordance with Article 371 PC, it is forbidden to process personal data with regard to the state of health, the medical examination, medical care and treatment. In certain European countries, special attention is given to processing data referring to cases of alcoholism and other intoxications.[238] There are exceptions to this rule. In accordance with Opinion 11/2011 of the Legal Council of the State, forensic physicians (who are also covered by medical secrecy since they have the status of a physician) are obliged to provide to the National Statistics Agency, upon demand, all data concerning the decease of a person, without the right to deny on the grounds of medical secrecy. Relevant provisions where medical secrecy is overridden also apply to independent agencies or public institutions such as the Citizen's Ombudsman, Agency for the Prevention of Financial Crime, etc.

361. Regulation (EU) 2016/679 known as the General Data Protection Regulation (GDPR) published in the Official Journal of the European Union on 23 May 2018 sets out detailed requirements on collecting, storing and managing personal data, recognizing data concerning health as a special category of data and provides a definition for health data for data protection purposes.

362. More precisely, Article 9 prohibits any data processing of special category of personal data such as genetic data, biometric data for the purpose of uniquely identifying a natural person or data concerning health, unless the data controller can meet one or more conditions in addition to having an appropriate legal basis for the data processing.

1. Special Written Consent

363. The data subject may consent in writing to the processing of personal medical data by anyone, not physicians only.

2. Processing by the Treating Physician

364. Without the special written consent of the patient, treating (attending) physicians may process personal medical data under their supervision and responsibility.

---

238. Nys, *supra*, para. 257.

B. *Guarantees with Respect to the Processing of Personal Medical Data*

365. Persons participating in the processing are to be appointed by name by whoever is responsible for the processing. Personal medical data can be communicated to a third party following the written consent of the patient or to a physician and his/her medical team to further the medical treatment of the patient.

C. *Rights of the Data Subject*

366. One of the aims of the GDPR is to empower individuals and give them control over their personal data. The GDPR has a chapter on the rights of data subjects (individuals) which includes the right to access, the right to rectification, the right to erasure, the right to restrict processing, the right to data portability, the right to object and the right not to be subject to a decision based solely on automated processing.

IV. Consent

367. On the one hand, consent may occur without information, as in, for example, emergency cases where the physician needs to take decisions and action quickly and/or the consent of the patient is presumed.

368. On the other hand, the duty to inform may go beyond that required to inform for purposes of consent: after an operation, the physician keeps the patient informed about the results, the prospects of recovery, etc. The duty to inform is less clear when it is a matter of prediction (prognosis) or when there is no further possible therapy for a patient's condition. However, in these cases too, the patient has the right to be informed.[239]

A. *Right to Information*

1. General Rules

369. The right to physical and mental integrity and the right to self-determination lead to the right to information. When there is a contract between physicians and patient, it is based on the general principle of good faith, which means that the physicians should inform their patients. Another physician who succeeds the first physician has a new contract relation with the patient and a duty to

239. A. Benaki-Psarouda *The Medical Duty to Patient's Information as a Precondition of His/Her Consent,* Poinika Hronika, t. KD, 1974, 642 et seq.

provide information, regardless of the kind of information the first physician has delivered to the patient. The second physician, especially when he/she is more specialized than his/her colleague, should always inform the patient.

370. The right of the patient to be informed is delegated to physicians and not to nursing or paramedical personnel. Physicians are always obliged to inform the patient in the sphere of the activities they may legally perform. All health providers should clearly guarantee that this right of the patient is in fact observed.

371. The contents of the information should be determined by the reason which made the patient turn to a physician when this reason is clear and the physician is in a position to discern in a general way the lines of his/her duty to inform his/her patient. Jurisprudence has not entered into how explicit this information should be. In certain European countries, great but exceptional risks need not be communicated to the patient, but the question remains if this is an example of 'medical disposition' and whether the right of self-determination of the patient is fully respected.[240]

372. In general, the information should encompass:

(a) therapeutic information, that is, information on the treatment prescribed and on any possible operation;
(b) information intended to secure the patient's consent and his/her protection from unconsidered medical interventions.

373. In accordance with jurisprudence, and more specifically under AP 424/2012, 'an operation on medical issues may only exist if the interested person provides the agreed consent, after relevant and previous information concerning the nature and the scope of the operation, and potential dangers that this operation may entail. The person may freely and at any point recall his decision'. These provisions entail that the execution of medical acts, regardless of their nature as simple, diagnostic or therapeutic, presupposes the free consent of the patient and after the patient has been informed on the nature and the scope of the medical action and any dangers that this operation may entail. The existence of a valid consent of the patient presupposes the previous full information, in accordance with the above definition, from the physician that will execute the medical action and the physician that diagnosed the need for the medical action and consulted it to the patient, since in both cases the dangers are the same and must be covered by the patient's consent.

374. AP 1741/2013 also states that the illegal and negligent behaviour of the physician is evidenced by the fact that he proceeded to the operation without mentioning the potential, although statistically low complications, that would provide to

240. Nys, *supra*, para. 220.

the patient the ability to balance his options and to proceed or not by being fully aware of all dangers that the operation may entail.

375. Consent entails the significant capability of the patient to make judgments and that, following this capability, the contents of his/her will shall be declared freely.

376. The above formulation of consent is of particular reference to risk-bearing therapies or major surgical operations, when the patient should be informed of the risk in the intervention, of the chances of achieving the desired outcome, and of other factors surrounding the intervention. There are a few exceptions to the patient's right to information, even when risk-bearing therapies are involved, such as when a mental burden would be placed on the patient, and as in emergency cases.[241]

2. Therapeutic Exception

377. There are cases when the physician acts in the perceived interest of the patient by withholding information: this exception should be applied strictly, and the physician has the burden of proving that this withholding of information was justified for therapeutic purposes.[242]

3. Sanction

378. The duty to inform the patient is well established, but it is difficult to sanction the physician who did not respect it. All the conditions for holding physicians liable must be fulfilled.[243]

B. Right Not to Know

379. A patient may refrain from his/her right to information if he/she does not want to be burdened with information about his/her illness, as sometimes this helps. But in certain cases (in a purely diagnostic context), the right not to know is not absolute when not informing would seriously cause harm to the patient or third parties.[244]

241. Kotsianou, *supra*, 149 et seq.; Karakosta, *supra*, 21; Art. 12, para. 3a of L. 3418/2005.
242. Article 12, para. 3b of L. 3418/2005.
243. *See also* Art. 25 of the PC and Art. 36 of L. 3418/2005.
244. H. Politi, *Information and Consent of the Patient*, Iatriko Vima, 1990, 42; Alexiadis, *supra*, 113 et seq. para. 2 of Art. 11 of L. 3418/2005.

C. Right to Consent

1. General Rules

380. Besides the right to consent of the patient that is a precondition of a contract for medical services, consent of the patient is also needed in relation to the infringement of the physical integrity of the patient caused by a medical intervention.

381. Any medical intervention that infringes the physical integrity of the patient could be a voluntary injury (Articles 308, 309 and 310 of PC). It is the infringement of the patient's person that forms the legal foundation of the physician's liability when a medical intervention is carried out without due consent; the medical intervention is considered as bodily harm, and the illegal character of this act is annulled only when the valid consent of the patient obtains. By Article 2 of Law 3418/2005, physicians are required to respect the patient's person and honour absolutely. Physicians are forbidden to carry out, unless indicated, any therapy, surgical operation or experiment that might affect the sense of individual liberty and free will of a patient who is of sound mind.

382. The physician owes unlimited care for the maintenance and preservation of human life. He/she is obliged to refrain from any action which might result in hindrance to the reproduction of, or might create hazard to, life; an exception is made only for indicated and unavoidable therapeutic needs. Article 25 of the PC states that no act is illegal which is executed in order to overturn a present or certain danger that threatens a person.

383. The question remains whether the legal justification is clear or if the physical integrity of the human body is a 'good' that can be disposed of freely by its 'owner'. It remains a fact that criminal law protects both the private and the public interest, so a criminal offence is not related to the consent of the individual.[245]

384. In medical and legal practice, the consent of the patient has become of great importance. According to certain authorities, a person's physical integrity is to a certain degree at his/her disposal. This opinion exempts from criminal liability action that, seen in an objective way, would amount to bodily harm, such as taking blood for a transfusion or cosmetic surgery. So with vasectomy: the consent of the patient is decisive because it does not have therapeutic but contraceptive purposes in most cases.[246]

---

245. Article 29, para. 3 of L. 3418/2005.
246. *See* definition of 'health' by WHO, Nys, *supra*, para. 197.

2. Presumed Consent

385. It is not right to think that consent of the patient is not required for a trivial diagnostic or therapeutic procedure without any risks and so commonly practised. Consent is always required, but it may be presumed in such as the above cases. A physician must consider the consent of the informed patient, who has the right to express his/her refusal of any intervention, trivial or serious. Physicians are to respect the informed refusal of the patient.

386. However, there is the case when patients show passive behaviour because they do not dare to say anything to the physician. Whether the implied or presumed consent of the patient exists in a case will depend on the nature of the medical intervention, its possible consequences and the attitude of the patient.

387. In order to exempt the physician from criminal liability, there should be proved written real consent and not merely passive endurance, coming from a person legally competent to consent, prior to the fact.[247] Oral consent does not safeguard the physician.

3. Scope of the Consent of the Patient

388. The consent of the patient is valid only for that medical intervention. However, should there arise during an operation the need for an extended intervention, unforeseeable and so not discussed with the patient, the important disadvantageous consequences for the patient shall be the critical element; in emergencies, the duty to help prevails. In such cases, the physician performs medical actions upon the patient without consent as he/she judges that immediate action is needed. Such have been described as 'independently-willed' actions by the physician, which follow decisions taken alone and with utmost care, when exceptional conditions apply, these being the existence of grave damage to health or the prospect of imminent death, the impossibility of delaying the particular medical act indicated, and the impossibility of securing consent from the patient or his/her relatives, because of his/her unconscious state or the impossibility of contacting the relatives. In emergency cases, the physician may act for therapeutic purposes even against the consent of the patients or their relatives, e.g., those whose religious doctrines are opposed to the physician's (medically accepted) therapeutic act.[248]

247. Alexiadis, *supra*, 116–117.
248. Alexiadis, *supra*, 119.

4. Sanction

389. The lack of consent is very difficult for a patient to prove. The obligation of the physician to ask for the consent of the patient has a rather wide sense. Moreover, it is up to the patient to prove the causal link between the damage he/she suffered and the omission of the physician, in order to hold the physician liable.

5. Formal Aspects

390. More and more often in cases lacking any medical indication, such as sterilizations or cosmetic operations, written forms of contract are signed by the patient and sometimes the physician, though they are not considered as a substitute for informed consent of the patient, especially when the 'technical' language of the contract is not fully understood by the patient.

V. Duty of Medical Secrecy

A. *General Principle*

391. Physicians are obliged to protect the confidences revealed by their patients. According to Article 5A of the Constitution (as revised in 2008), all persons have the right to information, as specified by law. Restrictions to this right may be imposed by law only insofar as they are absolutely necessary and justified for reasons of national security, of combating crime or of protecting rights and interests of third parties. Though the PC does not define medical secrecy, the fact remains that any illness comes under medical secrecy. Article 13 of Law 3418/2005 (previous Articles 22 and 23 of MA 1565/1939) establishes the obligation of the physician to abide by total secrecy concerning any data of the patient or his/her relatives and provisions for reasons to revoke this obligation. These reasons are the following: (a) the physician aims to fulfil a legal duty when it is imposed by a special law such as in the cases of childbirth, death, inflectional diseases and others or by a general law as in the obligation of early notification to the public authority when the physician in a trustworthy manner becomes aware of a felony, or that a felony is underway in such a time to prevent its execution or its result; (b) the physician aims to secure a legal or other justified substantial public interest or his/her own interest or someone else's that cannot be differently protected; (c) when a state of emergency or defence has been declared; (d) the obligation of medical secrecy is revoked if the person involved consents unless if his/her declaration is void such as in the cases of misleading, fraud, threat, physical or psychological violence, or if the revoke of the obligation constitutes a violation of human dignity; (e) physicians involved in public control service, inspection or expert appraisement are released of this obligation only towards their principals, and only on the scope of the mandate as well as on the rest of the terms of the mandate.

392. The Code of Medical Deontology includes additional provisions that safeguard secrecy, for third persons that work with the physician regardless of whether the physician has stopped practising or the patient has deceased.

393. In particular,[249] the physician is obliged to take every possible measure to ensure that indications that might lead to a breach of medical secrecy are not included in professional or scientific books or articles. The issue of certificates or any kind of medical opinion is forbidden if they do not include a clear reference to their purpose as well as the name of the recipient. It is forbidden to issue certificates or prescriptions for therapeutic procedures or appliances without including the name of the recipient as well as the written declaration that he/she recognizes the obligation not to make public the certificate, declaration or prescription in non-scientific periodicals, newspapers or leaflets, or another profit-making publicity medium.

394. Further, law[250] rules that the strict maintenance of medical secrecy is obligatory for all physicians serving in social insurance organizations or foundations under public or private law, of any kind or category. Physicians must be inflexible in their maintenance of medical secrecy. Any declaration contrary to the principle of medical secrecy is to be avoided. The only ones exempt from this obligation are those executing a task of inspection, certification or evaluation, and then only within the limits of their instructions and the specific task undertaken. Under no circumstances may a doctor undertake an assessment of a patient on behalf of a third party when that patient is or has been under his/her care.

395. Moreover, Article 371 of the PC imposes upon the physicians a legal obligation not to disclose confidential information on patients which they have learned in the course of their professional practice, not only from the patients themselves but also from other sources too. By Article 371,[251] physicians to whom personal information has been confided because of their profession or in their quality as professionals, as well as physicians' auxiliary personnel, may be punished by a fine or by imprisonment of up to one year, should they disclose such information. Proof against a physician of a criminal breach of secrecy requires that there should be (malicious) intention on the physician's part as well as the disclosure of the information. However, for tortious civil liability, it is sufficient to demonstrate carelessness on his/her part in order to prove tortious liability under Articles 914 (et seq.) of the CC.[252]

396. The duty of medical secrecy still falls within the margins of the mission of physicians, in cases where physicians medically investigate persons at the request of third parties, e.g., insurance companies. They should not disclose any other medical information found during the examination or in the course of their profession.

249. Article 8 of L. 3418/2005.
250. Article 20 of Act 3418/2005.
251. *See also* Art. 63 of L. 4170/2013.
252. *See also* Art. 36 of L. 3418/2005.

The same obligation rests with nurses and paramedical personnel who are also bound to their professional duty of secrecy on medical information circulating within the team. This is the 'shared medical secret'.[253]

B. Exceptions

1. Testimony in a Court

397. Physicians summoned to testify in court have a right to silence, or testimonial privilege, not to disclose medical information in court, as the right is expressly recognized by Article 212 of the Code of Penal Procedure (CPP). According to this article, the physician, having been sworn in, then maintains professional discretion. However, in cases of alleged wrongdoing by a patient, such as failure to pay medical fees, then the physician may disclose information that would normally breach secrecy, as well as other information already made public by the patient, in justification of the physician's claim. Anyway, testimonial privilege to confidential disclosures made to a physician is generally accepted. Physicians are to judge and to decide with due regard to the interests of the patient. But, there are circumstances in which the disclosure of medically confidential information is covered by particular legal provisions.

2. Statutory Obligations to Disclose Confidential Information

398. Law requires physicians to disclose information about a patient despite his/her refusal in certain cases. Moreover, by Article 212 CPP, medical secrecy is not annulled by the patient's waiver exempting the physician from the duty to maintain it; medical secrecy exists for the benefit of society, not of individuals.[254] Law 1193/1981 on sexually transmitted diseases compulsorily demands the notification of any confirmed or suspected case of a venereal disease, but only to the competent authorities. Paragraph 2 of Article 13 of Law 1193/81 states that any physician, midwife, pharmacist, civil servant, municipal employee, or employee of a legal person under private or public law, who, in the course of his/her duties, or through personal relations with the sufferer or infected person, discovers any case of sexually transmitted disease, and communicates this information to any unauthorized person, shall be punished in accordance with Article 371 of the PC.

399. Paragraph 4 of Article 371 of the PC includes provisions which annul the wrongness of breaches of the duty to discretion; the act is not wrong or punishable if the obliged person should observe, in the course of his/her duty or in the following of the law or for other sufficient reason, an essential interest of the public, of himself/herself, or of some other person, which interest may not be protected by other means. The reasons set out in the above law are:

---

253. Nys, *supra*, para. 263.
254. Article 16 of L. 3418/2005.

(a) the fulfilment of a duty (the obligation to declare births, deaths and transmissible diseases to the competent authorities);
(b) the protection of an essential duty (protection of the disabled, saving of the unjustly accused, avoidance of public danger, cases of accidents at work, cases of persons infected with HIV1);
(c) defence or state of emergency (Articles 22 and 25 of the PC).[255]

400. In health insurances (private and/or public), the physician seems to evade the duty to medical secrecy. For instance, the physician is obliged to record the diagnosis in the patient's insurance book, which in turn passes into the hands of third parties. There is a lacuna in Hellenic law as far as this matter is concerned.[256]

401. In the course of a criminal investigation, the investigator may obtain and certify documents from a physician, even though these may breach medical secrecy; such documents, without the investigator's gaining knowledge of their contents, are passed to the board of the local medical association; if the latter finds that medical secrecy is not involved, the investigator may then hold the documents.

402. The Code of Fiscal Procedure (paragraphs 1 and 3 of Article 155 of Law 4125/1960) and the Code of Civil Procedure (Articles 400, 401) accept the refusal of a physician to breach medical secrecy, and the competent judicial authorities must refrain from any form of coercion towards the physician. However, by PD 99/1977, on the Code of Fiscal Information, a fiscal officer making an investigation on professional premises into the exact destination of taxable materials, and suspecting that accounts books, documents, etc., may have been concealed, may call upon the assistance of other organs of the State to proceed with a search, which the physician may not seek to impede by invoking the duty to secrecy; rather, he/she must refrain from any attempt to hinder the task of the fiscal bodies, which are in turn obliged to maintain discretion regarding anything which comes to their notice in the course of their investigations.[257]

C. Notification of Criminal Acts

403. There is no legal obligation for physicians to notify a criminal act, whether the patient is the author or the victim of it. Exceptions may arise on grounds of justification, like the duty in a state of necessity, the right (not the obligation) to notify a case of child abuse to the competent authorities, or duties in other special circumstances. There are cases where higher values and interests prevail over medical secrecy.[258]

---

255. A specific exception to medical secrecy is made by Decision A1/6122/19 Sep. 1986 on the compulsory declaration by the diagnosing physician of any case of HIV to the competent administrative branch of the Ministry (Alexiadis, *supra*, 33–34).
256. Alexiadis, *supra*, 37.
257. *See also* Art. 371 of the PC; Alexiadis, *supra*, 37.
258. *See* Art. 23 of L. 1565/1939.

D. Consent of the Patient or Waiver

404. Physicians cannot be released from the duty of secrecy in front of a court of justice by the circumstance that the patient has consented to the disclosure of confidential information,[259] though the consent or the request of the patient enables a physician to disclose confidential information to a third party. However, action for breach of medical secrecy may follow upon a deposition by the person who confided in the physician, by the person who suffered harm by the revealing of the confidential information, or by a person who has an interest in maintaining that discretion the breach of which caused harm.[260]

E. Issuing of Medical Certificates

405. By Article 5 of Law 3418/2005 on the Code of Medical Deontology, it is forbidden to issue a medical certificate that does not bear the reason for its issue and the name of the recipient. The issue of a false certificate is a criminal offence. By paragraph 1 of Article 221 of the PC,[261] a physician, dentist, veterinarian, pharmacist or midwife who knowingly issues a false certificate[262] destined for a public service or an insurance enterprise may be punished by a term of imprisonment of up to two years, a fine, and dismissal from office or post of employment. A physician who is also a public servant may be punished more severely (Article 242 of the PC). Furthermore, the use of a false certificate by the patient is also punishable under paragraph 2 of Article 221 of the PC.

406. The validity of medical certificates delivered directly to a third party at the specific request or with the expressed consent of the patient is accepted. Certain courts in European countries considered a certificate as void because it had been delivered to the insurance company notwithstanding the duty of medical secrecy, though the insured had signed an insurance policy containing a clause relieving his/her physician of the duty to secrecy.[263] Moreover, the announcement of work-related illness on the part of the employer is considered to constitute a breach of medical secrecy. The law allows to physicians the decision on whether or not to deliver a certificate which may or may not be in the interests of the patient.

407. Certificates and opinions issued refer to the physician's specialization, and not to his/her employer (e.g., hospital, legal person under public law, etc.). By Article 122 of Law 2071/1992, legally issued prescriptions, certificates, etc., have the same standing and validity before all authorities, whether issued by private physicians or by those serving in hospitals.[264]

259. Article 212, para. 2 of the CPP.
260. Alexiadis, *supra*, 29.
261. *See* Art. 7 of L. 410/1976 and Art. 6 of L. 1941/1991.
262. Article 216 PC.
263. Nys, *supra*, paragraph on medical certificate (275).
264. *See also* Art. 175 of the PC and Art. 5, para. 1 of L. 3418/2005.

408. The attending physician issues the death certificate: his/her refusal to do so may be considered illegal (Article 48 of Law 344/1976). Any physician in the clinic may issue the certificate. Cases of sudden death are investigated by a forensic physician (Article 183 CPP).

VI. The Patient's Right to Complain

409. The right of a patient to complain was protected as it had been verified expressly in Article 1 of Law 2519/1997. The decision of the Minister of Health, Social Insurance and Social Solidarity which implemented the provisions of the above article established a service and the committee. A Communications Office, or the Secretariat for urgent cases, was constituted in each hospital. A three-member committee for the protection of citizens' rights is constituted following a decision of the board of the hospital. However, all the above provisions have been abolished under Article 32, paragraph 4 of Law 3868/2010. Now, all the complaints are managed by the independent authority of the Greek Ombudsman.

VII. Access to Medical Records

410. By Article 16 of Law 1599/1986 on Citizen/State relations, a subject may not have access to written documents covered by medical secrecy and which refer to third persons. Such documents are accessible only by persons to whom the information therein refers, and then only with the presence and assistance of a physician: or it is also possible to provide such information to legal or physical persons having a right or legal interest by following a procedure established by law.[265]

VIII. Medical Fees

A. *Right to Fees or Remuneration for Services*

411. In accordance with Article 19 of Law 3418/2005,[266] a physician[267] has a right to a fee or remuneration for services provided by him, with regard to the rules of professional medical conduct. A fee is payment for services; remuneration is a salary. No agreement is permitted between a physician and third parties (pharmacists, etc.) when it is connected with medical practice and is intended to be profitable to any of them.

265. Article 1460 of the C.C., Art. 14 of L. 3418/2005.
266. *See also* Art. 28 of CD 1565/1939 as completed especially by Art. 17 of CD 1843/1951.
267. *See* PD 98/1993 on fees for dental services (Arts 2 and 3).

B. Amount of the Fee

412. By a decree issued in consultation with KESY and on the opinion of PIS, there is drawn up a table of every kind of medical and forensic service and the fee which corresponds to each. Within these limits, the fee due to the physician is established with regard to the circumstances of each case, other circumstances, etc. The limits on fees may be altered by YA or by PD. The charging of a lower fee, or no fee, by a physician does not contravene these provisions, on the condition that there is no undesirable competition or advertising.

413. Physicians provide their services under a limited time or indefinite contract, or as entailed in a period of service (e.g., rural service), and are rewarded by act, or by case of illness, or by the piece, or by a monthly or yearly salary for each person whose care they undertake, or by monthly salary, or by hourly pay, or by a percentage of treatment and examination fees and other sums deposited or of the insured sum, as may be laid down in each case by the applicable agreement.[268] Agreements prior to treatment or between physicians and hospitals or clinics making the fee dependent on the outcome – 'no cure, no pay' – are forbidden by law. The so-called contingency fee is prohibited.[269]

414. The lower earnings limit for each type and category of care institution, physician's surgery (office), laboratory, service, organization of public utility, insurance fund, legal person under public law, or legal person under private law are laid down on the basis of the lowest price mentioned in the tables of the relevant decree in each case, in accordance with Articles 1 and 2 of PD 127/2005. As far as the provision of medical services to the destitute or to insured persons is concerned, this lower limit may be reduced by up to half, the amount of this reduction being established by common decisions of the Ministers of Health and Social Solidarity, Finance, and the supervising minister of the insurance provider.[270] The PIS is seeking the realization of those provisions of Act 2071/1992, which provide for the drawing up of a National Collective Agreement between the PIS and the State on medical fees and rewards; this has not yet happened.[271]

415. Suits brought by physicians demanding payment are heard by the local justice of the peace (magistrate) or by the first-level court, depending on the total amount sought. By Articles 677–681 of the Code of Civil Procedure which replaced Articles 35–47 of MA 1565/1939, the judge shall hold an immediate hearing and shall judge by free assessment. The provision of a medical subscription is always considered to have the aim of payment. An appeal may be lodged against the decision, but it is not permitted to bring any other legal means to bear against the appeal.[272]

268. L. 3623/1956. *See also* Art. 4, para. 4 of LD 4111/1960.
269. *See also* CD 1843/1951.
270. In accordance with Art. 29, paras 3 & 4 of CD 1565/1939, and PD 127/2005.
271. *Iatriko Vima*, March–April 1997, 10.
272. *See also* Decision of StE No. 368/1989, *Armenopoulos*, 1989, 171.

416. Hippocrates (4/7) advises physicians:

> 'Consider your fee only a means to satisfy your thirst for further knowledge. I instruct you to set your fee according to the poverty or the wealth of the patient, never demanding an excessive amount in an inhuman manner. At times you will even offer your services without payment, remembering past obligations or considering your present good name. When the opportunity presents itself, you will assist a stranger or an indigent person, this being an eminent demonstration of proper medical discernment. For where there is philanthropy, there is also the love of science.' Hippocrates further observes (4/4): 'We must add this advice: if at the outset you are preoccupied with your fee, you will cause the patient to suspect that you may abandon him, neglect him, or fail to suggest the correct course of treatment, because of disagreement over the fee. So I say that a physician must not worry about his fee. Such preoccupation is damaging to the patient, particularly if he is suffering from an acute illness, the rapid course of which does not allow time to the physician to consider his own interest when the interest of the patient must take precedence. It is preferable that the physician should consider, rather, his reputation; it is preferable that he should complain that patients whom he has saved have shown themselves ungrateful, rather than that he should exploit the seriously ill and squeeze money out of them.'

417. Law prohibits all fee-splitting in any form between members of the medical profession, unless it is in the context of group practice and is 'known to all interested parties'.[273] Fee-splitting, as prohibited by law, means the case where a physician refers patients to a colleague and the fee is divided with the first, referring, physician. If there is a lawful prestation, there is no fee-splitting, e.g., between a physician and a hospital.[274]

C. Unlawful Enrichment

418. The physician shall manage the matter of the medical fee with delicacy, discrimination and moderation, without taking any action or incurring censure for being motivated by profit or for profiteering.[275] Agreements between physicians or between a physician and a third party connected with the practice of medical profession and intended to be profitable directly or indirectly are prohibited.

419. Law prohibits those supplying pharmaceutical products from offering or allowing free gifts or benefits of any kind whatsoever, either directly or indirectly. Also, law prohibits manufacturers and importers of pharmaceutical preparations

273. Article 19 of L. 3418/2005.
274. Article 38 of L. 2519/1997.
275. Article 77 of L. 2071/1992 and Art. 19, para. 1 of L. 3418/2005.

from offering premiums or advantages to persons authorized to prescribe these products. The expenses for the promotion of these products are under the control of EOF.[276] Article 235 of the PC, in combination with Article 263a of the PC, prohibits the soliciting or accepting of free gifts and benefits by those physicians employed by legal persons financed by the State or National Banks (maximum of one-year imprisonment). Provisions to prevent unlawful enrichment by physicians may also be found in Articles 904 et seq. CC. Bonus payments for dangerous work made to certain specialist physicians are in general legal.

276. Article 49 of L. 2519/1997.

Chapter 2. The Physician-Patient Relationship in Specific Terms

§1. The Minor Patient

I. Legal Provisions

420. A patient who has not attained fully the age of 18 years is of minor age.[277] A minor lacks legal capacity, so may not contract with a physician or a hospital.

421. Law 3984/2011 on the removal or transplantation of organs in the Member States of EU contain some specific provisions concerning minors, making a distinction, contrary to the previous Law, between the transplantation of organs that is prohibited to minors and the transplantation of tissues or cells. A prior consent of a minor who has attained 15 years of age is required in the case that the substances removed are regenerable and the removal is intended for transplantation of tissues or cells to a brother or sister of the donor.

422. Any minor, regardless of age, may object to removal of his/her organs after his/her death since they are capable of making known their wishes. This is a more subjective criterion than the age limit.

423. Other capacities of minors in medical law exist, and they all depart from a certain fixed age limit. Substances derived from human blood can be taken from persons only 18 years or older. Law on the prophylaxis of sexually transmitted diseases obliges minors of 16 years of age and over to choose a physician and seek treatment.[278]

II. The Capability of Minor Patients with Regard to Medical Treatment

424. Minors lack the legal capacity to contract or give consent to a medical treatment or diagnostic procedure. The attitude of the associations of the Order of physicians on the treatment of minors is to distinguish two categories of minors: those who have attained the age of sound mind and the others. It is not expressed in terms of an age limit. The physician should decide considering the personality of the child, the medical treatment proposed, the family and social background, etc. Generally, the age of 15–16 years is considered as the turning point between legal incapacity and relative capacity.[279]

425. For the medical treatment of an immature minor, the consent of the parents is required, as a rule. The final decision belongs to the parents and not to the doctor,

277. *See* Art. 127 of the CC.
278. *See also* L. 1193/1981.
279. *See* Arts 128 et seq. of the C.C., as amended by L. 2447/1996.

who is liable if he/she carries out a treatment without the consent of at least one parent, except in cases of emergency.[280] In accordance with Decision 3/2008 of the Court of First Instance of Thessalia, there may be an emergent medical procedure due to danger of life or health to a minor without the consent of the parents. The Code of Medical Deontology stipulates that the physician may proceed, taking into account the situation of the patient, to the immediate medical procedure contra to the provision by Article 153 of the CC permit from the Public Prosecutor in accordance with the principle of *lex posterion derogate priori*.

426. A mature minor may give his/her consent alone, but the consent of his/her parents may also be required. The physician always has to evaluate the situation and to judge whether the consent of the parents will also be required. Sometimes, the parents' duties of custody and care (and the duty to pay the fee) conflict with the personal rights of the minor (the physician's duty of secrecy). The implied consent of the minor is considered as given to his/her physician in order to disclose to his/her parents the minimum information required to justify the fee. But if the minor expressly requests the physician not to inform his/her parents, this wish is to be respected as happens in other Member States of the EU.[281]

427. If the parents of a minor refuse to consent and the life of the minor is in danger, Hellenic medical common practice on youth protection gives an *ultimum remedium;* if the parents cannot be convinced to cooperate, in emergency cases, such as the refusal of a blood transfusion by parents who are Jehovah's witnesses, the duty of rescue obliges the physician to act on his/her own initiative. In non-emergency cases, the physician should inform the Public Prosecutor.[282]

§2. The Mental Patient

I. Legal Framework

428. LD 104/1973 on mental health and treatment of mental patients, in Article 4, foresaw the issuing of a YA for the placement of mentally ill patients in a hospital. The Decision, No. C2b/3036 of 20 November/31 December 1973, made a distinction between two categories of so-called hospital protective measures: 'voluntary placement in a hospital' and 'treatment in a hospital' (asylum). 'Treatment in a hospital' in the law means 'involuntary or compulsory placement in a mental hospital'. A little later Decision of the Minister of Health, Social Insurance and Social Solidarity No. C2b econ 6497 of 19 December 1974/15 January 1975 put under a new regime and defined all mental health institutions. In Hellas, there is also the development of non-hospital mental health Institutions, which avoid the conditions of 'hospitalization'. Hence, Law 2071/1992, in Articles 91–101, provides the following procedure on placement and treatment of mental patients.

280. Article 12, para. 3a of L. 3418/2005.
281. Nys, *supra*, para. 289.
282. Alexiadis, *supra*, 119 and sources there cited. *See also* Art. 2, para. 3 of L. 3418/2005.

429. In accordance with law,[283] a Sector of Mental Health is established in each prefecture. It includes mental health services, which are called mental health units. By a YA, mental hospitals, psychiatric youth homes, pedagogical youth homes, university mental clinics, private mental clinics, etc.,[284] dedicated to prevention, diagnosis, treatment, supervision or healing of mentally ill persons, are defined in each district. A Committee for Mental Health is founded to organize and supervise all activities of mental health units of the area. Law has not defined mental patient or mental disorder, but a negative definition of mental disorder exists. The inability or denial of a person to comply with social or moral or political values prevailing in the Society is not by itself mental disorder.[285]

II. Voluntary Placement and Admission for Observation

430. Voluntary placement is when a person requests to be admitted for therapy of his/her own free will to a proper mental health unit. The patient must be capable of judging his/her own mental interest, and the Scientific Director of the unit must agree. The patient has all the rights of a free person and may stop the treatment on his/her application or may leave if the Scientific Director or his/her replacement considers that no further treatment is needed.

431. A person involuntarily placed in a unit may ask to continue to stay voluntarily. In that case, two psychiatrists decide on his/her capability to know his/her mental interest, and a written document is sent to the Public Prosecutor who had started the procedure for the involuntary placement.[286]

III. Involuntary Placement in a Unit of Mental Health

432. Involuntary placement of a person in a mental health unit takes place without his/her free will. Moreover, law foresees the procedure for 'guarding' a patient[287] and the special procedure for combating drug users.

A. *Compulsory Admission for Observation*

433. The preconditions for compulsory placement are mental illness, incapacity of the patient to judge his/her health interest, deterioration of his/her mental condition, or when the patient may probably harm himself/herself or another person.[288]

283. Article 92 of L. 2071/1992.
284. Article 93 of L. 2071/1992.
285. Article 95, para. 3 of L. 2071/1992.
286. Article 94 of L. 2071/1992.
287. Articles 69 et seq. of the PC.
288. Article 95, para. 2 of L. 2071/1992.

434. In accordance with Article 96 of Law 2071/1992, an interested party, e.g., a relative of the patient, a treating physician or the Public Prosecutor, may request the admission for observation of a mental patient. This request, in order to be admissible, should be accompanied by two medical reports, by two psychiatrists or child psychiatrists, not relatives of the patient, from a list of names which the Medical Associations prepare for the courts every two years.

435. The reports are to be presented to the competent Public Prosecutor who orders the placement of the patient in an appropriate unit. If the psychiatrists are in dispute, the Public Prosecutor sends the case to the First Instance Court (*Polymeles Protodikeion*) and, in parallel, may order the placement of the person in a mental unit.

436. In 'emergency cases',[289] the Public Prosecutor may request the immediate placement of a mental patient in a mental hospital for mental examinations. During the examinations, all rights and the dignity of the person are safeguarded. In forty-eight hours, all the examinations of the patient must be concluded. Within three days, the Public Prosecutor must send the case to the court, and the court may decide. The procedure takes place in camera in order to protect the personal life of the patient.

437. In the case that there is still a dispute in the medical reports, the court may order examination by a third psychiatrist, a member of the Faculty of Medicine or a director of a mental health unit. The court may finally decide on the obligatory placement or the immediate release of the person. During the period of judgment by the court, the Scientific Director of the unit is responsible for the patient.

438. Decisions of the First Instance Court are subject to appeal or annulment in accordance with the provisions of civil procedure. The legal measure of annulment may also be taken by the Scientific Director of the unit where the patient is lodged, within two months of the publication of the court's decision. Appeals are heard in camera by a three-member tribunal within fifteen days. This tribunal may seek a new opinion or whatever else it deems necessary.

B. Prolonged Stay

439. The conditions of an involuntary stay must serve therapeutic needs. Measures of restraint must not preclude necessary therapeutic means such as leave of absence, organized excursions or supervised residence outside the closed institution. The conditions and the manner of application of such means are defined by the decision of the Minister of Health, Social Insurance and Social Solidarity. Respect for the patient's personality must be observed. The limits to be placed on personal freedom must be determined by the state of the patient's health and the progress of his/her treatment.

289. Article 96, para. 5 of L. 2071/1992.

440. An involuntary stay is terminated when its legal preconditions cease to exist; in this circumstance, the Scientific Director of the clinic must issue a discharge to the patient and inform the competent Public Prosecutor (Examining Magistrate). An involuntary stay may not exceed six months in length: at the end of the first three months, the director and another psychiatrist submit a report on the patient's state of health to the Public Prosecutor, who passes on the report to the regional First Instance Court, with an application to continue or to terminate the involuntary stay.

441. The patient or his/her relatives may seek the termination of the involuntary stay by an application to the Public Prosecutor, who immediately refers it to a First Instance Court; if it is not there accepted, then a new application may be made after three months.

442. The extension of the patient's stay beyond six months requires the approval of a three-member committee of psychiatrists, one of whom is the patient's attending physician and the other two of whom are appointed by the Public Prosecutor.

443. Should the patient who has been subject to involuntary admission suffer relapse, he/she may be readmitted provided that the legal preconditions are fulfilled.[290]

444. Private clinics and other legal persons under private law that provide care services for the mentally ill are subject to the provisions of this law on mental health units in the sector. The conditions, limits and procedure for application of these provisions to private care institutions are established by the decision of the Minister of Health, Social Insurance and Social Solidarity.[291]

445. In accordance with Article 9, 1 of Recommendation No. (83)2 of the Committee of Ministers of the Council of Europe, involuntary placement does not, by itself, restrict the legal capacity of the mental patient.[292]

C. The Quality of Non-hospital Mental Health Services

446. The development of non-hospital mental health services,[293] such as mental health centres, hostels, sheltered accommodations, cooperative units, etc., began in Hellas in the 1980s with EEC Regulation 815/1984 and continued with Regulation 4130/1988. The new services clearly compare favourably on cost, quality and service provided with the conventional closed psychiatric hospital.

---

290. Article 94, para. 2 of L. 2071/1992.
291. PD 235/2000 and YA DYd/30536/2005.
292. Nys, *supra*, para. 316.
293. G. Kaprinis, et al., *Evaluation of Quality and Financial Parameters of Non-hospital Mental Health Services Function*, Iatriko Vima, November–December 1996, 46–52; Iatriko Vima, September–October 2005, 84.

447. The care of the psychiatric patient used to be limited only to psychiatric hospitals, where large numbers of patients were frequently confined for life or for many years. During the last years of the 1980s, the provision of mental health services comprised eight hospitals/asylums, one department of a general hospital (in the Alexandroupolis Regional General Hospital), and four mental health centres. The 'psychiatric reform' was principally due to psychoactive medications, and to therapeutic techniques in the branches of psychiatry developed in general hospitals for long-term care, in the mental health centres, and in the centres for the training of the psychologically disadvantaged. A thorough centrally planned programme was put into action in 1991, and Hellas founded or reorganized:

- nineteen psychiatric departments in general hospitals;
- twenty-three community mental health centres;
- nineteen hospitals or day centres;
- forty-three units for the chronically ill (hostels, lodgings, sheltered accommodation);
- thirty-eight associated therapeutic units;
- twenty-two workshop units for the occupational training of patients with mental disturbances.

§3. The Dying Patient

I. Euthanasia and 'Comparable' Practices

448. Euthanasia in its classical form is defined as the deliberate shortening of a person's life by a physician by an act of commission or omission using technical means and without a person's consent at a time when that person is found already in the final death agony. This form has to be distinguished from other practices such as aiding suicide on this person's request, or accepting a patient's refusal of medical treatment with death as a consequence.

II. Euthanasia

449. As in other countries, the classical form of euthanasia is not rare; in the final stages of an illness, in all hospitals, such large doses of painkillers are administered that they may well bring life to an end more swiftly; this form of euthanasia is not punishable. It is regarded as assistance given in accordance with the patient's own wishes when the latter is no longer in a position to express these. In accordance with the principle that the patient's true interests must be served, and with the patient's assumed consent, this act cannot be considered wrong and should therefore remain unpunished.[294]

294. A. Katsaounis, *Euthanasia and Homicide*, Typos tis Kyriakis, 7 Apr. 1966, 84.

450. In general, the consent of the victim does not justify offences against bodily integrity because persons' lives are not at their own disposal.[295] The PC covering homicide (murder, assassination) applies to the physician who intentionally provokes the death of a patient even if the chief motive is to shorten the patient's pain and suffering and whether the physician acted by his/her own initiative and alone or after the consent of the patient. The physician has, besides the penal, civil liability.

451. If the physician has omitted a legal duty to act or not to act and there is also the intention of the physician to make an attempt, the physician may be declared guilty of homicide with the intention of causing death and treated as having committed murder under the Hellenic PC and the Code of Medical Deontology. However, the prosecution of a physician for murder remains a theoretical possibility in the case of withholding treatment, especially as to the point of proving the intention to cause death.[296]

452. The Code of Professional Deontology, in Article 8, states that:

(a) The physician owes absolute respect towards the honour and personality of the human being. It is forbidden to carry out any therapy, surgical operation or experiment that affects the sense of personal freedom and the free will of any patient who is of sound mind.
(b) Physicians must under no circumstances employ the means and the potentialities of medical science in the service of unfounded interests or abnormal appetites or passions.
(c) Furthermore, it is forbidden to cause disease or to aggravate a minor illness for experimental or any other reasons.
(d) Physicians are forbidden to cause drug addiction whether by negligence or for illegal profit.

453. Furthermore, the Code, in Article 9, states that physicians owe unlimited care to the maintenance and preservation of human life. They are obliged to refrain from any action which may stand in the way of the reproduction of life, or may place it at risk, with exceptions only those cases of proven and unavoidable therapeutic necessity. Hence, deliberately deciding on and causing the death of a patient for whatever reason, particularly out of compassion for one who is suffering from an incurable illness, is a criminal act, which is in no way justified by the victim's persistent and clear request.[297]

III. Withholding or Withdrawing (Cessation) of Treatment

454. Withholding or withdrawing ineffective medical treatment that is not in the best interests of the person shall not be punished. The PC sanctions anyone who

295. *See* the Hippocratic Oath, as quoted above in para. 37 and Art. 29, para. 3 of L. 3418/2005.
296. Nys, *supra*, para. 335.
297. Article 300 of the PC. *See also* Art. 29 of L. 3418/2005.

intentionally or negligently withholds food or care from a child or from an incapable person to the point of endangering his/her health or fails to procure assistance for a person in serious danger. But obstinate continuation of a pointless therapy or over-treatment may not be in accordance with medical practice or deontology. Physicians should be free from the fear of prosecution when they discontinue a treatment that has become medically useless or inappropriate, though in fact no physician has ever been found guilty of this. Though care does not only mean medical treatment (there is, e.g., artificial nutrition), and in incurable disease the health of the patient is not endangered by the cessation of a pointless therapy.

455. 'Orthothanasia' is a specific kind of treatment cessation. It consists in the non-application of difficult or particular form of care and the abandonment of the incurable patient to the natural approach of death. This type of omission by a physician does not constitute a punishable act. The physician has neither the right to curtail life nor the obligation to protract it.[298] The contrasting case is that known as 'dysthanasia', that is, the protraction of the life of a sufferer from an incurable disease by the application of expensive therapeutic care without which the person would die.

IV. Refusal of Treatment

456. It is difficult to speak of a physician's right to refuse a lifesaving treatment or of his/her respect (acceptance) of a competent patient's refusal of a treatment. The main justifying reason for the infringement of the bodily integrity of the patient is not his/her consent, but the so-called authorization by the law on the practice of medicine; thus, it is not a criminal offence on the part of the physician.

V. Assisted Suicide

457. Suicide is not an offence. However, in accordance with Article 301 of the PC, anyone who wilfully persuades or provides assistance to a person to attempt suicide, successfully or not, is liable to be punished by imprisonment.

298. Alexiadis, *supra*, 132, and sources there cited.

Chapter 3. Specific Activities

§1. Termination of Pregnancy (Abortion)

I. Short Overview of the Existing Legal Rules on Termination of Pregnancy

458. Articles 2–5 of Law 1609/1986 on the technical interruption of pregnancy and the protection of woman's health and other provisions, amending Articles 304–305 of the PC, have revised the legal disposition on the termination of pregnancy by a physician. Article 310 of the PC provides for more severe criminal sanctions. An abortion is considered legal because of the quality of the physician. There are penalties having to do with the advertising of abortions and abortive means (Article 305 PC up to two years' imprisonment).

459. Paragraph 2 of Article 305 PC provides physicians and other hospital personnel with technical and medical means to help women in critical situations or when they are unable to use contraceptive methods. According to paragraph 4 of Article 304 PC, physicians are obliged to perform an abortion only in certain situations described by law, in which the termination of the pregnancy should not be considered a crime.

II. Short Historic Overview of the Legislation on Termination of Pregnancy

460. In Hellas in recent years, there have been about 100,000 births per year. Fifty thousand of these are in Attiki, of which 30,000 are delivered in four big private clinics, 10,000 in smaller clinics and 10,000 in public hospitals. Problematic births in the provinces generally end up in State maternity units. However, the number of abortions carried out yearly is unknown; the estimated number of 200,000 is (most conservatively) correct. Hellenic Penal Law of 1834 was based on the 'Bavarian Code' of 1813. Articles 303–305 dealt with the termination of pregnancy, without including any of those conditions under which the termination of pregnancy is allowed today. Article 1492/1950 on the Ratification of the PC included, in Article 304, the provisions for abortion. A new period started in 1986 with the introduction of the bill to change the abortion legislation.

III. Termination of Pregnancy by a physician

461. Article 304 of the PC describes the situation when a pregnant woman requests a physician to terminate her pregnancy. This termination has to be performed under conditions described by the law.[299]

---

299. *See also* Art. 30 of L. 3418/2005.

462. The termination has to be accomplished before the end of the twelfth week of pregnancy (with possible exceptions).[300] It has to be practised by a physician and an anaesthesiologist under medical conditions in a healthcare institution where the pregnant woman is informed of all her rights and the possibilities of adoption. Social services shall advise her. The physician shall inform the woman of all the risks, remind her of all the possibilities she has, and make sure of the firm will of the pregnant woman to have her pregnancy terminated. After the woman's request and a written confirmation of her will, the physician terminates her pregnancy.

463. According to the same Article, even after the end of the twelfth week, but before the end of the twenty-fourth week, the pregnancy can still be terminated if all conditions are fulfilled as the law provides: there must be a serious danger to the woman's health (paragraph 4c of Article 304 PC), in which case the advice of a second physician is needed, or the child to come must be to known to suffer from an incurable serious condition (paragraph 4b of Article 304 PC). The advice of a second physician is needed.

464. There is a larger definition of abortion: the termination of a pregnancy, regardless of the stage of gestation and the viability of the foetus. Without this definition, the viable foetus would not be protected by law, as the law prohibits only infanticide. According to law, the physician and the consenting woman are liable to punishment if the above conditions are not met, on the grounds of paragraph 2a of Article 304 PC.

§2. Sterilization

I. Surgical Contraception

465. Article 308 of the PC considers any medical intervention that infringes the physical integrity of the patient as voluntary injury. Sterilization with no medical purpose is considered an offence by criminal lawyers. Neither male nor female sterilization has become common medical practice in Hellas. There is a slight chance that sterilization will not succeed, which is why the physician does not promise a result but only an effort. Negligence of the physician in performing a tubal (litigation) ligature or a vasectomy (male sterilization) is not allowed in accordance with Articles 26, 28 and 29 PC.

466. Contrary to fact, it is generally believed that sterilization results in infertility which is definite and irreversible, so the physician is obliged to inform the patients that after the intervention fertility may still exist or regenerate after a time, and the patient has to take additional measures (e.g., the contraceptive pill) to prevent the conception. In cases of accidental conception, the existence and the measure of damages are judged and special damages are allowed for the pregnant

300. Article 304, para. 4a of the PC.

woman, the costs of the birth of the child and the child-rearing costs. Family planning is now a right, and when it fails by someone else's mistake, that person has to pay damages on the grounds of public order or good morality.

II. Sterilization of the Intellectually Disabled

467. No cases of sterilization of the intellectually disabled have come to courts, and no specific legislation exists.[301] Physicians consider sterilization of retarded girls as unacceptable. This does not mean that sterilizations are not performed in the above cases. Legally no one is competent to give consent for the intellectually disabled over 18 years of age. The patient may be placed under a special protection regime, for prolonged minority, by a judge.

§3. Medically Assisted Reproduction

I. Legal Framework

468. YA 73/21.1.2017 established a Code of Deontology for Medically Assisted Reproduction (CDMAR) with the aim to respond to the growing needs of society concerning a scientific and legitimate framework of conduct by taking into account medical responsibility for both physicians who practise and those persons that pursue Medically Assisted Reproduction (MAR). In accordance with the Preamble of the YA, the Code signifies the importance of legal, environmental and societal concerns and the importance of MAR concerning the promotion of the institution of the family and the improvement of the quality of life.

469. CDMAR supplements the Code of Medical Deontology and is reviewed by the National Authority of MAR in accordance with Article 20, paragraph 1, section c of Law 3305/2005.

470. Article 3 of the CDMAR stipulates the protection of the rights of those involved in MAR in a manner that ensures the liberty of the persons and the right of personality as well as the satisfaction of the need for having descendants in accordance with current developments in medicine, biology and the principles of bioethics. All the above need to take into account the rights of the child to be born. MAR is allowed only in cases where childbirth is not possible in a physical manner when it needs to be ensured that the transmission of serious illness is avoided and when fertility of the persons is to be ensured in cases of serious illness.

471. The new Code, among others, further sets limits to MAR, defines which properties need to be established for the persons that are involved in MAR, which methods to be allowed, information to those willing to proceed to MAR and consent of the persons without faults to the medical actions involved in MAR. Also,

301. Articles 2, 8 and 15 of L. 3418/2005.

the new Code has provisions concerning the donation and surrogacy, multiple birth and cryopreservation of genetic material, protection of personal data and the promotion of MAR.

472. One of the most important provisions of the Code is the provision for the recording of data of third persons that are donors of genetic material before the first use-donation that are codified in a record by the National Authority for MAR.[302] MAR Units, during the selection of donors, must consult the record in order to examine possible excess of the number of children by the particular donor.

473. In accordance with Article 24 of the CDMAR, it is prohibited for any physicians or professionals in MAR, Cryopreservation Units, MAR Units, advertising companies and media to create any type of announcements or advertising to promote the supply of their services. It is therefore provisioned that information provided to the persons that are willing to proceed to MAR is specific concerning the possibility of success (compared to similar couples with the same method of MAR) without the aim to commercialize this service in violation of the principles of medical profession.

474. In Article 59, Law 2071/1992 provided the organization and functioning of units for MAR. Neither the Code of Medical Deontology nor the European Code of Medical Deontology created difficulties for MAR. There were also Recommendations of the Parliamentary Commission of the Council of Europe No. 934/1982 on genetic ethics and No. 1046/1986 which suggested rules on when it is and when it is not acceptable to make use of embryos for research and other purposes. Law 3089/2002, Law 3305/2005 and Law 4272/2014 issued rules for medically assisted human conception in Hellas. Recently, PD 10/2016 established provision for the functioning of MAR Units, while YA 73/24.1.2017 established the CDMAR.

475. The methods of MAR are artificial insemination and in vitro fertilization followed by embryo transfer. Techniques include the intra-fallopian transfer of gametes, zygotes or fertilized eggs (ova), the intra-ovarian infusion of sperm, the cryopreservation of genetic material or of fertilized eggs, assisted incubation, and pre-implantation diagnostic investigations. Research utilizing fertilized human ova is permitted under conditions laid down in Articles 11 and 12 of Law 3305/2005. Cloning for reproductive reasons is forbidden, as is the production of chimaeras and hybrids.[303] The selection of sex is also forbidden except for the avoidance of serious heritable sex-linked disease.[304] In the application of the above methods and techniques, what must be taken into primary account is the interest of the future child.[305]

302. Article 10 of the CDMAR.
303. Article 4, para. 3 of the CDMAR.
304. Article 2, para. 3 of L. 3305/2005.
305. Article 1, para. 2 of L. 3305/2005; Art. 4 of the CDMAR.

476. MAR, IYA, is defined as any instance of gestation or childbearing which is achieved by methods other than the physical union of man and woman, which methods are applied in special IYA facilities (MAR). MAR may be carried out under certain conditions; the woman may not be over 50 years of age;[306] when, in younger persons, genetic material or fertilized eggs are to be cryopreserved for future use,[307] it is obligatory to check for the presence of human immunodeficiency viruses (HIV1, HIV2), hepatitis B and C, and syphilis.[308] If the persons are HIV positive, then a previous licence by the National Authority of MAR is required.[309] These techniques are considered as a remedy against infertility, as a means for the prevention of genetic diseases, as an alternative to natural procreation and of course as a medical activity.

477. Artificial insemination with or without donor sperm, in vitro fertilization with or without donor sperm, and in vitro fertilization with or without donor eggs and/or sperm are applied by, or under the supervision of, a physician, though self-insemination is also possible. In a broad definition of health given by WHO, all the above techniques are considered medical activity. These techniques are now practised in Hellas.[310]

478. Persons resorting to MAR are to be informed of the legal and other consequences and of the risks involved in the application of the methods; then the written consent of the persons wishing to acquire a child must be given, by Article 1455 of the CC.[311] If the subject of assistance is an unmarried woman, both her consent and that of the person with whom she cohabits are given in a notarial document, and may be revoked by notarial document (CC Article 1456, with reservation to Article 1457).[312] If the man with whom the woman cohabited has deceased, a judicial decision is required in order to proceed with the fertilization technique. A parent, being the extramarital partner of an unmarried mother, may not dispute his paternity after having consented by notarial document to any act aiming at procreation. It should be noted that, by Article 14 of Law 3305/2005, the transportation of genetic material and biological constituents and their products may be carried out freely to and from other EU Member States only through the Medically Assisted Conception Facility and the Cryopreservation Banks which operate under licence of the constituted authority.

306. Article 4 of the CDMAR.
307. Article 4, para. 2 of the CDMAR.
308. Article 4, para. 5 of the CDMAR.
309. Article 4, para. 6 of the CDMAR.
310. *See* Art. 30 of L. 3418/2005.
311. Article 6 of the CDMAR.
312. Article 1456 of the CC with reservation to Art. 1457; Art. 6 of the CDMAR.

II. Use of Donor Gametes

479. Gametes from a lawfully informed donor may be used for MAR after his consent to their procurement and use. Responsible physicians should follow the legal provisions and the duty of professional secrecy.

480. More specifically, by Article 1459 of the CC, persons resorting to artificial insemination decide, in a joint written declaration to the physician and the director of the medical facility, before the procedure begins, that cryopreserved gametes or fertilized eggs that are not required for conception may be:

(a) made available without consideration or reward to other persons chosen by the physician or the medical facility;
(b) used without consideration or reward for purposes of therapy or research;
(c) destroyed.

481. In the absence of a joint declaration by the interested parties, gametes and fertilized eggs are kept for five years from the time of collection or production and after that either are used for therapy or research or are destroyed after a Decision of the National Authority for MAR and a previous application of the Cryopreservation Unit that must be submitted during a period of sixty days after the aforementioned period of five years.[313] Non-cryopreserved fertilized eggs are to be destroyed fourteen days after fertilization. Any intervening period of cryopreservation is not counted.

482. By Article 354 of the PC on impairment of family order, if insemination is carried out without the knowledge and consent of the husband, and with sperm from a third person, family order is considered to be harmed by the imposition of a child upon the husband, and penal sanctions may be incurred.

III. Surrogacy

483. There is the case of surrogacy, which is the practice whereby a woman carries a child with the intention that the child should be handed over after birth to a couple. For surrogate pregnancy, the use of artificial insemination or in vitro fertilization is enough, and no sexual intercourse is necessary. According to Article 1458 CC, specific provisions are registration and agreement without consideration or reward of persons who will acquire a child, of the wife and the husband, and the permission of the court. Article 9, paragraph 2 of the CDMAR prohibits the donation of gametes or fertilized eggs with the aim of any kind of exchange and defines that the necessary cost for acquiring and cryopreserving are not considered as exchange.

---

313. Article 21 of the CDMAR.

IV. Research Not Leading to Pregnancy

484. Research is permitted[314] utilizing superfluous human gametes, zygotes and fertilized eggs that have been kept for the purposes of therapy or research. Such research may be undertaken to extend knowledge of reproduction, to improve diagnostic or therapeutic methods in under-fertility and test contraceptive methods, to discover the reasons for spontaneous abortions (miscarriages) and to deal with these, to develop techniques for the control and therapy of heritable diseases, and to study the biology of the blastula cells. Such research is undertaken following the issue of a licence by the constituted authority, which is issued following approval of the research protocol, the written consent of the donors, and previous corresponding research on experimental animals (except where this is impracticable), in a suitable scientific facility; it is valid for fourteen days at most (excluding any period of cryopreservation). In accordance with Article 55, paragraph 2 of Law 3984/2011, a bank of tissues or blastula cells can be established after a permit is obtained by the Minister of Health, Social Insurance and Social Solidarity with a YA. So far, there are a few public hospitals that are undertaking storage of blastula cells (Herakleio, Biomedical Research Foundation of the Academy of Athens) and private units that operate in accordance with the provisions set in PD 26/2008.

485. PD 129/2016 incorporated into national Law Commission Directive 2015/565 of 8 April 2015 amending Directive 2006/86/EC as regards certain technical requirements for the coding of human tissues and cells and Commission Directive 2015/566 of 8 April 2015 on the application of Directive 2004/23/EC regarding procedures for verifying the equivalence of quality and safety standards of imported tissues and cells. In particular, the present provisions, on the one hand, seek to facilitate the traceability of human tissues and cells from the donor to the recipient and vice versa by establishing a unique identification code for tissues and cells distributed in the Union (single European code) and, on the other hand, to ensure the observance of the quality and safety standards of tissues and cells imported into the EU and the implementation of the uniform European code by defining the licensing conditions for the activities of Tissue Importing Institutions.

V. Research Leading to Pregnancy

486. With the aims of the successful implantation of fertilized eggs and the birth of a healthy child, it is permitted to undertake research on human gametes, zygotes and fertilized eggs that will be used in persons undergoing MAR.[315] Such research requires a licence from the constituted authority; the terms of Article 12 of Law 2619/1998 must be met; in particular, the research protocol must be approved, participants must give informed consent, there must be previous experiments on animals or on human gametes, zygotes and fertilized eggs that have not been used for

314. By Art. 11 of L. 3305/2005 and in accordance with Art. 1959 of the C.C; *see also* Art. 14 of the CDMAR.
315. Article 15 of the CDMAR.

the production of pregnancy, the expected benefits must exceed the possible risks to woman and child, while the research facility must possess expertise and be suitably equipped.

§4. Human Genetics

I. The National Authority of MAR

487. An independent administrative authority is constituted in order to supervise the application of Laws 3089/2002 and 3305/2005, with its headquarters in Athens. It is not subject to any administrative control, but is directly subject to the Minister of Health, Social Insurance and Social Solidarity. Chapter 5 of Law 3305/2005 (Articles 19–25) refers, in whole, to this National MAR Authority. The authority issues operating permits under conditions that it itself sets, draws up a specific code of ethics for MAR, informs, collects research results, allocates examinations, brings charges of breaches of law or regulation and imposes administrative sanctions. It draws up an annual Report, submitted to the President of Parliament and to the Minister of Health, Social Insurance and Social Solidarity, and which is communicated to the National Commission for Bioethics and Deontology. This Commission examines any charges of misconduct, issues opinions, cooperates internationally with corresponding authorities, issues regulatory acts, and maintains the National Register and archive relating to MAR, access to which is granted for justifiable reasons (for further information also Law 2472/1997). The Commission is composed of a President and eight further members, with their substitutes, serves for four years, and has its own Secretariat. The National Authority participated in the design of PD 10/2016 concerning the functioning of MAR Units, advocated for the YA 6901/2015 for the terms and conditions of Cryopreservation Units and concluded the CDMAR.

II. Units for Human Genetics

488. PD 10/2016, as supplemented by Laws 4633/2019 and 4958/2022, regulates the functioning of Units for MAR, meaning specially modified units that have the scope of pregnancy and childbirth with the use of methods other than the natural one. Beneficiaries of these Units, in accordance with P.D. 10/2016, are legal persons of public or private law that are established in accordance with current provisions of medical science and deontology and the provisions of the aforementioned PD.[316] Also, beneficiaries are natural persons provided that there is at least one competent physician, obstetrician or gynaecologist with the qualifications provisioned in Article 6, paragraph 1 of PD 10/2016. All the above types of beneficiaries can be of EU origin and from countries outside the EU in accordance with the principle of reciprocity.

316. Article 1, para. 2 of P.D. 10/2016.

489. The operation of MAR Units follows current national and European provisions, national and international codes of deontology, best practices and decisions of the National Authority of MAR. They are considered as Institutions using Human Tissues in accordance with PD 26/2008 and apply quality control systems in accordance with the provisions of PD 26/2008 and Article 1, paragraph 4 of PD 10/2016.

490. PD 10/2016 and Laws 4633/2019 and 4958/2022 also regulate issues such as the premises of these Units as well as necessary equipment and personnel, issuance or revoke of licence.

491. Records of MAR Units are connected electronically with the national records of the National Authority for MAR. This connection is protected by electronic codes, and the scope of these records is to ensure traceability in accordance with Article 8 of PD 26/2008 and Article 15 of Law 3305/2005.

492. The operation of MAR Units is controlled by the National Authority for MAR.

493. Units for human genetics operate today follow the requirements of the present law, which are Law 3089/2002, Law 3305/2005, Law 4272/2014 and PD 10/2016.

494. Cryopreservation Banks conserve and make available human gametes, ovarian and testicular tissue, zygotes and fertilized eggs which will be used for the purposes of research. They also hold blastula cells for research and therapy purposes. YA 6901/2015 regulates the framework of operation of Cryopreservation Banks in Hellas. Cryopreservation Banks are established under a licence from the National Authority for MAR. Their operations follow current national and European provisions, international codes of deontology, the CDMAR, best practices and decisions of the National Authority for MAR. They may operate independently with a permit issued by the competent agency, which permit is valid for three years and may be renewed. An archival record of all stored material must be kept.[317] MAR Facilities are obliged to inform the MAR Authority of any unusual occurrences during the distribution of material or in the course of their own operation.

495. Any person who breaches the stipulations of Law 3305/2005, the CDMAR and Article 1455 of the CC by engaging in reproductive cloning, selection of sex for non-medically indicated reasons, the creation of chimaeras or hybrids, the modification of genes, the transfer of a fertilized human egg to an animal or the development of a fertilized egg beyond fourteen days, is subject to a term of imprisonment of up to fifteen years. Any person who breaches the provisions of Article 8 by selling, buying, offering to sale or buy genetic material or fertilized eggs or material from fertilized eggs or mediates in the selling or buying of the

317. Article 17 of L. 3305/2005 as amended and complemented by Art. 19 of L. 4272/2014.

aforementioned or withholds or falsifies evidence with the aim to sell genetic material or fertilized eggs is punished with at least two years of imprisonment. If these actions are repeated or in an occupational manner, the person is punished with up to ten years of imprisonment.[318]

496. Any person who breaches the stipulations of the law, apart from the penal sanctions, is subject to the temporary withdrawal of the right to practise his/her profession, for at least two years, and a financial penalty of EUR 50,000 to EUR 100,000. A repeat offence leads to the permanent cancellation of the right to practise and a financial penalty of between EUR 200,000 and EUR 400,000. Any person who buys or sells genetic material or fertilized ova or acts as an intermediary in such sale, or who conceals or falsifies data in the medical record with a view to such sale, is subject to the withdrawal of the right to practise for at least one year and a financial penalty of EUR 30,000 to EUR 60,000. Any person who utilizes genetic material for purposes other than those permitted and referred to in the law is subject, apart from other penal sanctions, to a financial penalty of EUR 50,000 to EUR 100,000. Article 27 of Law 3305/2005 details and defines the unlawful actions related to MAR.

III. Genetic Testing and Insurance

497. Certain European Parliaments have approved legislative dispositions 'on the use of genetic testing to predict the future health status of applicants for (life) insurance contracts'. There are certain obligations of the insurance taker (beneficiary) to give 'accurate information of all known circumstances of which he can reasonably assume to be of influence on risk-assessment by the insurer, but genetic data, favourable or unfavourable, may not be communicated, in order to avoid discrimination between genetically fortunate and unfortunate insurance takers'. In EU countries, there are provisions relating to medical information and private insurances. According to these, a medical examination of a candidate to conclude an insurance contract may only depend on his/her 'anamnesis of his/her present health condition and not on genetic research techniques which are meant to determine the future health condition'.[319]

§5. Removal and Transplantation of Organs

I. Scope of the Organ Transplantation Laws

498. The clinical application of organ transplantation by Hellene physicians started in 1968, and since 1990, successful double organ transplants have been carried out. It may be mentioned that in 1903 Skevos Zervas, in Smyrna (Turkey), carried out transplantation of the testicles on experimental animals, and reported his

318. Article 26, para. 2 of L. 3305/2005 as replaced by L. 4272/2014.
319. Nys, *supra* (Chapter: *Genetic Testing and Insurance)* para. 369 and sources there cited.

work at the 1909 International Medical Congress in Budapest; 1910 saw the transplantation of monkey testicles into human subjects.[320] According to European figures, Hellas is falling behind the other EU Member States in the application of organ transplantation, in the number of organ donors and of transplants carried out, despite a fall in numbers observed in the EU over the last few years.

499. From a historical point of view, LD 3372/1955 on the operation of keratoplasty (corneal transplant) is the earliest legislation in the field. There followed Law 821/1978 (amended by Law 1023/1980) on the removal and transplantation of biological substances of human origin. Finally, Law 1383/1983 covered the removal and transplantation of human tissues and organs. Moreover, in accordance with YA A3a/Econ. 2715 of 28 February/1 March 1991, the National Transplantation Organization (EOM) was established. Certain decrees were awaited in order that the law might enter into full force, a situation which created some confusion. At the same time, the procedural organization of the competent authorities for the coordination of transplantation had no clear and intelligible definition in law. One of the basic failings of the law was that the executive orders anticipated in Article 4, on the Tissue Transplant Bank, had never been issued, neither had the YA under Article 3 on the procedures and criteria for the presumption of death in an organ donor. Failing this, physicians simply sought consent from the relatives of the deceased, and difficulties arose when there was disagreement among them.

500. A serious failing on the political side was the status of the National Transplantation Council, which had advisory and opinion-giving competencies but no power of decision. The Service for the Coordination and Control of Transplantation (YSEM) also lacked decisive authority, and coexisted with the Service for the Coordination and Control of External Kidney Cleaning (artificial renal dialysis): the two bodies had not yet been separated. They were to have been separated in 1993, but the separation had not been put into effect by 1996, in which year they were reunited.[321]

501. The anticipated establishment of a Transplant Coordinator had not yet occurred. By Article 6 of Decision A3a/1526/1991 of the Minister of Health, Social Insurance and Social Solidarity, this post was tabled once more, under the name of Health Professional. The coordinator may be a trained physician, social worker or care worker. It should be noted that the uncertainty which reigned in the field of transplantation created various situations, particularly in intensive care units, where physicians certify death only of brain-dead organ donors, ignoring non-donors with diagnosed brain death, as medical personnel is often afraid to switch off the cardio-respiratory support systems.[322]

320. Alexiadis, *supra*, 168.
321. The separation of the two Services was abolished by Ministerial Decision Y4d/8874/96, which also established a national waiting list for kidney patients.
322. K. Koniavitou & A. Varka-Adami, *National Policy in the Transplant Sector*, Iatriko Vima, January–February 1977, 46–50.

502. The removal of organs and tissues from the body of one person with a view to a transplantation of these organs and tissues for therapeutic purposes to the body of another person has been provided for by law. Law 2737/1999 reads that transplantation is allowed only when it has a therapeutic purpose and not for diagnostic or research purposes. It is evident that Hellas possesses the last place, on a European level, concerning the transplantation of organs, with an inadequate transplantation activity concerning the cover of its demands and with an increasing waiting time. Finally, the last place that Hellas keeps in the transplantation of organs on a European level, the low transplantation activity related to the needs of the country and the long waiting time, as well as the protection from the trade of organs or persons with the aim to trade their organs[323] and the harmonization of the Law of the Land to Directive 2010/53/EU of the Council of 7 July 2010 led to the vote of Law 3984/2011.

503. The donation of tissues and cells is regulated by PD 26/2008, and under the new Law, the existing legal framework is complemented, while the regulative framework of the removal and transplantation of tissues and cells is explicitly separated by one of the transplantations under Article 2, paragraph 2. Last, under the most recent Law 4272/2014, Directive 2012/25/EU of the Commission of 9 October 2012 laying down information procedures for the exchange, between Member States, of human organs intended for transplantation is incorporated into Law of the Land.[324]

504. The transfer of embryos or the removal and transplantation of testicles and ovaries and the use of ova and sperm is now foreseen by Law 3089/2002 and Law 3305/2005.

II. Removal of Organs from Living Donors

A. Under the Legal Provisions on Organ Transplantation

1. General Conditions

505. The removal of organs is undertaken in Removal Organizations that are hospitals, legal persons of public or private law, not-for-profit or private clinics that operate under the relevant purpose.[325] By paragraph 1 of Article 1 of Law 3984/2011, the removal of organs from a human, living or dead, for the purpose of transplantation into another human, may be undertaken exclusively for therapeutic reasons, as provided for by law. The stipulations of this law do not apply to autotransplantation except for the autologous transplantation of haematopoietic cells

323. Justificative Report of L. 3984/2011.
324. The Provisions of Arts 1–8 are applied to transnational exchange of organs with the aim of transplantation in the EU.
325. Article 13 of L. 3984/2011.

(bone marrow) and explicitly for therapeutic reasons,[326] to the donation, supply, control and coding of human tissue cells that are for applications on humans in accordance with the provisions of PD 26/2008 that incorporated Directive 2004/23/EC, to the removal and transplantation of testicles or ovaries, to the removal and transfusion of blood in accordance with PD 138/2005, or to the endometrial implantation of embryos, in accordance with Law 3305/2005. Removal is to take place without consideration of reward, but payment may be made for necessary expenses (medical, laboratory, travel, loss of income through absence from work, hospitalization and so on: by Article 4 of Law 3984/2011). Transplantation of organs may only be carried out in Transplant Units, specifically organized for this purpose, within hospitals or medical centres that are legal persons under public or private law, of public benefit and non-profit-making, operating under a three-year licence of the Minister of Health, Social Insurance and Social Solidarity, following a proposal by the EOM and the opinion of the KESY (Article 13). By Article 6 of Y4a/109058/2004, Transplant Units already in operation (for corneal and skin transplantation), within hospitals or medical centres that are legal persons under public or private law, of public benefit and non-profit-making, are obliged to take out a new operating licence in accordance with the law, or to cease operation.[327]

506. For the achievement of the objects of the EOM, there are available transplantation coordinators on a 24-hour basis and 365 days every year.

507. The EOM draws up a National Register of Volunteer Bone Marrow Donors,[328] keeps a National Register of potential recipients and is obliged to protect sensitive personal data (Article 9, paragraph 3).

508. Since the removal of organs from a living donor is unquestionably premeditated bodily harm, the physician is potentially liable for an act which constitutes an offence. When the donor has given consent, not contrary to morality, and the harm is trivial and without danger, the physician may be considered penally non-liable under Article 308 of the PC. Contrariwise, in cases involving grave bodily harm,[329] the criminal nature of the act is annulled only when the donor's consent, not contrary to morality, has been given, and the team of physicians who carry out the removal for therapeutic reasons inform the donor that in their judgment there appear to be no obvious serious dangers to the latter's life and health. The removal of organs from living donors for transplantation purposes is to be carried out exclusively for therapeutic benefit of the recipient, and on the condition that no tissues or organs are available from a deceased donor, up to the time of the transplantation. The removal of organs from living donors for transplantation purposes is permitted only if they fall into the widened circle of donors as defined by Law 3984/2011.

326. Article 43 of L. 4272/2014 which incorporated into national law Directive 2012/25/EU of 9 Oct. 2012 on the establishment of information procedures regarding the exchange between Member States of human organs intended for transplantation.
327. *See also* Art. 41 of L. 3252/2004.
328. Article 6, para. 4 of L. 2737/1999.
329. Articles 309 and 310 of the PC.

509. More specifically, in accordance with Article 8, paragraph 1 of Law 3984/2011, the circle of potential donors is widened and includes: (a) the spouse; (b) the partner in case of a partnership agreement of more than three years in accordance with Law 3719/2008; (c) every blood relative of fourth degree; (d) every marriage relative of second degree; (e) every person that the patient has a personal relationship or emotionally connected with a decision of a court after a control of all the prerequisites for the removal of an organ from a living person and the mental health of the potential donor, his/her personal relationship with the patient, the emotional bond and the voluntarily of the offer;[330] (f) if the spouse or aforementioned relative wishes to offer the organ but this is not compatible, then the organ is removed and the patient is taken precedence in the National Register, thus not violating the principle of equality on the treatment of potential recipients. If there is no compatibility between two potential recipients of a transplant and the living spouse or the aforementioned relatives, but they are compatible with a potential recipient, then there can be mutual donation under a decision of the EOM.

510. A living donor must have attained 18 years of age.

511. When the recipient's life is in danger and the transplantation of non-regenerable organs may not be performed from a deceased person, the decision for transplantation, which may seriously affect the donor (who must be over 18 years of age), needs more than the doctor's consent: medical ethics and deontology must prevail.

2. Consent from a Living Donor

512. Concerning the manner of consent for the removal from a living donor with the aim of transplantation, this is offered in accordance with Article 8 of Law 3984/2011 in the following ways:

(a) by notarial document;
(b) by a document on which the authenticity of the donor's signature is certified by the Police Authority.

The consent must be explicit and special. Documents from (a) and (b) are kept in the medical file of the patient.

513. The donor's consent is freely retractable up to the moment when the removal procedure is begun. Retraction may be made in any form whatsoever. All information relevant to the transplantation is transmitted to the EOM, where it is to be kept in a special archive.

330. Further provisions for the emotional donor can be found in Art. 260, para. 1 of Law 4512/2018 which requires for a permit by EOM after a proposal submitted by a commission comprised by a first instance judge, a representative from EOM and a psychiatrist or social worker in order to establish the emotional link between the donor and the recipient.

III. Removal from Deceased Donor

A. *Ways to Consent or Object*

514. The removal of organs from deceased donors is permitted only for therapeutic reasons.[331] Removal may be carried out only after the consent of death, though it is possible that the function of some organs of the body is being maintained by artificial means.

515. One of the major changes of the new Law 3984/2011 is the manner of consent in the case of the removal of organs from a deceased donor. Initially, Law 3984/2011 in Article 9, paragraph 2 stipulated that the removal of one or more organs from an adult, deceased person is made only if during his/her lifetime he/she had not expressed his objection in accordance with paragraph 3. This paragraph states that in the EOM, there is a record where the statements of the citizens concerning their objection to transplantation post-mortem. Any adult citizen may send to the EOM a relevant statement with his signature. This statement is revocable. The revocation is made with a new statement which is similarly sent to the EOM. The first statement is therefore deleted and is considered void.

516. The phrase 'after the consent of the family' was added under Article 55, paragraph 4 of Law 4075/2012 to paragraph 9 of Law 3984/2011. In any case, the absence of the explicit statement of the deceased is not considered as positive concerning the removal, but is dependent on the opinion of the members of his/her family.

B. *Establishment of Death*

517. When the physician in charge of the case has diagnosed death of the brain stem, and on condition that the function of some organs is being maintained only by artificial means, the death certificate is to be drawn up jointly with an anaesthetist and a neurologist or neurosurgeon. No physician belonging to the transplantation team may participate in the certification of death. If the potential donor had not expressed his/her written consent or refusal to removal, then the physician in charge of the case must inform the Services of the EOM without delay, and in cooperation with these informs the deceased's spouse or relatives of his/her death, as well as of the possibility of a donation for the purposes of transplantation, so that they may express their consent or refusal, as in Article 4. Artificial life support is now continued only if it is intended to carry out a transplantation. The removal of organs from a deceased donor is to be carried out with due respect to the dignity of the

331. Article 4 of L. 3984/2011.

donor's body. It is carried out in the place where the donor is located and under suitable conditions. The operation for the removal of transplantable material takes priority over any other operation. Immediately after death, potential donors who had given their consent to the posthumous removal of tissues or organs are registered in a catalogue drawn up by the EOM.

IV. Expenses and Compensation

518. In accordance with Article 6 of Law 3984/2011, both the expenses and the compensation of the donor or potential donor are regulated in case of death or disability. More specifically, the principle of the free donation does not limit the offer of compensation to the donor, under the precondition that this compensation is strictly limited to compensate for the expenses or the loss of income that are related to the donation, in order not to create an economic motive or gain for the potential donor.

519. Any expense for the removal of one or more organs from a living or deceased person, maintenance, transport and transplantation, the transport of the donor or the recipient is borne by the insurance organization of the recipient or the potential recipient. If the person is uninsured, then the expenses are covered by special credit that is written every year in the budget of the Ministry of Health, Social Insurance and Social Solidarity.[332]

520. Specifically concerning the living donor, the expenses of paragraph 2 mainly concern the medical and paramedical examinations before and after the removal of the organ, the pharmacological therapy, materials for the recovery of health or relief, hospitalization before and after the removal of the organ, occupation of a personal nurse, cost of transport to the Organization of Removal and subsistence of the donor, any positive damage because of his absence from work, remuneration for work lost in order to prepare and make the removal and to recover his/her health.

521. Concerning the deceased donor, the expenses of paragraph 2 mainly refer to:

(a) medical and paramedical actions before the removal of the organ;
(b) the necessary hospitalization and transport for the removal of the organ.

522. In case of disability or death of the donor or potential donor due to implications from the removal of one or more organs or due to the preparation and the related preliminary examinations, compensation, after a decision of the Ministry of Health, Social Insurance and Social Solidarity, is due to the donor or his maintenance creditors. This compensation is different to the benefits of paragraphs 2–4 by

332. Article 43 of L. 4272/2014.

the insurance organizations. This compensation is paid by the special credits of the budget of the Ministry in accordance with paragraph 1. After a decision of the Minister of Health, the required documents are defined in order to be submitted to the competent agency of the Ministry of Health, Social Insurance and Social Solidarity.

V. Information

523. Under Law 3984/2011, special attention is given to the content of the information, to the persons that offer this and the manner that this is offered (Article 7). Article 7 places attention to the information concerning:

(a) living persons who want to become donors;
(b) persons who have parental control of the deceased minor;
(c) all citizens who want to take specific relevant information.

524. The strict and exhaustive provision concerning the duty to inform is imposed given the widening of the circle of the potential donors and the rule of no opposition in post-mortem organ donation.[333] The offer of a full objective and comprehensible information contributes to the formation of free will and choice of persons.

525. Information on living persons that wish to become organ donors with the aim of transplantation is provided by competent persons (Article 7, paragraph 1) and include the nature of the operation, the necessary preparation of the donor, the procedure and the time for the recovery, the potential dangers for the life and health of the donor and the amount of expenses (Article 7, paragraph 1 case B). Information must be full, easily comprehensible, objective and has to be provided in discretion and respect to the freedom, personality, religious, social and philosophical beliefs of the person. Besides, it can be repeated many times and from different physicians.

526. The information concerning the parents or the parent or the guardian of the deceased minor, in order to have an organ removal, in accordance with Article 9, shall be provided by the physician of the minor or the physician or the medical group of transplant organizations or by the physicians of the Transplant Unit or Transplant Coordinators or specific for this purpose and specially trained employees of the EOM. Information includes the necessity of donation of organ and benefits for the recipient, as the urgency of removal. And in this case, information must be full, easily comprehensible, objective and has to be provided in discretion and respect to the freedom, personality, religious, social and philosophical beliefs of the person. The provision of information is proved through a special form, signed by the persons who consent on behalf of the minor deceased donor and the physician or physicians who provide it, and a copy is kept in the medical donor folder. This

333. Justificative Report of L. 3984/2011.

special form shall be made by the National Transplant Organization and distributed to all hospitals in the country and particularly in procurement organizations.

527. The request for the signing of a special document of information of the living potential donor or the persons with parental control of a deceased minor donor secures compliance with the information of a specific content.

VI. Duties of Physician Removing Organs

528. The physician shall have no doubt as to the altruistic motives of the donor, as to the clear and complete information given to the donor and the persons whose consent is required and as to the acceptably low unfavourable effects on the physical, mental, family and social well-being of the donor, the procedure may in any case take place only for therapeutic reasons.[334] Any advertising is prohibited, with the exception of that intended for the information of the medical profession.

VII. Blood Transfusion

529. Blood, red blood cells, sera, plasma, proteins and other derivatives and also any tissue or organ which is a constituent of the human body are therapeutic substances and their removal from a human body is not regulated by Law 3984/2011. Law 1620/1988 on blood transfusion organized the blood donation services which functioned in care institutions under Laws 2592/1953, 1397/1983 and PD 59/1990, in university and IKA clinics, and in blood donation units and posts (of first and second order). Law 3402/2005[335] on reorganizing the blood transfusion system states that blood and blood products of human origin may be removed, prepared, imported, stored, distributed, dispensed and supplied for therapeutic purposes. By Article 2 of Law 3402/2005, the EKEA is founded as a coordinating body and in the form of a legal entity under public law. The new Law provides for blood donation services[336] under the supervision of the EKEA. These services are named Blood Centres and Hospital Blood Donation Services. There is also the Advisory Council of Blood Donation, which last has the mission of assisting EKEA. Private clinics cooperate with the donation services, and compatibility checks are also carried out in clinics with the prior authorization of the donation services when the latter found that the former has a well-organized laboratory and suitably qualified staff. Blood transfusions incur to the physician both civil and criminal liability, chiefly in the case of the transfusion into a patient of incompatible blood.

---

334. Article 4 of L. 3984/2011.
335. *See also* L. 4272/2014.
336. Articles 9 and 10 of L. 3402/2005.

VIII. Other Cases of Removal of Organs and Tissues

A. *Examples: Biopsy, Amputation*

530. Autotransplantation (when the donor and the recipient are the same person), the removal and transplantation of testicles and ovaries, the use of ova and sperm, and implantation of embryos are not regulated by Law 1383/1983. Law 3305/2005 regulates the physician-patient relationship and governs certain medical acts, such as diagnostic acts (biopsy) or other therapeutic acts (removal of organs or tissues, e.g., appendectomy, amputation of a leg), and the careful disposal of their products.

IX. The National Transplantation Organization

531. Under Article 24 of Law 3984/2011, the EOM, a legal person of private law, is founded, which operates under the auspices of the Ministry of Health, Social Insurance and Social Solidarity. The object of EOM is the assistance to the Ministry of Health, Social Insurance and Social Solidarity for the design and implementation of the national strategy in the field of transplantation of organs, tissues and cells. The EOM may transfer to another agency, also supervised by the Ministry of Health, Social Insurance and Social Solidarity and deemed as competent, part or whole of his duties. This agency may also assist EOM in the implementation of its objectives.

532. For the achievement of its objectives, the EOM may undertake the following measures:

(a) proposes a quality and safety framework under Article 12, as well as the framework's adaptation to any given situation;
(b) proposes the issuance, renewal or recall of licences to Organization of Removal, Transplantation Units, Organizations for the Supply of Tissues, Banks of Tissues or Cells, Private Banks of Stem Cells, Banks of Stem Blood and Units of Tissue and Cells Applications as well as the preconditions for these licences;
(c) ensures that the Organizations of Removal, Transplantation Units, Organizations for the Supply of Tissues, Banks of Tissues or Cells, Private Banks of Stem Cells, Banks of Stem Blood and Units of Tissue and Cells Applications are regularly controlled in order to abide by the requirements of the Law;
(d) proceeds to an annual evaluation and assessment of the operation and the results of the Organizations of Removal, Units of Transplantations and Supply Organizations, Units of Tissue and Cells Applications and submits a report to the Ministry of Health, Social Insurance and Social Solidarity;
(e) applies a system of submission and management of all data concerning serious undesirable events and/or reactions in accordance with Article 20;
(f) provides the proper guidance to the hospitals, professionals of the fields and in any other agencies that operate in any stage of the transplantation process;

(g) participates, whenever possible, in the network of the EU in accordance with Article 32;
(h) supervises the exchange of organs with other Member States and third countries in accordance with Article 30;
(i) ensures that the fundamental right of the protection of private date is fully and effectively defended in any transplantation activity.

533. Articles 24–28 of the new Law regulate all other issues of the EOM. The EOM employs specialized scientific staff and Transplantation Coordinators for the administrative and technical support of the Organization. The Minister appoints an eleven-member Administrative Council, which serves for three years in accordance with Article 25 of Law 3984/2011. Article 26 defines the resources of EOM which are: (a) a subsidy from the budget of the Ministry of Health, Social Insurance and Social Solidarity; (b) donations, bequests, inheritances and any other donations from third parties; (c) receipts from any type of expenses for search, taking and transport of bone marrow from International Search Banks, insurance organizations or from the special credit concerning uninsured recipients; (d) participations in European or international funding projects. Article 27 stipulates all issues concerning the personnel of EOM, and Article 28 sets the regulation of the Organization.

534. Under a PD, that is issued after a proposal of the Ministers of Finance and Health, the regulation of operation of EOM is concluded which regulates the organization and the structure of the agencies of EOM, the distribution of the competencies of the staff, the scheduling of the on-call for the coordinators, the creation of a committee of deontology and the penal control of the personnel. Under a similar procedure, the administrative board may change as well as the personnel of EOM.

535. Under a common decision of the Ministers of Health and Finance, regional departments of EOM may be created with up to ten positions for medical or other staff for each department. A PD that is issued after a proposal of the Ministers of Finance and Health defines the headquarters, the competencies, the structure and the staffing as well as the competencies of the regional department, and the positions are distributed by category, sector and speciality.

X. Penal and Other Provisions

A. Penal

536. The shortage of transplants as well as the danger from their trade explain the increased protection from the penal legislator and the detailed provisions. Penal law concerning transplants is included in Articles 34–39 of Law 3984/2011.

537. Whoever intentionally proceeds to the removal of an organ breaching the provisions of Articles 4, 8 and 9 is punished with imprisonment of two years and with a fine of at least EUR 15,000. Whoever is subjected to removal of one or more organs with a financial benefit is also punished with imprisonment of at least four months. The court may judge the action without punishment. Whoever publicly announces the offer from his part of organs with financial benefit is punished with four months' imprisonment. Whoever agrees or receives financial benefit in order to mediate to a removal of another person's organs, no matter whether the transplantation is made, is punished with two years' imprisonment and a fine of at least EUR 15,000. Whoever receives or offers to receive with a financial benefit organs of human origin is punished with imprisonment of four months. If the purpose of the acquisition is the resale, then the person is punished with three years of imprisonment and a fine of at least EUR 15,000. Whoever orders, facilitates or participates in any way in the transplantation of an organ to a different recipient than the one in the list in the National Register, of Article 19, is punished with two years' imprisonment and a fine of at least EUR 15,000. Whoever orders, facilitates or participates in any way in the transplantation of an organ to a recipient that is not included in the National Register is punished with two years' imprisonment and a fine of at least EUR 15,000. Whoever composes the National Register of Article 19, by breach of the legally provisioned criteria, is punished with imprisonment of two years and a fine of at least EUR 15,000. Whoever in any way illegally hampers the removal of a transplant, its preservation, storage or transportation or transplantation is punished with one-year imprisonment and a fine of at least EUR 6,000. If the performance of the offence of the previous paragraph had as a result the non-utilization of the transplant, then the person is punished with two years' imprisonment and a fine of at least EUR 15,000. Whoever conducts a removal or transplantation of an organ by breaching Article 13 concerning the Organizations of Removal and Article 14 concerning Units of Transplantation is punished with imprisonment of two years and a fine of EUR 15,000. The punishments referred to in the previous cases are imposed unless they are not punished heavier with other legal provisions.

B. The Principle of Anonymity and the Principle of Equal Treatment

538. The identity of a deceased donor is not to be revealed to the recipient or his/her family. Equally, the identity of a recipient is not to be revealed to the donor's family. This can be revealed only after the success of the transplantation.[337]

539. Article 11 ensures the principle of equal treatment of the potential recipients with the prohibition of indication of a certain person.

C. Donation to a Named Person

540. Law[338] forbids the donation of tissues or organs to a specific, named person after the donor's death. Any indication by the donor of a favoured recipient for his/her tissues or organs is not to be taken into account; the predetermined order of priority must be followed.

337. Article 10 of L. 3984/2011.
338. Article 11 of L. 3984/2011.

XI. Regulations Concerning the Removal, Donation, Control, Maintenance, Treatment, Storage, and Distribution of Cells and Tissues

541. The new Law explicitly distinguishes the regulatory framework of the removal and transplantation of tissues and cells from one of the organs' transplantation, while under Law 2737/1999, these provisions were common.

542. All issues concerning donation, maintenance, control, storage, and distribution of human cells and tissues that are intended for applications on humans, as well as processed products that origin from human cells and tissues, are regulated by PD 26/2008. Article 42 distinguishes the legal framework concerning the removal of organs from the removal of tissues and cells and by clarifying the concept of cells states that these include stem cells, placenta, which are extracted from stem blood, cells from bone marrow, reproductive cells, foetal tissues and cells as well as stem cells of embryos and adults.

543. The same principles, as in the case of the transplantation of organs, also apply concerning the transplantation of tissues and cells. Transplantation is allowed for therapeutic reasons (with the exception of reproductive cells) in accordance with Article 43. However, in that case, storage and usage of cells and tissues that have been removed from a living donor with the intention of transplantation are allowed for research reasons if the preconditions of information and consent are met, in accordance with Law 2619/1998 which ratified the convention of the Council of Europe on Human Rights and Biomedics (Oviedo 1997). Specifically for the donation of cells and tissues from a living donor with the intention of transplantation, this is conducted if there are no available tissues or cells from a deceased donor, until the moment of the removal and there is no alternative therapeutic method or this does not entail serious danger for the donor.

544. Article 44 stipulates that the expenses for the donation of tissues and cells are borne by the insurance organizations with special provisions concerning the search of bone marrow (with the exception of reproductive cells). Any expenses related to the search, receipt and transport of bone marrow from non-relative donors through the International Search Banks may be borne from EOM and afterwards from the insurance organizations or the Ministry of Health, Social Insurance and Social Solidarity for uninsured patients. EOM may receive funding from the International Search Banks for search services of bone marrow that he or related services provide.

545. In accordance with Article 45, the rule of anonymity applies, while under Article 46 of Law 3984/2011, the donation to a defined recipient is prohibited (with the exception of reproductive or placenta cells). Concerning the information of a living or deceased donor of tissues or cells (Article 47), Article 7 of Law 3984/2011 will apply in combination with PD 26/2008 (with the exception of reproductive or placenta cells). Article 48 extensively regulated the duty to inform concerning the collection and storage of placenta blood for future use.

546. The donors of cells and tissues are living or deceased persons under the preconditions provisioned for the donation of organs (Articles 8 and 9), meaning the widened circle of potential donors and the establishment of a system of no objection of the adult donor to post-mortem transplantations (Article 49) with the exception of reproductive or placenta cells.

547. The procurement of tissues and cells is taking place on 'Organizations of Procurement' (with the exception of reproductive cells Article 51). These Organizations can be hospitals, NPDD or NPDI, public benefit and non-profit or private clinics and are required to obtain permission for adversarial application of Article 5 of PD 26/2008. Article 52 stipulates that monitoring activities, maintenance, storage, etc., are taking place in the tissue establishments and are divided into Banks of Tissue and Cells in Private Banks of Cord Blood and Cord Blood Banks.

548. Concerning the collection of bone marrow, the provisions of Article 8, paragraphs 1 and 2 are not applicable, concerning the circle of donors, and the removal is made only from an adult person.

549. The collection of bone marrow is only allowed from an adult donor when this is a transplantation to a sibling or a blood relative of up to second degree if there is compatibility, the collection is necessary for the life of the donor, there is no other compatible donor who has the contractual ability to provide in time his consent and both parents consent even if only one of them has the parental control. If there are no parents, or both of them have lost parental control, consent is provided by a commissioner after a decision of the supervisory council. The minor that has completed the 12th year of age also consents to the removal. Consent of all involved persons is provided in accordance with Article 8, paragraph 4. All documents concerning the relation and the consent of the above persons are kept in the medical record of the donor.

550. The new Law also deals with a major issue that had not been dealt in the past. This is the operation of private banks for the storage of cells of placenta blood, meaning stem cells. Article 54 regulates the legal personality of the banks which are legal persons of private law; however, the preconditions for the licence are very strict (Articles 54–57). Article 58 repeats the principle that EOM concludes a National Registrar of Volunteers Donors of Bone Marrow.

551. Article 59 regulates penal provisions that apply concerning the removal and transplantation of tissues and cells.

§6. Research with Human Beings as Subjects

I. Legal Framework

552. Prevention, diagnosis and the treatment of the patient are underpinned by research and experiment, which must not place a patient's life in immediate danger.

The Code of Medical Ethics forbids any experiment which might affect the sense of personal liberty and free will of a patient who is of sound mind.[339] It also prohibits the experimental causing of disease in the course of scientific research or the prolongation or aggravation of an occurring disease for experimental or other purposes. This means that if a physician uses a method that is still in the experimental stage or if the method is tested on the patient and fails, the physician is criminally liable under Article 308 of the PC, which liability is aggravated if he/she failed to take all indicated due measures in accordance with the rules of medical science.

553. Non-therapeutic research or non-therapeutic biomedical research involving human subjects (non-clinical biomedical research) can be classified in legal terms as voluntary injury, and the consent of the patient cannot justify this research. The Hellenic State, in its pursuit of the recognition of the experimental methods of physicians who aim at the relief of the sick or the advance of medical science, passed Law 1316/1983, which provided for the foundation, organization and competencies of the EOF, while the Minister of Health, Social Insurance and Social Solidarity had laid down a clear and detailed framework for the conduct of any kind of permissible clinical trial.[340] By Article 2 of Law 2519/1997, a National Commission for Bioethics and Deontology had been set up, to which had been transferred the competencies of the National Medical Council of Medical Ethics and Deontology that had been established by paragraph 1 of Article 61 of Law 2071/1992. Today, in accordance with Article 40 of Law 3204/2003, the National Medical Council of Medical Ethics is renamed at ESIHD.

554. The YA determined the general conditions under which clinical trials (under the notion of medical research combined with professional care) with pharmaceutical products may take place. In particular, clinical trials of pharmaceuticals are permitted only by authorization of the EOF, granted on the signed application of all parties involved, and when all procedures have been followed and recorded in a protocol. The EOF observes, checks, modifies the protocol and has the right to terminate the trial (Article 7 of the YA).

555. There are various international agreements, covenants, etc., that include principles and provisions for medical research on humans. In the 1964 Helsinki Declaration of the WMA, on human experimentation, revised in 1975 (Tokyo), 1983 (Venice), 1989 (Hong Kong), and 1996 (South Africa), it is declared that progress in medicine is founded on research which must consist in part of experimentation upon human subjects, which in turn is founded on experimentation upon animals, etc. At the 1975 Tokyo meeting, certain principles were reviewed while new principles were introduced, first among these being the consent of the human subject. The EU standing committee of physicians, in its principles of European medical deontology in 1987, provided for general regulations for human experimentation. Consent is to be granted by the person or by his/her legal representative and remains valid as long as there is full information on the subject, importance and

339. Article 24 of L. 3418/2005.
340. Ministerial Decision 10983/1984.

risks of the clinical trial. According to Article 7 of the International Covenant on Civil and Political Rights of the UN (N.Y., 19 December 1966), 'no one shall be subjected without his/her free consent to medical or scientific experimentation'.

556. The physician remains responsible, despite consent, for any damaging consequence of the application of his/her experimental method. The physician remains responsible for the offence, civil or criminal.[341] Some studies consider that experimentation without consent falls under the definition of torture and as such is forbidden by Hellenic legislation, such as the Constitution (paragraph 2 of Article 7), the UN Declaration of Human Rights (Article 5) and the European Convention on Human Rights (Article 3 of PD 53/1974).[342]

II. Requirements for Research with Human Beings

557. The Code of professional ethics and the new legislation contain certain requirements.[343] By paragraph 2 of Article 2 of Law 2519/1997, a decision of the Minister of Health, Social Insurance and Social Solidarity was taken on an opinion of KESY and an introductory study by the National Commission for Bioethics and Deontology. These specified the limits and preconditions for the application of experimental methods and clinical research, and laid down a framework for the functioning of the committee. Hellenic law, by issuing Law 3204/2003, complies with the stipulations of Directive 2001/20/EC on correct clinical practice for drug testing on humans, and of Directive 2003/63/EC on the creation of a code for drugs intended for human use. The above Law 3204/2003, in Article 20, introduces the new organ, the ESIHD, which replaces The National Commission for Bioethics and Deontology. By 'correct clinical practice' in research into pharmaceuticals, into the identification of their counter-indications and the evaluation of their effectiveness and safety (as distinct from noninterventionist study, such as the normal prescription of medicines, which is determined by current medical practice), there is to be understood the whole body of internationally accepted requirements as to quality in research, of a scientific and ethical nature, which are to be adhered to during the design and conduct of studies as well as the recording of results and the publication of findings. Adherence to correct clinical practice ensures protection of the rights, the safety and the integrity of the individual, as well as the reliability of the results. The principles of correct clinical practice are reviewed and adapted by the EU on the basis of progress recorded in the field.[344]

558. A clinical trial may begin after the National Commission for Deontology for Clinical Trials and the EOF have agreed on its utility, once they have examined all the information, and have found that the participants' rights to respect for their

341. *See* Art. 458 of the PC.
342. *See also* PD 2400/1996.
343. Article 5 of L. 2345/1995. *See also* Arts 24–27 of L. 3418/2005. M.D. 316/2004. M.D. (Y.A.) DYG 3/89292/2003. *See also* PD 160/1991 on Protection of Animals used in experimental research.
344. Article 1 of YA DYG/2003.

mental and physical integrity and the protection of personal data will be ensured. There must be insurance coverage by an insurance agency for any possible injury or disability that may be caused by the participation of the individual in the clinical trial.[345] Medical research may be freely conducted, with respect for the person and his/her dignity, and is permitted when the subject has been informed of all his/her rights, including that of immediate withdrawal of consent, and has given his/her unreserved and specific consent, and, furthermore, when the dangers are disproportionately small in comparison with the possible benefits, and the research programme has been approved by the competent bodies.[346]

559. Clinical trials on underage persons (minors) require that further conditions be met, such as his/her own assent having received information, to the extent that she/he is able to understand, as to the risks and the benefits, while she/he may choose to withdraw at any time. Furthermore, it is required that the research could not be carried out effectively without using underage subjects.[347] The same procedure as for underage subjects applies in the case of adults who are incapable of legal consent. Both the subject and the person responsible for the care of the subject must be informed. The study must be essential to the verification of data, and must be designed in such a way that it guards against, and does not cause, harm or serious disturbance. A text must have been drawn up, describing the aims, design, methodology, statistical tests and organization of the study, of its modifications and of its formulation. This text is known as the Research Protocol.[348] By paragraph 4 of Article 24 of Law 3418/2005, any diagnostic or therapeutic method which is not applied internationally is characterized as experimental, and its application is permitted only following approval by the KESY; contravention is subject to the penalty of permanent cancellation of the right to exercise the profession. By Article 25 of Law 3418/2005, clinical research involving new pharmaceuticals and new diagnostic or therapeutic methods is permitted on condition that EU standards are adhered to, that there are indications of improvement to patients' health, and that the benefit to the health of the patients always takes priority over the advance of scientific knowledge. Article 26 of Law 3418/2005 deals with non-therapeutic biomedical research, which is permitted with human subjects for clearly scientific purposes, on condition that all preconditions are met, and that the protection of the life, health and dignity of the person always takes precedence over the interests of science or the community. The researcher-physician is responsible for the continuation or termination of such a study. The physician is obliged to make the results known to the medical community.[349]

560. The National Commission for Deontology for Clinical Trials[350] functions as an independent opinion-giving body, headquartered within the EOF NPO. The Administrative Council of the EOF makes proposals to the Minister of Health,

345. Article 3 of Ministerial Decision DYG 3/2003.
346. Article 24, paras 1 & 2 of L. 3418/2005.
347. Article 4 of Ministerial Decision DYG 2003.
348. *See also* Art. 24, para. 3 of L. 3418/2005.
349. Article 27 of L. 3418/2005.
350. Article 6 of Ministerial Decision DYG 2003.

Social Insurance and Social Solidarity, who is responsible for its composition. There are nine members, of whom six are from the health field, one is a lawyer, one a theologian, and one a scientist (academic) specialized in bioethics. The members and their substitutes serve for a three-year term, renewable. The Commission gives opinions on the realization and success of every clinical trial conducted in Hellas.

561. Departments of hospitals may be designated as Special Centres for Research, among other things. All relevant aspects of the functioning and work of such centres, their progress in the assigned field of research, their cooperation with others, their obligations, and their funding, are governed by YAs. Such YAs take into account relevant international agreements, etc., such as the Declaration of Helsinki of the WMA of 1964, as revised, the Recommendation No. (90) 3 of the Committee of Ministers of the Council of Europe to Member States, adopted on 6 February 1990 and the document 'Good clinical practice for trials on medicinal products in the European Community', put into operation within EEC on 1 July 1991[351] and the latest Directives 2001/83/EC and 2003/63/EC.

§7. Professional Freedom

I. Legal Framework of Professional Freedom

562. The diagnostic and therapeutic freedom or professional freedom of a physician are found in legal acts.[352] Part of this freedom is the freedom of choice of legally circulating medications.[353] In June 1993, the Council of the Ministers of EU adopted Regulation 2309/93/EEC which, together with Directives 65/65/EEC and 75/319/EEC as they have been revised or replaced, constitutes the basis of the system of approving medications in the EU countries.[354] In Hellas, this new system of approving medications for human and animal use has been in use since 1 January 1995. By the above Regulations, the European Agency for the Evaluation of Medical Products was established. A physician is free to choose what procedures will be adopted, whether in establishing a diagnosis or drawing up and applying a course of treatment. Any limitation of this freedom is legal without effect. Diagnosis and treatment by a hospital physician is an expression of this professional autonomy.

II. Control over Professional Freedom

A. *Control by the Councils of the Order of Physicians*

563. Intentional or unintentional misuse of professional freedom is considered an abuse of this freedom punishable by the disciplinary councils of the Order.

351. *See also* Nys, *supra*, paras 418 et seq. *on clinical trials*.
352. Articles 2 and 3 of L. 3418/2005.
353. YA 316/2004.
354. Council Directives 2001/83/EC and 2003/63/EC.

B. Control by Supervisory Committees

564. For a long time, the Order of Physicians had the legal monopoly of supervision of all the physician's activities. A physician, according to social insurance law, provides skilful medical treatment in the interest of the patient while bearing in mind the economic conditions of the insurance fund. Expensive examinations should be avoided if there are more economical alternatives practised by another physician under the same circumstances. Thus, supervisory committees propose a list of medications for physicians of the insurance fund to choose from.

565. There is a conflict when administrative bodies (e.g., the administration of a public insurance fund such as IKA) take official or unofficial decisions to issue lists of drugs: such lists limit the professional freedom of a physician working for that fund. The Administrative Court (Council of State) annulled one such official decision of IKA, on the grounds that it was, on the one hand, an individual act and, on the other, a merely regulatory measure. But now, in accordance with Article 45 of Law 2519/1997, a catalogue of medications that may be supplied is to be drawn up by the Ministry of Health, Social Insurance and Social Solidarity for all patients in hospitals.

§8. PRESCRIBING DRUGS

I. Prescription of Drugs

566. The current legal framework in Hellas for the distribution of narcotic substances is Law 1729/1987 on the combat against the supply of narcotics and the protection of young people, as amended and complemented by the provisions of Law 2161/1993, Law 2443/1996 and Article 23 of Law 2948/2001.[355]

567. Since antiquity, narcotic substances have been irreplaceable for therapeutic and other purposes. Nowadays, the enormous increase in their use and addiction to them are considered major problems in our societies. According to Article 3 of Law 5539/1932 and paragraph 1 of Article 4 of Law 1729/1987, drugs are all medicines that contain soporific, narcotic or psychotropic substances, that is to say, all artificial or natural substances that act upon the human central nervous system and cause dependence. Drugs (narcotics) are placed in four categories, each with its particular means of confrontation. By paragraph 3 of Article 7 of Law 1729/1987, a physician who prescribes or supplies narcotic substances for therapeutic reasons must use a two-part official prescription pad provided by the Administration or the Health Department of the local prefecture, and must retain his/her copy for three years. A licence to import or export narcotic substances is to be issued by the competent Directorate of the Ministry of Health, Social Insurance and Social Solidarity following an opinion given by the Narcotics Commission.

355. *See* L. 3459/2006 and the Code of Laws on Drugs.

II. Sanctions

568. In accordance with the law, severe penal sanctions are provided for any physician who commits an abuse when prescribing or administering drugs. The physician is punished with a term of imprisonment of at least ten years and a fine of at least EUR 3,000 as well as the withdrawal of the right to practice, following incarceration, for between one and five years. The same punishment applies to the pharmacist or the employee of the pharmacist who knowingly supplies narcotics without the correct prescription. Graver penalties are incurred by those who abuse an official position in order to supply narcotics. Law 2161/1993, which amended 1729/1987, introduced a more severe legal framework with even greater liabilities for physicians and pharmacists.[356]

569. The objective foundation of the offence requires the knowing commission of the act; if this is not proved, the court may not find criminal liability by negligence, as anticipated by Article 11 of Law 1729/1987, nor may a lesser penalty be imposed.

570. There are in Hellas special units for the treatment of dependence, which are supervised by the Organization for the Combating of Narcotics (OKANA). Within these units, the supply of substances to combat dependence is permitted.

---

356. I. Sigalas, et al., *The Law Governing the Distribution of Narcotic Substances in Hellas Today*, Iatriko Vima, July–August 1995, 40–46.

Part III. The Physician and the Healthcare System

Chapter 1. Relations with Other Healthcare Providers

§1. PHARMACISTS

I. The Practice of Pharmacy

571. There are many laws which have regulated the practice of pharmacy in Hellas. A basic law is Law 206 of 14/17 January 1947 on the practical exercises (examinations) of candidates in pharmacy. LD of 7/15 October 1925 on the national register of physicians, dentists, veterinarians and midwives considers all the aforementioned as 'medically professionalized'. Pharmacy is one of what are known as healing arts.[357] By YA No. A4/5226 of 6/10 November 1987, the practice of pharmacy is provided for in Article 2.[358] Now, PD 38/2010, which abolished PD 213/2003, harmonized the national legislation with Directive 2005/36/EC of the European Parliament and the Council of 7 September 2005 concerning the free movement of professionals and other provisions.

572. Persons practising pharmacy should have acquired a legal diploma as pharmacist, according to national legislation on the award of academic degrees or should have been legally exempted therefrom (Article 13 of Law 206/1947). They should have received a licence, after examinations according to Article 12 of Law 206/1947, from the competent administrative organ of their place of practice and should be inscribed on the list of the Order of Pharmacists. Law 3601/1928 on the establishment of provincial pharmacist boards, as revised and supplemented, states that in the area of each Hygienic Centre, a pharmacist board is established. Article 51 of Law 3601/1928 deals with the Panhellenic Order of Pharmacists, which is comparable to the Order of Physicians in many ways, as regards structure and responsibilities. The Panhellenic Order of Pharmacists is a special legal person under public law, it is located in Athens and its administrative board is composed of member-representatives elected by their respective provincial boards.[359] Its term of office, as

357. By Dioscorides, Hellene botanist of the first century AD, author of 'On Medicine Content'.
358. *See also* provisions of L. 2251/1994.
359. *See also* PD of 4/6 Apr. 1929 and Laws 328/1976, 1539/1985 and 1963/1991.

well as that of the Supreme Disciplinary Council of Pharmacists, is three years. There are disciplinary councils in each provincial board of pharmacists.

573. Until 2017, the practice of pharmacy was a legal monopoly of pharmacists.[360] Illegal practice of pharmacy was detected by the Pharmacists' Inspection Service, which had, in each region of the country, Inspectors of Pharmacies, who carried out thorough and regular checks on pharmacies.[361] After 2017, Article 64 of Law 4509/2017 introduced a new framework where non-pharmacists may acquire a pharmacy permit under the precondition that no other pharmacists have applied for the permit.

574. The simultaneous practice of pharmacy and medicine is forbidden by Article 6 of Law 3418/2005. The Law provides that in emergency cases the provision of initial medical assistance (and medicaments) by a physician may be without any fee or reward. Physicians may supply free samples of medicaments in accordance with the pharmaceutical legislation. For the control of sexually transmissible diseases, the physician may supply medicaments prepared by a pharmacist with the pharmacist's label.

575. PDs deal with the personnel of pharmacies. Furthermore, pharmacy assistants qualified in recognized private schools within the country, as well as other matters and provisions concerning pharmacy assistants, are covered by PD 103 of 17/21 February 1977 as supplemented by PD 705/1977. Moreover, by Decision D.Y. 13B/27782/1995, turns of duty (duty roster) were defined.

II. Professional Relations Between Physicians and Pharmacists

576. The competent provincial medical commission is informed by the physician if a pharmacist has prepared the formula inadequately. Every prescription has to be signed and dated by a physician. Prescriptions of soporifics and narcotics under certain preconditions and the special procedure including the sealed prescription are in accordance with Law 1729/1987. The Law, in Article 7, foresees penal sanctions for malpractice of physicians and pharmacists concerning drugs.[362] Pharmacists must guarantee the quality and conformity of the medicines they supply, as they have the legal monopoly to supply them. PD 340 of 25 August/2 September 1993 on the Hellenic Code of Pharmaceutical Deontology defined professional relations between pharmacists, physicians and dentists:

(a) The pharmacist is obliged to make every possible endeavour to promote affection, esteem and trust for the other medical professions, taking every opportunity to demonstrate courtesy towards them.

360. L. 1667/1986.

361. *See also* the following Laws on Inspection Committees of EOF on pharmaceutical products: 1316/1983, 1965/1991, Arts 45–51 of L. 2519/1997 and L. 2539/1997.

362. Decision No. 4216/1996.

(b) In their professional relations with physicians, dentists and midwives, pharmacists shall respect the independence of the former.
(c) Pharmacists must refrain from any action that might damage the physician's standing with his/her clients.
(d) Pharmacists must demonstrate concern but must refrain from giving medical advice on any matter within their pharmacy.
(e) Before entering into a partnership, pharmacists must deposit a draft plan and declarations with the pharmaceutical association so that the observation of the provisions of law and ethics (deontology) may be certified.

577. The State and other public insurance providers and branches are obliged to see to the financial clearance of their insured persons' prescriptions. The law does not demand that the pharmacist should demand authentication of prescriptions written by insurance fund physicians before acting upon them, irrespective of the sum of money involved. Only in exceptional cases may the competent minister determine specific pharmaceuticals or classes of prescription for which authentication by a competent body may be demanded before their execution. It is anticipated that there will be a single, unified form of prescription, machine-readable and processable, which will be used by all insurance funds in Hellas. Each insured person has a pad of prescription forms, which he/she presents to the physician, along with her/his health insurance book, so that the physician may write down the medication prescribed. The quantity of medication prescribed on a single prescription may not be greater than that required for thirty days of therapy. The Minister of Health, Social Insurance and Social Solidarity may, by decision, determine certain pathological conditions for which prescriptions may be issued only by physicians with a specific specialization. Physicians and pharmacists acting as inspectors are to exercise a check or restraint on the issuing of prescriptions. Those responsible for breaches of the regulations are subject to penalties under PD 67/2000.

578. By Article 13 of Law 3457/2006, on the protection of health and the appropriate distribution of pharmacies within the national territory, limits are placed for municipalities, communities and community subdivisions on the basis of the populations recorded in the last census. A newly licensed pharmacy must be located at least 100 metres from any other pharmacy in municipalities, communities and community subdivisions with up to 5,000 inhabitants, 180 metres where the population is between 5,001 and 100,000, 200 metres where the population of the area is between 100,001 and 200,000, and at least 250 metres in municipalities with populations of 200,001 and over. The distance is measured between the nearest points of the premises on a map or topographic plan authenticated by the competent authority. A licence to set up a pharmacy is issued by the Prefect after seeking an opinion from the local pharmaceutical association.[363]

579. Paragraph 1 of Article 13 repeatedly raised constitutionality issues; therefore, the Council of the State under Decisions 420/2014, 422/2014 and 423/2014 regulated that the population criterion for the granting of a licence of a pharmacy is

363. Articles 13 and 14 of L. 3457/2006.

not a limitation of the freedom of those possessing the licence of a pharmacist and does not violate Article 1, paragraph 5 of the Constitution nor the principle of proportionality under Article 25, paragraph 1 passage d of the Constitution.

§2. Dentists

I. Practice of Dentistry

580. Dentistry is a part of medicine, and its practice is regulated by the law. Law 3038/1922 on practising the dental occupation in Hellas stated in Article 1 that no person may practise dentistry henceforth unless he/she holds the diploma of licentiate in dental science, obtained in accordance with the legislation on the award of academic degrees of the national university. The practice of those having previously acquired the licence continued, and they were legally exempted therefrom. In areas where there are no dentists, physicians may practise acts of dentistry. Holders of diplomas of foreign university dental schools have to follow the legal stipulations (Article 2) in order to receive their licence. All dentists, within two months of receiving their licence, are to be inscribed on the list of the provincial dental board competent for the place where they intend to practise. Certain disciplinary[364] and penal sanctions for dentists were provided by law.[365]

581. Law 1026/1980 provides for the provincial dental boards, the Hellenic Dental Federation (EOO) (which is assimilated into an Order of Physicians) and other relevant topics. Article 1 states that the act of the dentist is the prevention and cure of irregularities and diseases of the teeth, mouth, jaw and their associated tissues. Specifically, and in accordance with dental science, the work of the dentist with patients may be analysed as any intraoral operation or manipulation effected on patients, the purpose of which is the preservation, cure, straightening or replacement of teeth, this term including the alveolar tissue, and particularly in connection with operative dentistry, orthodontics and bucco-dental prosthetics. Dentists have a legal monopoly for practising dentistry. Law considers as illegal practice of dentistry and absolutely forbids even dental technicians from carrying out any dental manipulation whatsoever upon patients.[366]

582. Those who legally exercise the profession of dentist[367] in the region of each prefecture constitute a Dental Association.[368] These associations are legal persons under public law (compulsory associations, not syndical), and all dentists practising in the region are obliged to be members (Article 4, Law 1026/1980). Each Dental Association maintains a register, and each member is obliged to present a yearly

364. RD 11 Jul./5 Aug. 1950 on the Code of Deontology of Dentists.
365. Articles 111 and 112 of CD 1565/1939, RD of 11 Oct./7 Nov. 1957. *See also* Art. 38, para. 13 of L. 3418/2005 and PD 84/2001.
366. Article 4 of L. 3038/1922.
367. Decision A4/1777/1990 of the Ministers of National Economy and Health and Social Solidarity; *see also* LD 4111/1960.
368. Article 2 of L. 1026/1980; Art. 5 of L. 2430/1996.

declaration of his/her exercise of the profession (Articles 6 and 7). By Article 35 of Law 1026/1980, the EOO is the central coordinating body and supervisory organization for all dentists and dental associations in the country; it is a legal person under public law with its seat in Athens. By paragraph 2 of Article 6 of Law 1425/1984, which amended Article 38 of Law 1026/1980, the General Assembly of the EOO is composed of the presidents (chairpersons) of the dental associations, of the members of the board of the EOO, and of representatives of the associations elected for this purpose.

583. Disciplinary committees are constituted within the larger associations and regionally for the remainder; members are elected at the same time as the members of the administration of the association (Article 55 Law 1026/1980). Appeals may be made, within thirty days of the communication of a decision to the interested parties, to the Supreme Disciplinary Council for Dentists (SDCD) in Athens (Article 66).[369] By Article 44 of Law 3370/2005, which replaced paragraphs 1–4 of Article 6 of Law 1026/1980, the Supreme Disciplinary Council for Dentists has five members including its President, who is a judge of an Administrative Appeal Court, while the members are dentists who are elected together with their substitute members. Each regional disciplinary council has seven members, and its President is a magistrate of the Administrative Court of the First Instance. The members are dentists elected along with their substitutes. Decisions of the SDCD are executed by the President of the Association (Article 71 of Law 1026/1980) and may be taken on appeal to the Administrative Appeal Court of Athens. The following penalties may be imposed by the disciplinary council: (a) written reprimand, (b) temporary suspension from the practice of the dental profession for between fifteen days and six months, (c) permanent expulsion from the dental profession. Any unqualified person exercising the profession is subject to at least six months' imprisonment and a financial penalty of EUR 2,000.

584. Law provides for the exercise of the right of establishment and free provision of services on the part of dentists who are citizens of EU Member States, and for other related matters, in accordance with Directives 78/686/EEC of 25 July 1978 and 81/1057 of 14 December 1981 of the Council of European Communities.[370]

585. The laws on the practice of medicine provide that dentists, like physicians, may prescribe medicines and soporifics and narcotics for the treatment of mouth and tooth diseases. They should seek their dental fee with delicacy, discrimination and moderation.[371]

---

369. *See also* Art. 38, paras 10, 11 and 12 of L. 3418/2005.
370. PD 98/1986.
371. PD 141/1989 and Decision No. 17/202 of 15 Feb./21 Apr. 1993 of the Minister of Health and Social Solidarity.

II. Professional Relations Between Physicians and Dentists

586. The professions of physician and dentist are separated, and physicians are not competent to practise dentistry, even when they hold a diploma that enables them to practise both medicine and dentistry, unless the law provides for it.[372] Physicians holding a diploma of dentistry (or pharmacy) are not permitted to maintain a functioning dental practice or pharmacy or similar establishment, unless they cease to practise medicine and to employ the title of physician.[373]

587. There are certain problems on delimitation of dentistry and medicine. Mouth diseases, blood-releasing acts other than those concerning the mouth and associated tissues, and the performance of full anaesthesia for dental surgery are considered as not belonging to the practice of dentistry. At a European level, there is also the question of whether stomatologists are physicians whose qualifications permit them to practise dentistry.[374]

§3. Midwifery

I. The Practice of Midwifery

588. The earliest law in which reference to midwives is made is Law 356/1856 on 'practical midwives' (i.e., those who had learnt the job in practice without formal qualifications). There followed Law 5474/1932 as amended which founded the school of midwifery in the Athens maternity home, and Law 2448/1940 on the exercise of the profession of midwife and the training of midwives, which has been amended and supplemented. Holders of diplomas from State-recognized schools of midwifery, following successful completion of a three-year course and the diploma examinations, as well as a year's service in the institution in which they were trained (at a stipend determined by a decision of the Ministers of Finance, and Health and Social Solidarity, No. 173103/9175/81 of 26 January/10 February 1982) must take out a licence issued by the Minister of Health, Social Insurance and Social Solidarity or the authorized competent administrative body, the decision to be published in the State Gazette.[375] For holders of diplomas from equivalent schools of midwifery in foreign countries, other than those from EU Member States, practical and theoretical examinations for the acquisition of the licence are conducted by a three-member committee of PD 266/2003, as amended by PD 262 of 17 December 2004, on the adaptation of Hellenic legislation to Directives 89/594, 89/595, 90/658 and 2001/19 EC. By Article 6 of PD 262/2004, Polish qualifications as midwife are to be accepted with acquired rights.

372. For example, Art. 1 of L. 3038/1922.
373. L. 1666/1986.
374. Nys, *supra*, para. 505.
375. Article 2 of RD 206/1996.

589. By paragraph 1 of Article 11 of LD 2593/1953, the duties of a midwife are preparation for natural childbirth, the observation of the course of pregnancy (the giving of general and specific guidance), attendance at delivery (natural only), and the instruction of the mother for the healthy development of the infant. By paragraph 2 of the same article, midwives are forbidden to carry out any obstetric or gynaecological operation. Graduates of three-year courses in midwifery at recognized schools are entitled to use the title 'Qualified Midwife' after their names (Article 14). Midwives who are established or who legally exercise their profession in an area are obliged to place their names on the register kept by the Hygiene Centre (Article 15). The illegal exercise of the profession by those with no diploma (paragraph 1 of Article 16) or who, holding a diploma, have no licence (paragraph 2), or who exercise the profession in an area other than that inscribed on the licence (paragraph 3), or who have not placed their names on the register within the time prescribed under Article 15 (paragraph 4), may suffer imprisonment and financial penalties.

590. Article 19 of LD 2593/1953 was applied by RD of 15/28 December 1955 on the Association of Professionally Trained Midwives, which was amended and supplemented by RD 206/1966 which imposed rural service on midwives. By Article 1 of the above RD of 1955, an association of professionally trained midwives was to be established in each judicial district, with compulsory membership for all trained midwives, practical midwives and foreign midwives who legally exercise the profession in that district. Each association keeps a register, copies of which are deposited with the Hygiene Centre of the district and with the Athens Association of Professionally Trained Midwives, which oversees all the regional associations (Article 29 of the 1955 RD), while the general supervision of all the associations is a competence of the Minister of Health, Social Insurance and Social Solidarity. Disciplinary authority is wielded by the disciplinary council of the regional medical association, two out of three members of which in these cases are to be professionally trained midwives, while the same general provisions apply as to the disciplinary councils for physicians.[376]

591. RD 686/1960 deals with the code of ethics (deontology) for midwives. A midwife is obliged, in accordance with her oath, to work devotedly, to lead a virtuous life, to make every possible endeavour to raise the esteem in which the profession is held, to maintain absolute discretion concerning that which she discovers or is told in the course of her duties, and to assist the physician faithfully (Article 2). In case of urgency, she shall offer her assistance without regard to wealth or poverty and without charge to poor families; those in paid employment with the State, with municipalities or with other organizations are forbidden to accept gifts in money or in kind over and above their salary (Article 3).

592. By RD 687/1960, professionally trained midwives are permitted to prescribe only such drugs and analgesics and to make use only of such equipment as is listed in the decree.

376. Article 35 of the 1955 RD as replaced by para. 8 of Art. 1 of RD 206/1966.

593. The exercise of the right to free establishment and provision of services by midwives being citizens of EU Member States, and related themes, following Directives 80/154/EEC and 80/155/EEC of 21 January 1980 and 80/1273/EEC of 22 December 1980 of the Council of the European Community, was regulated by PD 97/1986, as amended by Decision 14/1666 of 28 March/6 April 1990 of the Ministers of National Economy, Health and Social Solidarity, and National Education and Religions and by Article 9 of Decision A4/2557 of 30 July/7 August 1991 of the Deputy Ministers of National Economy and Health and Social Solidarity. Now, Directives 89/594, 89/595, 90/658 and 2001/19 EC, as well as PD 266/2003, regulate the rights of midwives.

II. Professional Relations Between Physicians and Midwives

594. Midwives are forbidden to issue prescriptions, or to administer drugs except under the instructions of a physician, or to stop administering drugs being used under a physician's order, with the exceptions allowed in Article 11 of LD 2593/1953 (paragraph 3). Midwives are forbidden to carry out any obstetric or gynaecological operation (paragraph 2), and in cases of problematic birth are obliged immediately to hand the pregnant woman over to a physician (paragraph 1c). A midwife may not criticize the treatment prescribed by a physician or influence the choice of physician (paragraph 4), and above all is required to act as the physician's faithful assistant.[377]

§4. Physiotherapists

I. The Practice of Physiotherapy

595. One of the earliest laws that makes reference to 'manipulators' is the RD of 18/24 May 1914. LD 775/1970 established, and regulates the functioning of a tertiary School of Physiotherapy in the Athens General Hospital, offering a three-year course open to graduates of full six-year high schools (Articles 9 and 10). On successful completion of the course, the school issues a diploma, to be validated by the competent ministry, which then issues a licence to practise (Article 12). By Article 17, existing graduates of the school for physiotherapy assistants under Act 2048/1952 may use the title of physiotherapist and are in every way equal with the above graduates. Those who have graduated from a non-equivalent school abroad may obtain a diploma in physiotherapy by attending certain classes at the above school, after the examination of their qualifications. RD 411/1972 regulates the rights and duties of physiotherapists.

377. Article 2, para. 2 of RD 686/1960.

II. Professional Relations Between Physicians and Physiotherapists

596. By the single Article of RD 411/1972, those holding a licence to practise as physiotherapists, with respect also to the provisions of Articles 2 and 13 of LD 775/1971, may apply only those physiotherapeutic means and methods specified by the law, and only following the written instructions of the physician in charge of the patient's case. Those actions which physiotherapists are competent to perform are determined by RD 411/1972, PDs 29/1987 and 90/1995, and are costed in the chapter 'Physiotherapies' of PD 157/1991. By Article 33 of Law 3329/2005, which supplements Article 13 of Law 2071/1992 as amended and complemented by Laws 4025/2011 and 4093/2012, these actions may be carried out only by graduates and in those places which the law determines as suitable for physiotherapy services. Actions within the competence of physiotherapists may be prescribed by insurance funds, using a special form of referral. The Minister of Health, Social Insurance and Social Solidarity covers the cost of new physiotherapeutic services on condition that four years have passed since the registration of the applicant physiotherapist in the Physiotherapy Department of a Technical Educational Institute.

§5. The Nursing Profession

I. The Practice of Nursing

597. CD 613/1937, on the establishment and functioning of a school for home and hospital nurses, was in force until 1948, when it was repealed by Article 31 of LD 683/1948, which law defined matters concerning qualified home and hospital nurses. The exercise of the profession and the use of the title of qualified nurse require a diploma certified by the competent organ and a licence to practise in accordance with provisions of the above law. By Article 4, the training of nurses is to take place in State schools and in schools functioning within care institutions: these schools may be of higher or lower level. The higher level schools issue a diploma of hospital nurse or home nurse, while the lower level schools issue a diploma of nursing auxiliary.

598. Articles 23pp of LD 683/1948 anticipated transitional provisions and regulated matters concerning schools and serving practical nurses, auxiliary nurses, nurses who had followed courses of one or two years' duration and assistant health visitors; essentially, they were obliged to assimilate themselves to the ranks of the holders of a legal licence to practise.[378]

599. By LD 781/1970, the schools offering a three-year course for hospital and home nurses and midwives, requiring basic secondary education for entry, as well as the Ministry of Health, Social Insurance and Social Solidarity's school of physiotherapy, were reclassified as lower tertiary institutions. The duration of studies for home and hospital nurses was set at four years, while the three-year diploma course

378. *See also* Art. 17 of LD 4111/1960.

was assimilated into the new four-year course. The fourth year was dedicated to specialization in public hygiene for the acquisition of the diploma of home nurse (health visitor), and the programme of studies was adapted to that of similar schools within tertiary technical colleges (TEI). Graduates of the above schools or other equivalent schools within the country or abroad were offered specialized training in various branches of nursing, such as:

(a) pathological and surgical nursing, including specialized units such as those for laryngology, cardiology, thoracic surgery, neurosurgery, etc.;
(b) paediatric nursing;
(c) psychiatric nursing;
(d) operating theatre methods and asepsis;
(e) rehabilitation.

600. Those trained abroad in a specialized branch of nursing (rather than general nursing) may acquire a licence to practise their specialization under the provisions on graduation of Article 5 LD 781/1971. By Article 6, graduates of the military academy for officer-nurses are assimilated with nurses qualified in schools under LD 683/1948, as they have completed an equivalent three-year course requiring basic secondary education for entry. PDs and YAs have regulated the selection criteria, terms and preconditions for practical nurses wishing to study in secondary technical-vocational schools of nursing, and the conversion of lower tertiary institutions into secondary technical-vocational schools.[379]

601. By Article 20 of LD 683, whosoever uses the title of home or hospital nurse, who wears the uniform of a nurse (Article 21), or who practises the profession of nurse, without being a graduate of a school functioning under 683/1948, is guilty of the illegal exercise of the profession. LD 683/1948 remains in force as amended and supplemented, particularly by the following legislation: paragraph 1a of Article 6 of Law 1579/1985, Article 12 of LD 3057/1954, RD of 17/19 December 1951, Article 14 of Law 4053/1960, RD 196/1969, LD 781/1970, Law 1076/1980, PD 375/1990, and others.

602. According to the Governmental Act No. 82/1962, persons holding the diploma for midwives, permanent residents of foreign countries and having a foreign nationality are eligible to acquire the diploma for nursing after following courses (for one year) and practical exercises in a school for nurses and a hospital, and *vice versa* for persons holding the diploma for nursing. The exercise of the right of establishment and free provision of services by nurses responsible for general care being citizens of EU Member States, and related matters, following Directives 77/452 and 77/453 of 27 June 1977 and 81/1057 of 14 December 1981 of the Council of the European Community, is regulated by PD 40/1986 as amended and complemented by YAs A4/4910 of 3 October 1990 and A4/2557 of 30 July/7 August 1991.

379. PD 199/1988, PD 375/1990 and others.

603. In accordance with the laws on the practice of medicine, nursing is a profession apart from the paramedical professions, and as such, it is regulated by the above and other laws. Article 3 of Law 683/1948 determined under what circumstances and conditions certain medical activities may be performed by persons entitled to practise nursing. Hospital and home nurses are obliged to confine their activities to the administering of therapeutic means and the provision of assistance as these were taught in their schools. They must maintain strict discretion as to what they see, hear, learn or deduce in the exercise of their profession and which constitutes confidential information for the patient and his/her family, with the exception of cases in which provisions of law require the disclosure of such information. Hospital and home nurses who fail in their duty or display inexcusable negligence are sanctioned by the competent authority.[380]

604. According to Article 1 of LD 683/1948, no person might practise nursing or use the title of nurse or visiting nurse, unless the person holds the diploma of graduate nurse, or the equivalent certificate on nursing from a school abroad and fulfils the other conditions of the law. The Minister of Health, Social Insurance and Social Solidarity or the replacement administrative organ (Prefect) certifies the diplomas, as well as the qualifications of the persons coming from abroad and determines their equivalence in accordance with the categories of diplomas and certificates found in law.[381]

605. There is now an Order of Nurses established by Law 3252/2004. Nevertheless, according to Article 30 of LD 683/1948, Hygiene Centres maintained classified registers in which all those serving in any care or health institution of any physical or legal form were obliged to be inscribed. Those engaged henceforth, as well as those not serving in an institution, are under the same obligation. The hygiene centres deposited their registers with the competent ministry, where a general register is kept. Paragraph 4 of the same article lays down the penalties for whosoever exercised the profession of nursing in contravention of the article and for those who employed nurses who did not appear in the registers of the Hygiene Centres, the State or the Medical Associations.

606. In medical science, the persons referred to in the law as nurses may perform the following activities, in the meaning of nursing:

(a) observation and detection of both physical and psychological symptoms in the patient to assist the physician to establish a diagnosis or to apply medical treatment. Continuous care and assistance to healthy or sick persons to prevent, restore or preserve their health or to support them in their distress;
(b) performance of technical nursing procedures in order for physicians to establish their diagnosis, or application of medical treatment or measures of preventive medicine prescribed by a physician;

380. *See* L. 3252/2004, *see also* Art. 25 of L. 4272/2014.
381. L. 3252/2004, *see also* Art. 25 of L. 4272/2014.

(c) performance of medical procedures delegated to them by a physician.[382]

II. Professional Relations Between Physicians and Nurses

607. In accordance with paragraph 2 of Article 3 of LD 683/1947, a list of technical nursing procedures and the medical procedures that nurses are not allowed to perform was prescribed. Nurses are forbidden to administer any form of therapy which has not been delegated to them by a physician, apart from the dressing of unimportant injuries, the use of enemas, the application of simple or blood-drawing cupping vessels, the administration of first aid in situations in which the delay in the physician's arrival may put the patient at risk, and the administration of injections in urgent cases. Moreover, by paragraph 3 of the same article, nurses may not criticize the medical treatment chosen by the physician or seek to influence the patient's choice of physician. Finally, it is forbidden to administer drugs or terminate their use without the instructions of a physician (paragraph 4).

§6. The Transformation of Nursing Personnel into Care Personnel

608. Chapter 2 (Articles 5 & 6) of Law 1579/1985 is dedicated to the education and training of care personnel. Among the nursing personnel who provide first, second or third-level health care, there are:

(a) graduates of higher tertiary (university) level nursing schools (AEI);
(b) graduates of the departments of home and hospital nursing and midwifery of the tertiary technical/vocational colleges (TEI);
(c) graduates of the tertiary schools for hospital nurses, home nurses and midwives of the Ministry of Health, Social Insurance and Social Solidarity that have been incorporated into the tertiary technical/vocational schools (TEI);
(d) graduates of the tertiary technical colleges nursing/midwifery schools;
(e) graduates of the nursing departments of technical/vocational secondary schools;
(f) graduates of the secondary technical/vocational schools of nursing;
(g) practical nurses (those who have learnt the job while carrying it out, without formal training or qualifications).

609. On the publication of Law 1579/1985 and during the old regime, the use of the title of nurse *(nosokoma/os)* was reserved for holders of graduates or diplomas from:

(a) university departments of nursing;
(b) nursing departments of tertiary technological colleges (TEI);
(c) former tertiary schools for hospital nurses, home nurses and midwives of the Ministry of Health, Social Insurance and Social Solidarity and of KATEE;

382. *See also* Art. 3 of LD 683/1948.

(d) after compulsory education (completed three years of high school) schools for nurses;
(e) equivalent schools abroad corresponding to any of the above.

The meaning of the term 'nurse' was established in accordance with international Labour Agreement 149 of the International Labour Organization.

610. Article 6 enables the possible conversion of tertiary schools for nurses and home and hospital nurses under the authority of the Ministry of Health, Social Insurance and Social Solidarity into secondary technical/vocational schools of nursing by PD emanating from the jointly competent Ministers, those of Health and Social Solidarity and of National Education and Religions. As for practical nurses serving in hospitals or social welfare institutions or services, they were obliged to undergo rapid training by the time of the final abolition of their sector.

611. By Decision A4/203/of 20 January/25 February 1988, there were established the conditions for the issue of the title of 'specialized nurse' in one of the categories of specialization referred to in Article 5 of Law 1579/1985. Qualification in a nursing specialization may be offered by any of the hospitals or other institutions legally recognized as offering full specialization to physicians. The duration of practical work for all specializations is twelve months. The competent authority for the selection of candidates is the Health Authority responsible for the hospital to which the interested party has made an application.

612. The curriculum for pathology nursing (general syllabus, intermediate syllabus and programme of studies) is described in Article 7 of Decision A4/203/1988. The other specializations, in the order described, are surgical nursing (Article 8), paediatric nursing (Article 9), mental healthcare nursing (Article 10) and nephrology nursing.[383]

613. Successful candidates for specializations receive their qualifications from the Prefect of the place of establishment of the institution, after successful examination by a three-member examination board, composed of three nurses and assembled by decision of the competent minister on the initiative of KESY in Athens or Thessaloniki.[384]

614. Law 3252 of 16 July 2004 set up the Union of Nursing Personnel of Hellas (ENE). By Article 1, the Union is a legal person under public law, headquartered in Athens, with regional groups in each health region of the country. The aim of the ENE (Article 2) are: the promotion of nursing care as an independent and autonomous science and art for the good of the public; the research and study of matters pertaining to nursing care with the consequent drafting of scientific studies; the

383. Decisions A4/2450 of 1 Jun./1 Jul. 1991 and A4b/1614 of 29 Apr./18 May 1992 of the Minister of Health and Social Solidarity. *See also* Decision Y7/econ. 3841/1996 on the specialization of oncology.
384. Article 11 of Decision A4/203/1988.

identification of questions to be put before the Ministry on matters of education and training: participation in EU programmes; the issue of certification to its members: the keeping of a register; cooperation with other agencies; the participation of its members in other bodies; proposals for the establishment of costing for nursing practices; and advice on the protection of the health of the Hellene people.

615. Membership of the ENE comprises all graduates of relevant schools and departments in Hellas or of equivalent schools and departments abroad who practise the nursing profession in Hellas, who are obliged by Article 4 to register with the regional branch of the ENE in the health region in which they practise their profession. Licences to practise the profession of nursing are issued by the competent Prefect (Article 31). The ENE may also have as honorary members persons who have promoted the nursing profession; these are elected by the fifteen-member Administrative Council of the ENE (Article 9).

616. Article 25 (Law 3252/2004) defines as a disciplinary offence any breach of duties and obligations as established by law and by the decisions of the Administrative Council of the ENE and the regional councils. Furthermore, demonstrable negligence in the exercise of nursing duties is considered a disciplinary offence. Article 26 (Law 3252/2004 as complemented by Article 25 of Law 4272/2014) refers to the disciplinary penalties that may be imposed by the disciplinary council and the higher disciplinary council. These are: reprimand; a financial penalty of between EUR 60 and one-third of the basic salary; temporary suspension for not more than six months; definitive expulsion of the offending member. Disciplinary offences are expunged from the record three years after the act. Final decisions are carried out by the President of the Regional Council. In any case of the practice of the profession of nursing without a licence, Article 458 of the Criminal Code applies, which provides for criminal prosecution and a financial penalty.

§7. Aestheticians (Beauticians)

617. By Article 38 LD 361/1969 as amended by Article 38 of Law 4058/2012, an aesthetician is considered to be one who has graduated from a State-recognized school or from an equivalent school abroad, provided that the diploma is recognized in Hellas. The acquisition of the diploma requires at least one year's theoretical and practical training and practice in accordance with the law. The exercise of the profession requires a licence from the competent ministry or the prefecture.

618. The task of the aesthetician is to care for and maintain the pleasing state and appearance of the healthy individual by the application, necessarily external, of the following natural and artificial means and methods:[385]

385. Article 4 of LD 361/1969, Arts 1 and 2 of Directive 76/768/EEC as revised and Arts 2 and 3 of YA DYG/2005.

(a) the care of the face and skin by means of creams, moisturizers, make-up and so on, the use of which has been authorized by the Higher Hygiene Council;
(b) the massage of the face, neck and body by hand or with the assistance of electrical appliances that do not cause damage to the cells of the skin;
(c) hot or cold spraying of the skin with a spraying device;
(d) beauty face masks using harmless substances;
(e) the aesthetic care of the breasts, by means of special appliances, massage, hydrotherapy and legal compounds, provided that these cause no damage to the glandular substance and are medically approved;
(f) relaxation of the body by means of sauna baths, subject to medical approval;
(g) adornment of the face or body;
(h) steam treatment for the care of the face;
(i) depilation of the facial skin with wax or with substances authorized by the Higher Hygiene Council, or by means of electrical appliances provided that the operator has been specifically trained as laid down by a decision of the Minister of Health, Social Insurance and Social Solidarity;
(j) the care and dying of the hair of the head;
(k) the care of the eyelashes.

619. The aesthetician is forbidden to employ any title other than that of aesthetician, to offer advice on the state of the body, healthy or otherwise, or any medical opinion, to carry out any designated medical act, to cooperate with any physician of any specialization, to make use of pharmaceutical compounds that cause skin damage (peeling, etc.), to use electrical (faradic or galvanic) appliances delivering a current of greater than 4 milliamps, to use ultraviolet appliances more powerful than 350 watts, to use X-rays, to use the appliances or instruments of physiotherapy or to use infrared radiation without being specifically trained in accordance with a decision of the Minister of Health, Social Insurance and Social Solidarity, to use lamps of various colours in machines for the absorption of applications, or to use masks that emit ultraviolet radiation. For the functioning of the aesthetician's place of work, an operating licence is needed.[386]

620. Whosoever exercises the profession of aesthetician without the qualifications laid down by provisions of this law will be sanctioned under Article 458 of the PC, or, if so provided for, by graver punishment and by the withdrawal of the licence to practise as an aesthetician. The EOF is to take all necessary measures to ensure that there are in circulation to only those beauty products that measure up to the stipulations of YA DYG/2005 and its extensions.[387]

§8. Psychologists

621. Law 991/1979 deals, among other provisions, with the exercise of the profession of psychologist, which requires a licence to practise issued by decision of

386. Decision Y7/econ. 3971 of 30 May/9 Jun. 1994 (FEK B' 433).
387. Article 3 of Directive 76/768/EEC as in force. *See also* Directive 95/17/EC as in force.

the competent Minister following a favourable opinion from the Special Assessment Council within the Ministry of Health, Social Insurance and Social Solidarity.[388] The candidate must hold a degree in psychology from a Hellenic higher tertiary institution, or a foreign institution of the level of master, or licence, where licence is considered the final degree from university studies or equivalent. The recognition of the equivalence of foreign qualifications is the responsibility of the Inter-University Centre for the Recognition of Educational Qualifications (DOATAP).

622. The law foresees particular qualifications for the exercise of the psychologist's specialization in particular branches of psychology (educational, clinical, industrial and others). As far as the putting of the law into practice is concerned, there are: Decision A2/3823 of 30 July/21 August 1981 of the Minister of Health, Social Insurance and Social Solidarity, which establishes the specific qualifications of the clinical psychologist, and Decision A2/4258 of 16 October 1981 of the jointly competent Ministers of Health and Education, establishing the specific qualifications of the educational psychologist.[389] With reference to the particular qualifications of the clinical psychologist, and specifically to the practice of psychotherapy with methods and techniques emergent from the science of psychology, the precondition is the corresponding specialization, that is, preparatory instruction in theory and practice corresponding to the specific method certified by official documentation. When psychotherapy is to be accompanied by the simultaneous administration of drugs, the cooperation of a psychiatrist is required.

623. By Article 43 of Law 2519/1997, a sector for psychologists was established within the ESY, with posts graded as C, B, A or Director-Psychologist (Consultant Psychologist). The posts in this sector are apportioned to hospitals, mental health centres, health centres, psychiatric units and other similar units attached to hospitals. By Article 44, the posts are established by common decision of the Ministers of the Interior, Public Administration and Decentralization, Economy, and Health and Social Solidarity. By PDs issued on the proposal of the above ministers, the following are established: the announcement and filling of the above-mentioned posts, the qualifications needed, the conditions and procedure for promotion, and the procedure for recruitment under the publication of the above act.

388. *See also* Art. 33, para. 1 of L. 1193/1981.

389. *See also* Art. 7 of L. 2519/1997, on the school health services and socio-psychological support of children.

Chapter 2. Relations Between Healthcare Providers

§1. Hospitals

624. Hellenic hospitals are autonomous, self-administered bodies within the public (State) sector. Until Law 2519/1997, there was some confusion as to their role and competencies, while their functioning was qualitatively inefficient, through the lack of professional management. The level of fees, economic viability, efficiency and the quality of service offered had been provided for by the previous legal regime. All hospitals face grave financial problems, which are referred to as 'the hospital crisis'. The crisis has been described as the result of the rising cost of care combined with public expectation of better services. Many experts believe that the reason should be sought in the weaknesses of hospitals' organizational functioning, with their undefined aims and administrative incoherence, their characteristic lack of management and their bureaucracy.[390] It should be noted that the yearly budget for the nation's hospitals was GRD 800 billion in 1996, while the accumulated debt stood at between GRD 140 billion and 170 billion. Law 2889/2001 represented an attempt to overcome the problems confronted by ESY hospitals. These were converted into decentralized facilities of the Regional Health and Welfare Groups; this did not meet with success. Recently, the political government converted the hospitals from decentralized facilities into self-reliant legal persons under public law within the ESYKA.[391] ESYKA hospitals are fully subject to the control and supervision of the Head of the DYPE, are governed by the stipulations of the present law (Law 3329/2005 as amended and complemented by Laws 4052/2012 and 4118/2013), and have their own budget, protocol, official stamp, archive and tax registration number. Each hospital has a Manager and an Administrative Council (with seven members for hospitals of up to 339 regulated beds and nine members for those with over 400) (Articles 7 and 8), and also a Scientific Committee (Article 9).

625. After the liberation, the first hospital was established in the island of Syros in 1827, and the second known hospital was I ELPIS in Athens in 1836. The earliest hospitals were founded principally on private initiative or on that of municipal authorities. There began to appear the first large hospitals which still exist today. Since 1983, when the ESY was passed into law, adjustments to the organization and administration of hospitals have been made by Law 1397/1983 and later by Laws 2071/1992 and 2194/1994. PD 87/1983, applying Law 1397/1983, set out a uniform framework for the organization of Hellenic hospitals, defining the limits of the competencies and functioning of hospitals. PD 87/1983 was considered insufficiently comprehensive and effective, so it was repealed by Law 2190/1992, in anticipation of a new law. In fact, Law 1519/1997 and Law 2889/2001 endeavoured to develop and modernize the ESY through the reorganization of health services, reforms concerning drugs (pharmaceuticals) and so on. However, these Laws

390. I. Sigalas, *Organizational and Administrative Reality of Hellenic Hospitals Today*, Iatriko Vima, March–April 1995, 42–45.
391. L. 3329/2005.

required, for their being put into effect, the issue of a large number of PDs and YAs, a fact which tended to limit the high expectations and enthusiasm of the experts.

626. Now, hospitals may be established only as legal persons under public law. The foundation, closing or integration of hospitals, or the transfer of their place of functioning, is carried out by PD on the suggestion of the Minister of Health, Social Insurance and Social Solidarity and, where applicable, another competent minister in the cases of transfer or integration, following an opinion from KESY. The use of the denomination hospital – *nosokomeio* in Hellenic – or similar by private clinics is forbidden. For private clinics (private hospitals), the use of the denomination 'private clinic' – *idiotiki kliniki* – is compulsory. Hospital units in any way funded by the State, or whose running costs are borne by a legal person under public law (such as an insurance fund) are now converted into legal persons under public law. A group of hospitals is treated separately and specifically. By paragraph 1 of Article 12 of Law 3329/2005, the hospitals named AHEPA, Agios Savvas, Andreas Syngros, Korgialenio, Agia Eleni, Asklepiio Voulas, the children's hospital P. and A. Kyriakou, Pammakaristos,[392] Dromokaitio, Karamandaneio, the Institute for Research into Chest Diseases, Health and Safety at Work, and the hospital I ELPIS, keep their former status, and are linked functionally but not by organizational regulation with the DYPE. Articles 7, 8, 9, 10 and 11 of Law 3329/2005 apply to these facilities, as do Articles 6, 7, 8 and paragraph 10 of Article 13 of Law 2889/2001.

627. Hospitals may be either general or special. A general hospital is one which has departments for more than one specialization. General hospitals are either regional – *periferiaka* – or provincial – *nomarchiaka.* A regional hospital is situated in the administrative centre (regional capital) of each health region, and covers the needs of that region, offers medical training in all or most medical specializations, and takes part in the advance of medical research. There is a provincial hospital in each province, which mainly meets the needs of the population of that province, offers medical training and takes part in the advance of medical research. Special hospitals come under the supervision of the DYPE for their health region and may, by decision of KESY, serve the needs of several regions. The hospitals of each region cooperate on care and on teaching, either scientifically or functionally, as and when treatment needs impose this.[393] Furthermore, Articles 23 to 34 of Law 3370/2005 open the possibility of cooperation between ESYKA hospitals and not-for-profit hospitals of public benefit which are legal persons under private law, chiefly for care in intensive care units.

628. University hospitals provide highly specialized tertiary care. University hospitals undertake most of the medical research and are responsible for the most highly regarded provision of both basic and specialist training for doctors and other paramedical personnel. In Hellas, all hospitals are equipped for emergency care, some of them during mornings, and others in afternoons and nights, in accordance

392. By Art. 12, para. 2 of L. 3329/2005, the stipulations of Art. 13, para. 10 of L. 2889/2001 do not apply to the two hospitals Kyriakou and Pammakaristos.
393. *See* Art. 12, para. 7 of L. 1579/1985.

with their turn of duty for certain days (and holidays) each month. Certain Special hospitals are equipped for emergency care twenty-four hours per day, others through the day until 8 o'clock in the evenings. It should be noted that primary health care has up to now been undertaken by the hospitals on duty; this situation still pertains. Law 3235/2004 provides for the functioning of health centres, operated by the ESYKA and by social insurance organizations, providing primary health care on a twenty-four-hour basis. In this way, the functioning of hospitals as secondary and tertiary (university) level health providers will be facilitated. Law 3235/2004, in Article 7, makes reference to the family or personal physician, defines the task of nursing personnel in primary health care (Article 8), and promotes the development of electronic medical records (paragraph 5 of Article 9), simultaneously ensuring the secrecy of data (Article 10), while providing for criminal sanctions for those in breach (Article 11).

I. Relations Between Physicians and Hospitals

629. About the relations between physicians and hospitals, *see below* as quoted in paragraphs 637 et seq.

§2. Private Clinics and Laboratories

630. Private clinics and laboratories need an operating permit,[394] which is personal but transferable. The law anticipates that the establishment, extension or conversion of private clinics, as well as the conditions under which they may be transferred, will be stipulated by PD on a proposal of the Minister of Health, Social Insurance and Social Solidarity. Moreover, operating standards for private clinics are established by decisions of the Minister of Health, Social Insurance and Social Solidarity, following an opinion from KESY. PD 247/1991 was issued in order to put into effect rules, conditions and procedures for the establishing, functioning and conversion of private clinics.[395] Provisions of Law 2071/1992 defined health units in which health and treatment services are offered to patients in accordance with accepted modern opinions and methods in medical science, outpatients may be treated, and departments and laboratories may function where suitable space for these is available. Physical or legal persons may hold one or more permits for the establishing and operation of a private clinic. Now, PD 235/2000 refers to specific reforms aiming at the modernization and better functioning of private clinics (private hospitals). All private clinics whose operation predates PDs 247/1991 and 517/1991 and the coming into force of Article 149 of Law 2071/1992, are obliged, in order to continue to function, to adapt themselves to the stipulations of PD 235/2000, lodging an application for a new operating licence with the Prefect.

394. Article 53 of Law 1892/1990 and Art. 8, para. 2 of L. 2345/1995. *See also* Art. 33, para. 2 of L. 3204/2003.

395. *See also* Art. 32 of L. 3305/2005.

631. At the administrative seat of each prefecture, a Committee for Private Clinics is created, and gives opinions on the granting of permits, etc., while in the central service of the Ministry of Health, Social Insurance and Social Solidarity, there is a second-level Committee for Clinics. A private clinic that takes out a permit for establishment is obliged also to take out an operating permit, also supplied by the Prefect, after hearing the opinion of the local committee. Article 9 of PD 235/2000 distinguishes three classes of private clinic: General, Mixed and Specialized. Paediatric and psychiatric clinics constitute a separate category. In any case, all may allocate beds of all classes, with a defined minimum number of beds. For instance, for Mixed clinics the minimum number of beds is thirty-five in the Attiki and Thessaloniki prefectures, twenty elsewhere. A table of medical fees has been issued by a joint decision of the Ministers of Health and Social Solidarity and Finance and by the approval of KESY. Law concerns the criminal arraignment of those who hold establishment and operating licences and breach the provisions of the PD on private clinics. Private clinics may operate out of working hours, all week or on certain days only, offering medical services in any specialization mentioned in the permit for its establishment and operation; while so operating, outpatient attendance must be offered in its specializations. In exceptional cases, an obligatory out-of-hours roster may be imposed on private clinics by a reasoned decision of the Prefect. Law permits the incorporation and operation, within a private clinic, of one or more units for specialized health services of a diagnostic or therapeutic nature which belong to other physical or legal persons.[396] The operation of laboratories and specialized departments of a diagnostic or therapeutic nature requires specific separate operating permits.

I. Relations Between Physicians and Private Clinics and Laboratories

632. The Scientific Director,[397] appointed by the owner or his/her legal representative, bears the scientific and professional responsibility for the clinic. Such responsibility for each department or laboratory is borne by the physician who directs it. The Scientific Director also chairs the Scientific Committee, which is a committee of director-graded physicians heading the departments or laboratories. This committee is also the committee for in-hospital infectious diseases. Any change of director must be made known to the prefecture and communicated to the local medical association. The Scientific Director is responsible for the diagnosis and treatment of patients, distributes tasks among the medical and other personnel, and coordinates patient care. He/she is also responsible for the keeping of patient records and files, which must be retained for twenty years, and must include the following:

(a) personal details of the patient;
(b) admission documentation and the diagnosis;

396. *See also* Arts 32, 33 of L. 3370/2005 and Art. 8 of L. 3527/2007.
397. Articles 6 and 7 of PD 198/2007.

(c) a copy of the treatment sheet and of the patient's personal treatment record book;
(d) various examinations/tests;
(e) a report on the care given and the progress of the state of the patient's health, signed by the director of the department of the clinic;
(f) discharge documentation and a copy of the informatory discharge note.

633. The Scientific Director of a laboratory is responsible for the investigation and diagnosis of the diseases of patients referred to the laboratory, and for the full and correct keeping of the laboratory findings record book. The responsibilities of all medical and other staff are laid down in the code of internal operation of the clinic. Directors who are scientifically and professionally responsible for clinical departments or laboratories must be qualified in the relevant specialization and must have exercised their specialization for at least three years or in case that this qualification do not exist, then the Scientific Director may be a physician who has exercised his speciality for at least twelve months.[398]

§3. Health Insurance

634. *See above* as quoted in paragraphs 99 et seq.

398. Article 7 of PD 198/2007.

Chapter 3. Relations Between Physicians and the ESY

§1. The National Healthcare System

635. In 1983 by Law 1397/1983 the National Health Care System *(Ethniko Systima Iyeias*, in Hellenic: ESY, now ESYKA) was constituted by law. The institution was found lacking from the very beginning, with the result that many changes have been made, for a variety of reasons. It has undergone many alterations and improvements, in particular by Laws 1579/1985, 2071/1992, 2194/1994, 2345/1995, 2519/1997, 2889/2001, 3106/2003 and Law 3204/2003. Law 3329/2005, as amended and complemented by Law 3868/2010, has been in force since 4 April 2005 and aims at the development and modernization of the ESYKA, the organization of health services, etc. Two previous bills concerning the ESY had not passed into law. In accordance with PD of 31–29 January/13 February 1986, Hellenic territory had been administratively divided into nine Healthcare Regions for the implementation of the healthcare system. Now, the Healthcare Regions are seven. By Law 3329/2005, as amended by Article 1, paragraph 1 of Law 4052/2012, Articles 1 to 6 inclusive, in each of the seven Healthcare Regions, there is to be formed a legal person under public law named DYPE, to which is added the name of the Health Region. Each DYPE has its own budget, protocol, archive, official stamp and tax registration number, and has four Directorates of Health Care (management sections). The mission of the DYPE is the planning, coordination, supervision and checking of the functioning of health agencies within its region. The agencies providing healthcare and social solidarity services in each region are: (1) Hospitals, Health Centres and Community Care Facilities; (2) Centres for Mental Health and (Drug) Dependence; and (3) other legal persons under public or private law of the State sector which are active in the healthcare and social solidarity sectors and which come under the supervision of the Minister of Health, Social Insurance and Social Solidarity. The administrative organs of the healthcare region are: (a) the Head of the DYPE and (b) the seven-member Administrative Council of the DYPE. A Central Council of Health Care Regions is set up within the Ministry of Health, Social Insurance and Social Solidarity, in order to coordinate the work of the DYPEs. This Central Council is comprised of the Minister or his/her representative substitute, the General Secretary of the Ministry or his/her substitute and of the Heads of all the healthcare regions. A SYPE is established in the headquarters of each healthcare region; its role is to give opinions to the Minister on matters pertaining to development. The SYPE may meet in plenary form (the Head, the hospital managers, a representative of the prefectural administration, a representative of a medical department, and others), but there is also a Coordinating Committee (the Head, the Managers of the hospitals, and the directors of the four management sections of the DYPE).

636. Law protects citizens' rights vis-à-vis health services. For the protection of rights of hospital patients as well as of those who receive PFY, there are provisions on the protection of every citizen's basic right to health. Law establishes an autonomous service for the protection of the rights of patients, at the level of a ministerial department, and a control Commission at the level of the Ministry, whose aims are the checking of complaints and the taking of independent action by the authorities.

Moreover, the board of every hospital organizes an Office of Communication with the Public (public relations office), which during duty turns functions as a Secretariat for Urgent Incidents, which is a three-member committee for the investigation of patients' complaints and of questions concerning patients' rights.[399] Law 3329/2005 establishes a Citizens' Service Centre for Matters of Health and Social Solidarity in each DYPE (Article 4). The Centre operates as an independent department that is directly subordinate to the Head of the DYPE. Its organization and operating regulations are determined by the Head's decisions.

637. By Article 2 of Law 2519/1997, the ESIHD foreseen by Article 61 of Law 2071/1992 was renamed as the National Council for Bioethics and Deontology, for the defining, for instance, the limits and conditions for the application of new experimental methods and clinical applications. Now, the Council has been renamed again as ESIHD.[400] The ESIHD is also competent to investigate, from the point of view of medical ethics, events or acts which appear to be of great importance, either by their own nature, or by the significance they have acquired in public opinion. The National Council is further competent to set in motion a preliminary administrative investigation; this may result in conclusive findings. These findings may include a recommendation, directed to the authorities (bodies, services or unions) which are competent for the imposition of sanctions, that disciplinary proceedings be initiated.

638. Public health services of the Ministry of Health, Social Insurance and Social Solidarity, of the regions, and of the prefectural administrations, have as their aims the prevention of disease, the improvement of health, the furtherance of social equality, and the planning, organization and development of public health services with the assistance of any methodology, means or science that has to do with public health. The ministerial level General Directorate of Health is renamed as the General Directorate of Public Health,[401] and is restructured to include the Directorates of Public Health, Environmental Health, Health Education and Information, as well as the School Health Directorate.[402]

639. Article 4 of Law 3329/2005 deals with the organization of public health services in each region and provides for the setting up of four Directorates of Health Care and Welfare, by common decision of the competent Ministers, as management sections, in each DYPE: (1) the Directorate of Planning and Development of the Provision of Civil Services of the Ministry of Health, Social Insurance and Social Solidarity; (2) the Directorate of Financial Organization and Support, (3) the Directorate for the Development of Human Resources in Health-Care Facilities of the Ministry of Health, Social Insurance and Social Solidarity; and (4) the Directorate for Information Technology. There are also three offices: the Office of the Head of the DYPE, the Office for Legal Assistance and the Press and Communications

399. Chapter 1 of L. 2519/1997.
400. Article 40 of L. 3204/2003.
401. *See also* Art. 4 of L. 2519/1997.
402. Article 7, para. 1 of L. 2519/1997.

Office. The Supplies Department of the Directorate of Planning and Development of the DYPE has the task of integrating the separate supply programmes of the DYPE, and all agencies providing services under the Ministry of Health, Social Insurance and Social Solidarity in its region, into a single programme, which is to be placed before the Ministry of Development. Each directorate is headed by a public health physician or other ESYKA scientist, and is staffed by physicians, dentists, public health engineers, pharmacists, specialists in social and economic sciences, technicians and so on. These directorates cooperate with the departments of health services, the regional welfare departments, the public health services of the prefectural administrations, and the Ministry.[403]

640. Posts as public health physicians are created within the ranks of ESYKA physicians, in the central services, in hospitals and in health centres. A public health physician holds a qualification specializing in social medicine, occupational medicine, general medicine, or a postgraduate qualification from a university, or has at least five years' attested experience in matters of public health. They are evaluated by the Assessment Council and appointed in the first instance for three years, after which they are re-evaluated and either dismissed or given tenure: promotion to a higher grade may follow later. The same provisions apply to dentists. Public health physicians and dentists employed by the ESYKA are eligible for promotion to a higher grade as follows: from grade B to A on completion of five years' service, and from A to director on completion of seven years' service. Promotion depends on evaluation by the Council for the Selection of Public Health Physicians, in which the following are taken into account: the in-service performance of the physician under consideration for approval: his/her professional and scientific training; his/her scientific, educational and research work; his/her administrative abilities. In the case of a negative evaluation, the candidate is not promoted.[404]

641. Law provides for a Directorate of School Health (Services) within the Ministry of Health, Social Insurance and Social Solidarity, with Departments of programming, statistics and research. Law also provides for a School Health Office within the departments of public health of the directorates of health and welfare of each region under the new reorganization. The offices are staffed by public health physicians specialized in paediatrics or general medicine, dentists, psychologists, health visitors, social workers, nurses, etc. Their mission is the observation and improvement of children's health, as well as psychological support. The physicians are assigned to directorates of primary and secondary education.[405]

642. Article 8 of Law 2519/1997 created Regional Public Health Laboratories in the administrative centre of each region and as a decentralized Service of the Ministry with competencies as in paragraph 2 of Article 4 of PD 138/1992. The Central Public Health Laboratory (KEDY) coordinates, supervises and inspects the

403. Article 5 of L. 2519/1997.
404. For further information also the stipulations of Arts 23, 24 and 25 of L. 3370/2005.
405. *See also* Art. 7 of L. 2519/1997.

work of the Regional Laboratories and carries out the investigation of water supplies, checks on foodstuffs and drinks, etc. Each laboratory is headed by a public health physician.[406]

643. An independent unit under the name of the Institute for Health Service Quality Research and Control (IEEPYY) was formed within the National Centre for Health Research (EKEY).[407] The Institute's aims are the evaluation of health services, the statistical analysis and economic evaluation of medical acts and health services, quality control and assurance, and the issue of certificates and declarations of assured quality to hospitals, health centres, private providers of PFY, laboratories, clinics and any kind of medical establishment.

644. A General Directorate for the organization and coordination of health services has been formed within the Ministry. A ministerial advisory body exists under the name of Council for the Coordination of Unified Action by Health Services (SYSEDYPY). A Special Supreme Scientific Health Council (Aesthetician) has been formed within the Ministry, as a twenty-one-Member State advisory body on major matters of public health.[408] The KESY[409] has been reorganized with new competences.

645. Laws have foreseen the supervision, administration, organization and functioning of hospitals. In particular, Chapter B of Law 3329/2005 (Articles 7 et seq.), as amended and complemented by Law 3868/2010, defines the provisions on the supervision of ESYKA hospitals by the Ministry of Health, Social Insurance and Social Solidarity, the composition of ESYKA hospital governing bodies (boards), the competencies of which, and of the Manager (Governor) of which, are reanalysed, the institution of the position of Manager in each ESYKA hospital, the conversion of the technical service into the Directorate of Hospital Technical Services, the statement that medical services in each hospital shall be directed by a physician,[410] the creation in hospitals of centres for specialized care in certain branches of medical and care science, for the specialization of personnel and the advancement of research following an opinion from KESY, and the consultation of the governing board with the Scientific Committee of the hospital.

646. In law,[411] reference is made to the functioning of committees for the training, further training and specialization of physicians and other healthcare professionals or scientists, to the evaluation of all departments offering specialization to physicians and dentists, the criteria for the selection of candidates and the assignment of specialists to units, their cyclical training in their specialization in the departments, the exemption from rural service of certain categories of specialist, the procedure for the granting of certificates of specialization in intensive therapy in

406. Article 8, para. 7 of L. 2519/1997.
407. Article 9 of L. 1579/1985.
408. Article 4 of L. 1965/1982 is replaced. *See also* Arts 10–13 of L. 2519/1997.
409. It was established by Arts 2, 4 and 5 of L. 1278/1982.
410. *See also* Art. 28, para. 8 of L. 2646/1998.
411. Article 20 of L. 2519/1997.

intensive care of the newborn[412] and of specialization in occupational medicine.[413] Moreover, the afternoon opening is instituted for departments, units and surgical units of ESYKA hospitals, as well as home care by hospitals and health centres.[414]

647. The organization and functioning of rehabilitation and post-therapy units in ESYKA hospitals are provided for. In hospital groups, within the framework of paragraph 4 Article 5 of Law 2194/1994, hospitals of the group may be converted into such units, in whole or in part. Rehabilitation and post-therapy units in private clinics are appointed by the ESYKA to work as satellite units of the hospital group. A daily treatment fee is established, dependent on the nature of the care provided and on the level of the respective rehabilitation or post-therapy unit, which is collected by the hospital from private individuals or from the insurers. The recruitment procedure and manner of evaluating candidates for ESYKA and EKAB physicians and the manner of functioning of ESYKA hospitals as centres for the professional development to meet the needs of ESYKA and EKAB staff, following YAs, are laid down.[415] Hospitals of the same group are permitted, on a YA, to transfer staff to cover needs. University hospitals keep their former names. The governing bodies of an ESYKA hospital are the Administrative Council and the Manager of the hospital. Hospitals with more than 399 beds, as counted by official regulation, have also a Deputy Manager. The Manager and the Deputy Manager are in full-time exclusive employment, are appointed by decision of the Minister of Health, Social Insurance and Social Solidarity for a period of two years, renewable and have competencies as are determined by law. A Scientific Council is formed in each ESYKA hospital, with nine members, of whom five are physicians and four are drawn from the other health sciences. The President of the Council is chosen by a secret ballot of the members. The Council is an opinion-giving body of the ESYKA physicians of the hospital. The Ministry of Health, Social Insurance and Social Solidarity draws up a list of auxiliary, substitute physicians by specialization, in order to cover urgent staffing needs, independently of the existence or otherwise of vacant positions. Since 2002, ESYKA hospitals have been permitted to run afternoon clinics or surgeries, after regular working hours, and to carry out diagnostic and therapeutic acts at such times.[416]

648. The Community Care Facilities listed in paragraph 2 of Article 15 of Law 3329/2005, as well as the legal persons under public law, the 'Centre for the Education and Rehabilitation of the Blind' (PD 265/1979) and the 'National Foundation for the Deaf' (Order 2.6.1939 and RD 703/27.10.1972), are to have both a Manager and an Administrative Council. There are also community care facilities administered by their Administrative Councils and the President of the Administrative Council, with competencies as determined by law.[417]

---

412. Article 84 of L. 2071/1992.
413. In accordance with the provisions of PD 213/1986 and PD 415/1994 and after the replacement of Art. 134 of L. 2071/1992.
414. Article 21 of L. 2519/1997.
415. Article 7 of L. 3329/2005.
416. Articles 9 and 10 of L. 2889/2001 as complemented by Art. 62 para. 1 of L. 3918/2011.
417. Articles 21–25 of L. 2519/1997. *See also* Art. 5, para. 4 of L. 2194/1994.

649. Many Laws refer to the much-needed upgrading of PFY in the provinces. Physicians (generalists) are taken on, preferably in positions as provincial (rural) physicians which are ESYKA positions. In this way, it is anticipated that the institution of compulsory rural service for newly qualified physicians (LD 67/1968 as amended and complemented) will be phased out. Moreover, decisions of the competent ministers establish regional medical offices in those islands lacking a health centre. These offices, classified as Multi-capable Medical Offices, function daily and keep a duty roster out of working hours. They are assisted by hospitals and by health centres and their sub-offices, with which they are linked and to which they belong organizationally. The organization and functioning of first-level (primary) health care are placed within a unified framework, in the direction of the functioning of a Single Health Care Body (EFY). EFY deals with the organization, functioning, and functional and scientific integration of the ESYKA PFY units, of the insurance funds and organizations, of the Local Administrative Organizations and other legal persons under public law, with ESYKA hospitals, ESYKA Health Centres and of Social Insurance Organizations.[418] Within this framework, services will also be offered by family physicians and personal physicians.[419]

650. A permanent problem of ESYKA functioning is the funding and financial management of health services. Law[420] describes the financial sources/resources of hospitals and health centres (as did Law 2592/1953) and states that hospitals and all other health bodies employ double-entry bookkeeping with analytic cost accounting.[421] Insurance providers work together, through common action or a union of insurance organizations and funds, in order to cooperate with the Minister on the setting of fee levels according to the category of hospital, or to negotiate the conclusion of agreements with private clinics and hospitals abroad, with the approval of the competent ministers.[422]

651. Family physicians are specialized in general medicine, pathology or paediatrics, and it is anticipated that they should offer general services within PFY networks in urban and semi-urban areas, each family physician having a list of not more than 2,000 patients. Family physicians sign yearly contracts with the responsible body within the network and provide services daily, mornings and afternoons, and make home visits to those on their list at any time of the day or night. They may refer patients to specialists or to laboratories within the network or to outpatient departments or laboratories in hospitals. The supervision and functioning of PFY networks come under the aegis of the Ministry of Health, Social Insurance and Social Solidarity, no matter which body they may belong to. Law[423] provides for the electronic medical file and the electronic health card for each citizen, securing also personal data (Article 10), and lays down the penal sanctions for evaders of law (Article 11).

418. Article 31 of L. 2519/1997.
419. Article 32 of L. 2519/1997; Arts 6 and 7 of L. 3235/2004.
420. Article 28 of L. 2519/1997; *see also* Art. 3 of L. 4118/2013.
421. Article 29 of L. 2519/1997.
422. Article 30 of L. 2519/1997.
423. Article 9 of L. 3235/2004.

652. Vacant posts for ESYKA are publicly announced with all particulars, including the grade, the hospital or health centre, the specialization, etc. The auditing of ESYKA physicians is carried out in accordance with the law. Law 3329/2005 deals with the responsibility and the evaluation of the medical work of ESYKA physicians, with yearly evaluations and reports which are held in the physician's file. Law describes the Councils for the Assessment and Selection of Medical and Dental Personnel in Care Institutions (SKEIOPNI), and refers to the manner of their composition and function.[424] Law allows the possibility that an ESYKA physician or other professional may take part, for reward, in research and educational programmes in the wider public sector. Permission from the board of his/her hospital is required for this.[425]

653. The disciplinary sanctions for ESYKA personnel are:[426]

(a) written warning;
(b) a fine of up to ten months' salary;
(c) the loss of the right to be considered for promotion to a higher grade, for between one and five years;
(d) temporary suspension from duty, for up to two years;
(e) permanent suspension from duty;
(f) the withdrawal of the professional licence (visa), temporarily for up to two years, or permanently.

By Article 11 of Law 3329/2005, the Manager of a hospital, the disciplinary supervisor of all staff, including that of regional surgeries and health centres within his/her area of competency, may impose on any staff member, with the exception of a physician, the penalty of a reprimand or a financial penalty up to half of a monthly salary. The same right is held by the President of a community care facility. The Administrative Council of a hospital or a community care centre, the collective disciplinary body, may impose on any staff member, apart from a physician, a reprimand or a financial penalty of up to one month's earnings. The Head of a DYPE may also impose a reprimand or a financial penalty of up to half-monthly earnings, and may also instigate a preliminary investigation and an Administrative Investigation under Oath against managers, and forward the findings to the Minster of Health and Social Solidarity.

654. Although appeals to the second instance against final judgments in the first instance were allowed (Article 163 of Law 2683/1999 as valid), this was abolished under Article 8, paragraph 3 of Law 4057/2012.

655. The Manager of a hospital and the President of the Administrative Council of a community care facility, qua disciplinary supervisors, may impose on ESYKA medical personnel (not specialists) the penalty of a reprimand or a financial penalty

424. *See infra* para. 672.
425. Article 38 of L. 2519/1997.
426. Article 39, para. 1 of L. 2519/1997.

of up to half-monthly earnings. The Administrative Councils of hospitals or community care facilities, qua collective disciplinary bodies, may impose on physicians the penalty of a reprimand or a financial penalty of up to one monthly salary. The Head of a DYPE may also impose on medical personnel a reprimand or a financial penalty of up to half-monthly earnings. The disciplinary authority which is exercised over ESYKA physicians is provided for in the stipulations of Laws 1397/1983, 2071/1992, 2519/1997 and 2889/2001. The provisions of the disciplinary code for civil servants are also applicable. By decision of the Minister of Health, Social Insurance and Social Solidarity, in each DYPE, a disciplinary council of the first instance is set up to deal with disciplinary matters concerning physicians (apart from those practised in medicine). It has five members and has jurisdiction of both the first and second instances. As a first instance tribunal, it may impose penalties as in Article 39 of Law 2519/1997 (first to third points). Acting in the second instance, it may bring a plea against the Manager of a hospital, the Administrative Council of a hospital, or the DYPE itself. Accused parties may not sit on the disciplinary council. Appeal to the Central Disciplinary Council may be made in cases where the First Instance Disciplinary Council has imposed a penalty of loss of four months' earnings or greater, or the penalty of disbarment from candidacy for promotion. The Central Disciplinary Council acts as a first instance tribunal in cases in which the penalty may include the withdrawal of the right to practice, and as a tribunal of appeal against first instance decisions where financial penalties of the loss of four months' earnings or more were imposed, up to disbarment from candidacy for promotion to a higher grade. Appeal to the Administrative Court may be made against final decisions of the First Instance Disciplinary Council and against definitive decisions of the Central Disciplinary Council, within thirty days. The disciplinary supervisor of DYPE Heads and of Managers of hospitals and community care centres is the Minister of Health, Social Insurance and Social Solidarity.

656. Law establishes a branch (of employment) for hospital pharmacists, into which those already serving in ESYKA hospitals are incorporated, and refers to the other branches of hospital scientists: hospital physicists, radio-physicists, clinical chemists, biochemists and biologists in hospital medical laboratories, and ESYKA psychologists.[427]

657. Articles 45 to 51 of Law 2519/1997, in Chapter 9, are dedicated to matters concerning drugs (pharmaceuticals) and the EOF. For the needs of patients in all the care institutions under the supervision of the Ministry of Health, Social Insurance and Social Solidarity, a catalogue of drugs that may be supplied is drawn up by a special committee of the Ministry in the EOF. The catalogue is revised yearly. This is the Hospital Drug Prescription List. The EOF is consulted by the Minister, who has the power of decision on all matters concerning drugs, such as the manner of controlling for quality, for authenticity, etc. Law adds and alters further provisions on drugs, such as the duties and competencies of the committees of the EOF, the scientific commissions for the assessment of drugs and so on. Law treats the expenses for the promotion of drugs, regulates limits which are placed by decisions

427. Articles 40–44 of L. 2519/1997.

of the jointly competent Ministers. Law provides for pharmacists' partnerships, operating licences for pharmaceutical warehouses and so on. The EOF assigns a code number to every pharmaceutical licensed for use in Hellas. This code is to be printed on the authentication tape and is compulsory and binding upon all public services, health funds, and private enterprises that produce, distribute, utilize or in any way have anything to do with branded, packaged pharmaceuticals.[428]

658. Further provisions of law (Article 52 of Law 2519/1997 as complemented by Article 39 of Law 4085/2012) refer to slimming and diet units, the operation of which requires a licence issued by the Prefect.[429]

659. The fact is that many provisions of law require PDs or YAs to put them into effect; this applies to the plans for the remaking of public health and most particularly of the public sector in health care. To date, this has been proceeding slowly, and the reforms after the economic crisis of 2010 have made things worse. The criticisms of the Law are focussing on the upgrading to be carried out by it, and the manner foreseen for its execution, which makes it hard to turn it into reality. The means of handling patients remains uneconomic, raising the cost of hospital care, while at the same time, the application of the Law's provisions on hospital stays will require significant new financial resources.

§2. Physicians of the ESY

I. Physicians' Selection and Employment

660. Positions in the physicians' branch of the ESYKA are filled, at all grades, after public announcement. Those selected are appointed to positions as Directors or Superintendents for a period of five years.[430] Law provides for Regional Councils for the Selection and Evaluation of ESYKA Physicians of Grades Superintendent A and B, corresponding to each grade, specialization and area of responsibility, and for similar Councils for the Selection and Evaluation of Physicians with the grade of director, again as corresponding to each specialization.

661. Positions in the physicians' branch of the ESYKA are created and announced henceforth by hospital or health centre, by grade and by specialization. Physicians who are appointed are placed in hospitals or health centres, respectively. Placement into departments, units, etc., is by decision of the board of the hospital following an opinion of the director of medical services, as concerns their numerical distribution between departments, laboratories and units. In the departments that comprise the sectors, specialized physicians are placed the object of whose knowledge corresponds to the contents of the medical task of the department. Specialists

428. *See also* YA DYG/8 Aug. 2001.
429. Article 23 of L. 3204/2003. *See also* YA DYG/18 Mar. 2005.
430. *See* Art. 11, para. 7b of L. 2889/2001.

are appointed with the creation of the positions.[431] The number of organic positions in the physicians' branch of the ESYKA at the grade Superintendent First-Class may not exceed 50% of the total of positions at the grade Superintendent Second-Class for each specialization in each hospital. Exceptions are provided for unproductive positions and specializations.

II. Physicians' Promotion

662. The title of Substitute Manager is established with reference to the auditing (supervision) of physicians in the ESYKA branch. The title is allotted, after assessment, to Superintendents First-Class who have completed thirteen years of service in the branch, of which at least six must have been at the grade Superintendent A. Vice presidents of the Administrative Councils of local DYPEs sit as presidents of the Councils for the Selection and Evaluation of Physicians with the grade of Director and of Physicians of Grades Superintendent A and B in Community Care Facilities. Their substitutes are the presidents of the Administrative Councils of the local Community Care Facilities.[432] Already-serving ESYKA physicians who fulfil certain preconditions are exempt. To each physician bearing the title of Substitute Director, a particular clinical, laboratory, research or teaching task is assigned, by decision of the hospital board on opinions from the Head of the corresponding unit or department, the Director of Medical Services, the director of the corresponding sector and the Scientific Committee. The execution of their task is coordinated by the Head of the department.

663. All physicians in a department take part in the unified programme of functioning of the department and of the outpatients' department, as well as in the department's duty roster, as is established by YA. Tenured physicians of the grade of Superintendent C, who hold a specialization in general medicine and who are still in service having served fifteen semesters (six-month periods) at their present grade, are considered for promotion to Superintendent B. Any further time period served at their present grade counts towards their promotion to the next grade.[433] Promotion assessments of serving ESYKA physicians occur once a year after a relevant evaluation and assessment by the local SKEIOPNI and a decision of the Minister of Health, Social Insurance and Social Solidarity. In the assessment and evaluation of candidates, special attention is paid to their scientific constitution and education, to their scientific research and, above all, clinical work, to administrative capability, to their spirit of cooperation, to their behaviour towards patients being treated or examined and generally their respect for the rights of patients and citizens who call upon

431. Article 34, para. 5 of L. 2519/1997.
432. Article 8, paras 2 and 3 of L. 3329/2005.
433. Article 21, para. 5a of L. 3293/2004.

the services of the hospital, as well as all the data in their service file. For the granting of the title of Substitute Director, great attention is paid to research and published work, training in special centres within the country or abroad, and demonstrable work experience in a particular area.[434]

III. Physicians' Responsibilities and Medical Work

664. As far as the responsibility and the evaluation of the medical work of ESYKA physicians are concerned, the execution of the duties of hospital physicians is connected with the conditions pertaining to the particular hospital or situation and is established under the responsibility of the Director of Medical Services, the chief criterion being effective service to patients. Service files are kept about ESYKA physicians, concerning the evaluation of their clinical work and medical work in general, their adherence to orders concerning medical functioning and to their obligations, and their service performance and productivity in general. These files are the responsibility of the director of the department in which the physician serves. They must contain yearly evaluation reports, and are to be produced by the end of the first half of February each year by two directors; the contents are made known to the evaluated physician, who may also submit a report on his/her own work.[435]

665. The annual evaluation Report may be re-examined, upon petition by the evaluated person deposited within thirty days of the disclosure of the report, by the Administrative Council of the hospital, apart from petitions for re-examination deposited by physicians in health centres, which have been transformed into decentralized and independent service facilities of the Regional Health Directorate; their reports are examined by the Administrative Council of the DYPE.[436]

IV. Physicians' Assessment and Selection Councils

666. For each member of the selection council, a substitute is appointed by the same procedure. In any special or exceptional case, the final assessment rests with the Minister. For the comparative evaluation of candidates for a position, the SKEIOPNI consults the above-mentioned appointees and the data in the personal file. The assessment procedure follows stages described by law, and the subjects of assessment have all the rights recognized by law, by the code of employment, etc.

667. Appeals against first-level decisions are lodged with the Regional Councils for the Assessment and Selection of Physicians. Any gaps or delays in the appointment of members are remedied by the Minister, who may personally appoint members. For the assessment of dentists, the same procedure is followed. These

434. Article 36 of L. 2519/1997.
435. Article 36, paras 1, 2, of L. 2519/1997.
436. Article 22, para. 2 of L. 3402/2005.

committees hear appeals within six months of their composition, and are then dissolved.[437] By decision of the Minister on advice from KESY, it is possible to alter the hierarchy of criteria and the system of grading for the comparative evaluation of candidates for posts in the ESYKA physicians' branch, and also for the individual assessment of ESY physicians. ESYKA public health physicians are exempt, and are assessed by other criteria (to be found in Article 6 of Law 2519/1997 on the creation of positions as public health physicians).[438]

V. Physicians' Participation in Research and Educational Programmes

668. ESYKA physicians and other scientific or professional staff, with the approval of the board of the hospital, may offer their services for reward, outside their regular working hours and their turns of duty, to research and educational programmes in the wider public sector, receiving a proportion of the earnings for post-hospital and special care offered by hospitals. There are also services offered by the afternoon and early evening opening of hospital departments, units or laboratories.[439]

669. Paragraph 1 of Article 39 of Law 2519/1997 provides for disciplinary sanctions for ESYKA physicians, as already mentioned. The main disciplinary organs for ESYKA physicians are the Head of DYPE, the Manager of the hospital, the President of the Administrative Council of the hospital or of the community care facility according to law, as already mentioned.[440]

437. *See also* Art. 37, paras 6 and 9 of L. 2519/1997.
438. Article 37, para. 13 of L. 2519/1997.
439. Article 21 of L. 2519/1997. *See also* Chs 6 and 7 of L. 3418/2005.
440. Law 2889/2001 and Art. 11 of L. 3329/2005.

Annexes

Annex 1 Hospitals, Beds, Physicians and Caring Personnel by Specialty 2015

Speciality of hospitals	*Hospitals (1)*	*In care Beds*	*Outpatient Beds/ Seats*	*Physicians*	*Midwives*	*Nurses*				*Health Visitors*	*Rest Caring Personnel*
						Professional nurses	*Associate nurses (4)*	*Practical nurses (5)*			
						University Degree (2)	*Techno-logical Degree (3)*		*Second Degree Education*		
Total	**283**	**45,945**	**3,764**	**23,669**	**2,602**	**1,256**	**18,001**	**14,975**	**1,024**	**486**	**4,964**
General	172	34,056	3,220	20,147	1,936	1,041	15,509	12,277	559	384	4,189
Combined Specialities	8	247	35	69	19	1	20	41	8	0	5
Cancer	4	1,151	161	939	22	47	603	434	3	21	152
V.D. and skin diseases	1	74	33	104	0	1	28	51	0	5	11
Infectious diseases and leprosy	0	0	0	0	0	0	0	0	0	0	0
Obstetrical-Gynaecological	25	1,193	104	533	614	16	119	255	27	4	111

Speciality of hospitals	Hospitals (1)	In care Beds	Outpatient Beds/ Seats	Physicians	Midwives	Nurses				Health Visitors	Rest Caring Personnel
						Professional nurses	Associate nurses (4)	Practical nurses (5)			
						University Degree (2)	Techno-logical Degree (3)		Second Degree Education		
Neuropsychiatric	50	6,983	48	777	5	63	706	1,293	399	48	236
Orthopedical	0	0	0	0	0	0	0	0	0	0	0
Ophthalmological	3	64	10	42	0	8	18	30	1	0	8
Pathological	10	557	25	75	0	4	52	92	24	0	18
Paediatrics	5	1,252	119	815	6	43	683	384	2	23	140
Tubercular	1	50	0	18	0	0	16	20	1	1	2
Physical & Rehabilitation Medicine	1	127	0	28	0	0	14	28	0	0	22
Surgical	2	159	1	118	0	32	229	60	0	0	70
Otorhinolary-ngological	1	32	8	4	0	0	4	10	0	0	0

Source: Hellenic Statistics Authority, available at http://www.statistics.gr/el/statistics/-/publication/SHE06/-.

Annex 2 Inhabitants per Doctor and Bed Average Duration of Treatment per Patient[1]

Year	*Inhabitants per doctor*	*Inhabitants per bed*	*Average duration of treatment per patient (in days*[2]*)*
1998	242	206	6
1999	236	212	6
2000	231	212	6
2001	228	209	6
2002	218	212	6
2003	211	213	6
2004	205	213	6
2005	200	211	6
2006	187	208	6
2007	180	208	N/A

1. NSSG, CSYG 2009, Pireas 2011, p. 93.

2. Excluding patients with mental disorders.

Selected Bibliography

Legislation: Codes (In Hellenic)

ISA (Medical Council of Athens). *Collection of Legislation, for Practising the Medical Profession and Legal State of Medical Councils*. Athens, 2018. Available at https://www.isathens.gr/nomika-themata/nomothesia/57-isa/nomothesia/404-syllogi-nomothesias.html.

Panhellenic Medical Association. *Syntaxis of a Planned New Code of Medical Deontology (proper conduct)*. 1989.

Raptarchi, P. (special cooperation: Katsini N.). *Continuous Code of Legislation*. Vols 34, 34A and 34B: Public Health Law, 1938.

Rigatos, G. *Codes of Medical Ethics*. Epsilon, 1991.

Skordakis, D. *National Health System*. Jurisprudence, 1988.

Sourlas, G. *Health Legislation: Laws, Presidential Decrees*. Vols A+B, December 1992.

Books: Articles (In Hellenic)

Alexiadis, A. *Introduction to Medical Law*. M. Dimopoulou, 1996.

Anapliotou-Vazaiou, E. *Abortion and Medical Deontology*. Archives of Hellenic Medicine. V.B., 1985.

Anapliotou-Vazaiou, E. *General Principles of Medical Law*. Sakoulas, 1993.

Argenti Ph. & Rose H.J. *The Folklore of Chios*. Vol. I, II, Cambridge University Press, 1949.

Avraam, K. *Medical Diagnosis and Penal Liability*. 1957.

Ayioutanti, G. *Coroner's Themes* Parisianos. Penal Chronicles, 1980.

Epivatianos, P. *Medical Law, Deontology and Problematics*. University Studio Press, 1984.

Fragkos, K. *Medical Responsibility, Criminal Offences of Physicians*. Sakkoulas, 2018.

Galani, D. *The Terminal Patient, the Doctor, the Fear of Death*. Iatriko Vima, 1989.

Gbanti-Kaiafa, M. et al. (eds). *Contemporary Issues on Medical Law*. Nomiki Vivliothiki, 2012.

Gbanti-Kaiafa, M. et al. (eds). *Medical Liability from Negligence*. Nomiki Vivliothiki, 2013.

Gritzalis, D. et al. *Study: Safeguarding Medical Confidentiality in the Information Systems of ESY*. Computers Department, 1990.

Granitsa, D. *Medical Deontology*. Iatriko Vima, Part A: 1991, Part B: 1992.

Selected Bibliography

Hamlatzis, P. et al. *Neurologische Ausfallserscheinungen bei Podophyllin-Vergiftung* (in German) *Neuropsychiatrie*, Band 5, Heft 3–4/1992.
Hortarea, K. *Medical Liability and Medical Legislation*. 1975.
Nockels Fabbri, C. *History of Medicine*, Papyros EEE-Fratelli Fabbri Editori, 1968.
Karlovassitou-Koniari, A. *Electroencephalographic Findings in the Elderly*. Aristotelian University of Thessaloniki, 1986.
Kazis, A. et al. *Temporal Slow Activity of the EEG in Old Age*. Archives of Psychiatry and Neurological Sciences, 231, 1982.
Kolympari, A. *Comparison Between the New Law on Transplantations and the Old Law, Contemporary Issues on Medical Law*. Nomiki Vivliothiki, 2012.
Koniaris, T. *The Usefulness of Welfare Social Indicators for Measurement of the Quality of Social Insurances Schemes*. Kyriakidi Brs, 1978.
Koniaris, T. 'Greece'. In R. Blanpain ed., *International Encyclopaedia of Labour Law and Industrial Relations*. Kluwer, 1st edition 1982, 2nd edition 1990.
Koniaris, T. *Social Policy and Administration*. Aristotelian University Publications Service, 1984.
Kopanaris, F. *Public Health in Hellas*. 1933.
Roy, K. *Greek Magical Amulets: The Inscribed Gold, Silver, Copper and Bronze Lamellae*, Part I. Published text of known provenance, Westdeutscher Verlag, Opladen, 1994.
Kotsianou, S. *The Legal Problems of Transplantations*. Nomiko Vima, 1969.
Kotsianou, S. *Medical Liability, Civil and Penal*. Digital Repository of Historical and Cultural Archives of S. Kotsianos, 1977.
Koutselini, A. & M. Mihalodimitraki. *Medical Liability*. Gutenberg, 1984.
Krug, A. *Heilkunst und Heilkult: Medizin in der Antike* (in German), 2d ed., Beck, 1993.
Mabel, L. *Cure and Cult in Ancient Corinth*. Princeton, 1977.
Liourdi, A. *Medical Penal Liability*. Nomiki Vivliothiki, 2014.
Manousou, O. & T. Mountokalaki. *Introduction to Clinical Medicine*. Parisianos, 1980.
Nys, H. in Herman Nys (Volume Editor), Roger Blanpain (General Editor), Frank Hendrickx (General Editor), *Belgium, IEL Medical Law*, Kluwer Law International, 2017.
Nys, H. *La médecine et le droit*. Diegem, Belgique, Kluwer Edit. Juridiques, 1995.
OECD. *Health Care Systems in Transition*. Paris, 1990.
Politi, C. *Enlightenment and Patient's Consent*. Iatriko Vima, 1990.
Rigatos, G.A. *The Medicine of Antiquity in Our Popular Traditions*. Vita Editions, 1999.
Rovithi, D. *Forensic Medicine*. Sakkoulas, 1960.
Tahou, A. *The Competence of Doctors and Biochemists of the National Health System* EDKA, 1993.
Vavouskou, K. *The Physician's Liability under Civil Law*. Sakkoulas, 1995.
WHO. *Health for all by the Year 2000*. World Health Organization, 1985.
Yfantopoulos, I. *The Programming of the Field of Health in Hellas*. EKKE, 1988.
Zafeira, T. *Medical Legislation*. 1966.
Zilidis, C. *The Medical Centres in Northern Hellas*. University Studio Press, 1995.

Index

The numbers here refer to paragraph numbers.

Index

www.ingramcontent.com/pod-product-compliance
Lightning Source LLC
Chambersburg PA
CBHW071444230926
51846CB00001B/334
9789403534862